The surname detective

From the author of the best-selling *Family tree detective*, this helpful guide provides the amateur genealogist or family historian with the skills to research the distribution and history of a surname.

Colin Rogers uses a sample of 100 names, many of them common, to follow the migration of people through the centuries. If you have one of the 100 or so sample surnames, the book maps out your surname distribution through the centuries. If not, you can still learn how to find out where your namesakes live now, how they have moved about the country through time, and how the name started out – quite probably in the medieval period as a placename, a nickname or Christian name, or as a name based on your ancestor's job (like Carpenter or Smith).

Colin Rogers finishes this fascinating book by showing how the distribution of surnames can be studied irrespective of the size of the surrounding population, and reaches some interesting conclusions about which names are more reliable guides to migration since the fourteenth century.

The surname detective is a must for genealogists and surname study addicts, but it also has much to interest the professional historian, population geographer and geneticist.

Colin Rogers is Head of Overseas Liaison at Manchester Metropolitan University; he also has a consultancy for tracing missing beneficiaries.

The
surname detective

Investigating surname distribution in England, 1086–present day

Colin D. Rogers

Manchester University Press
Manchester and New York

distributed exclusively in the USA and Canada by St Martin's Press

Copyright © Colin D. Rogers 1995

Published by Manchester University Press
Oxford Road, Manchester M13 9NR, UK
and Room 400, 175 Fifth Avenue, New York, NY 10010, USA

Distributed exclusively in the USA
by St. Martin's Press, Inc., 175 Fifth Avenue, New York, NY 10010, USA

Distributed exclusively in Canada by
UBC Press, University of British Columbia, 6344 Memorial Road,
Vancouver, BC, Canada V6T 1Z2

British Library Cataloguing-in-Publication Data
A catalogue record for this book is available from the British Library

Library of Congress Cataloging-in-Publication Data
Rogers, Colin Darlington.
    The surname detective : investigating surname distribution in
England, 1086–present day / Colin D. Rogers.
        p.   cm.
    ISBN 0–7190–4047–7 (hbk).—ISBN 0–7190–4048–5 (pbk)
    1. Names, Personal—England—History.   I. Title.
    929.4'2'0942—dc20   94–24441

ISBN 0 7190 4047 7 *hardback*
     0 7190 4048 5 *paperback*

First published 1995

01 00 99 98 97   10 9 8 7 6 5 4 3 2

Typeset in Great Britain
by Northern Phototypesetting Co Ltd
Printed in Great Britain
by Biddles Ltd, Guildford and King's Lynn

Contents

Maps

Abbreviations

ESS English Surnames Series:

    ESS 1 Redmonds, G. (1973) *Yorkshire West Riding*
    ESS 2 McKinley, R. A. (1975) *Norfolk and Suffolk surnames in the Middle Ages*
    ESS 3 McKinley, R. A. (1977) *The surnames of Oxfordshire*
    ESS 4 McKinley, R. A. (1981) *The surnames of Lancashire*
    ESS 5 McKinley, R. A. (1988) *The surnames of Sussex*

OES Reaney, P. H. (1967) *The origin of English surnames*
PRO Public Record Office
VCH Victoria County History

Glossary

byename   a second name given to an individual, not inherited
hypochoristic a diminutive or pet form of a personal name
locative   surname based on the name of a place
metronymic   surname based on a woman's Christian name
patronymic   surname based on a man's Christian name
polygenic   surname having arisen in different places
ramification branching out, becoming more numerous
surname   a second name which is inherited
toponymic   surname based on a natural, or man made, object

Acknowledgements

A number of people have assisted in this project by supplying information and ideas, including Dr Paul Booth, Dr Iain Bride, John H. Sagar, Judith Small, and Dr John H. Smith.

Apparently unoffended by already having had their brains picked, Professor David Hey and Eric Banwell devoted some time to looking through an initial draft, suggesting the elimination of the more unfortunate passages, and the incorporation of some sensible ones.

Acknowledgement of the work of those who have gone before me in this fascinating field will, I hope, be all too clear in the text.

Ebenezer Chapel
Tintwistle

Introduction

When I was a child in Prestwich, four miles to the north of Manchester, a man called Prestwich lived close to the chapel I attended. This coincidence of placename and surname fascinated me even then – was his family the present or original owner of the town, or was his presence coincidental? Was the town called after the family, or the family after the town?

Since then, my archival, genealogical and forensic interests have never strayed far from names in one form or another. How inadequate they are as a system for identifying individuals; how lax a system which allows people to change their name, almost at will – and yet how personal they feel to us all. When we meet someone new, and ask a friend 'Who's that?', the first answer is normally a name, rather than an occupation, a relationship, a place of residence, or a physical attribute. It is as if our whole essence has been crystallised into two words which have no intrinsic meaning beyond ourselves.

The only predetermined part of the name, of course, is the surname or family name, inherited in England and Scotland since the Middle Ages. In Scotland, inheritance was neither as early nor as straightforward as in England, with complications resulting from the clan system and the anglicanisation of names well into the eighteenth century. In Wales, surnames did not start to be inherited among the Welsh, as opposed to English immigrants, until the sixteenth century, a process which was not completed until the nineteenth. Indeed, Morgan and Morgan (1985) indicate that some of these settlers abandoned English practices and adopted the Welsh patronymic system.

This book is largely concerned with surnames *in* England; it therefore deliberates on names originating in other countries without pretending in any way to be knowledgeable about their earlier history. Some recent English writers without the necessary understanding of Celtic languages have rightly been attacked for reaching uninformed conclusions, and I still have enough trouble with English itself to risk putting my head above that particular parapet. However, when sources are available for other countries now part of the United Kingdom, I have tried to use them in order to provide more rounded conclusions about the whole area. I should also question whether it is fair to encourage novices in linguistics and medieval history to investigate names in the Middle Ages by following me into Part 3. Weekley in 1916 criticised some earlier writers as exhibiting a 'confident imbecility', being 'untrustworthy', even 'crazy', and it does seem as if the subject is peculiarly prone to wild theorising.

Since the fifteenth century a surname has normally been changed only by daughters at the time of their marriage – or at least after the signing of the register following the wedding ceremony. This inheritance of surnames through the male line, however objectionable to feminists, is very useful historically because the name can then be exploited as a surveillance bug or barium meal, enabling genealogists to trace the descent of individual family trees, the social historian to follow movements of population over long periods of time, and the biologist to explore the spread of genes and the extent of inbreeding amongst human beings.

The surname detective is interested in three main aspects of a name's history – its meaning, the pattern of its spread over the centuries since it became inherited, and its present distribution. It is the second and third of these with which this book is primarily concerned. I wanted to find out how far a study of surnames can help in tracking geographical mobility. Are some surnames more useful than others for doing so? Do the sources of information open to the general public allow the relevant measurements to take place, and do they provide unequivocal data which can be used in evidence?

Can the modern distribution of surnames throw *any* light on their origin, challenging some commonly held views, or resolving some of the disputes and mysteries, concerning those origins? We get little encouragement to believe so from one of the most erudite of recent writers who argued that 'the modern distribution of surnames is no safe guide' to their history (OES, p. 321). On the other hand, Lasker and Mascie-Taylor (1990, p. 2) believe that the most significant factor in that distribution is typically their 'circumstances of origin'.

Genealogists are never far from my mind. It is useful for them to know where families of particular surnames are located since the Middle Ages, at the micro-county if not the macro-country level, for which identifying the most reliable sources is a prerequisite. There is an important distinction to be made, however, between

- byenames, non-inherited second names commonly added in England in the early Middle Ages;
- surnames which are inherited;
- the genetic descent of particular individuals.

This book is largely concerned with the second of these three subjects of study.

You are therefore invited to join me in an exploration of those sources as vehicles for answering the sort of questions listed above and a host of side issues which they will undoubtedly throw up. That exploration is in three parts, each written in turn so that our starting-point, the description of the modern distribution of surnames (Part 1), was written before the research which lies behind Part 2, their distribution since the end of the Middle Ages; correspondingly, that was researched and written before Part 3, which tries to answer questions about origins, and their relationship to later distribution. Thus, questions and theories raised are genuinely those which occurred at the relevant stage, uncontaminated by, or not judiciously forgotten as a result of, later discoveries, and readers can be assured that the journey back in time is a genuine exploration, with little or no foreknowledge about what lies ahead. Useful insight may be gained by those who wish to start jumping to conclusions without an appropriate consideration of the lessons of earlier periods. Readers might also notice (and critics delight in finding) 'loose ends' when questions asked in Part 1 cannot be answered later.

Each Part will try to describe, in three main chronological periods, sources of information and techniques available to the surname detective, conclusions which earlier researchers have reached, and the application of all three to the study of surnames drawn from a sample group of one hundred listed in Appendix 4.

To start our journey, we will be armed with three weapons – the full set of UK phone books, a number of books about surnames, and some gazetteers which show the location of placenames. The first will help to suggest subjects and questions for research; the others will begin to try to solve them. The second brings into our armoury an impressive display of scholarly research from the last hundred years, some of the more modern ones examining the history of individual counties, together with articles about how to study the subject. Gazetteers are useful because so many of our surnames, perhaps up to half, are based on a place, but they need to carry a warning – in many cases, the places on which they were originally based might have changed their spelling quite dramatically. I have not met Macclesfield as a surname, for example, but plenty of Maxfields, an earlier version of that placename. Some places have been eroded by the North Sea, or (like Lomax, Hemingway or Wolstencroft far inland) abandoned for other reasons as places of human habitation, their placenames disappearing with them, leaving only the surnames like light still travelling from stars long dead.

Twentieth-century writing about British surnames has produced some interesting developments; there has been a regular stream of dictionaries which purport to show their original meaning. More recently, that market has been dominated by the excellent *Dictionary of British Surnames* by P. H. Reaney, which has been reissued several times since its first appearance in 1958; the latest, expanded, posthumous edition came out in 1991. Additionally, there is the *Penguin Dictionary of Surnames* (Cottle, 1978), and Hanks and Hodges (1988) which includes many names from continental Europe. At the same time several authors, including Reaney himself, have tried to generalise about the different ways in which surnames were created in this country, usually calling on a large and impressive range of specific examples (see, for example, Addison, 1978; McKinley, 1990; OES; Weekley, 1914).

The father of another group of writers interested in the geographical distribution of individual surnames was H. B. Guppy, whose *Homes of family names* (1890) was based on his extraction of the surnames of the farming community, whom he considered to be the least geographically mobile in his society, from entries in county directories. For an analysis of Guppy's work, see OES, pp. 323-7. (Henry Brougham Guppy was interested in this subject not, as one might suppose, because of his own name, but as a naturalist who wrote extensively on the distribution of flora.) Almost a century later, his work has been taken forward by a group of geneticists and biological anthropologists (particularly G. W. Lasker and C. G. N. Mascie-Taylor) who see advantage in using surnames in order to study the movement of the gene pool over several generations. 'Knowledge of the geographical distribution of surnames may provide insight into the genetic structure and evolution of populations' (Mascie-Taylor and Lasker, 1985). They believe that 'the effects of past migrations on distributions of surnames and on distributions of genes must have been similar' (Mascie-Taylor and Lasker, 1990). This study is still in its infancy as techniques are being refined, and work for this purpose on distributions earlier than those of the last hundred years has scarcely begun. It is hoped that research into earlier periods might be stimulated by Parts 2 and 3. Surprisingly, studies so far seem to have been concentrated on the migration of *any* name, whereas a careful examination of those arising from genetic causes (e.g. Redhead), having the advantage of an association with the current project for tracing Europe's genetic history, might prove far more revealing.

Geneticists have been assisted by the Guild of One Name Studies, formed in 1979, which caters for genealogists with a passion for the history of all persons who have held a particular surname. The Guild now includes well over 2,000 distinct names being researched (a register is available) and has greatly increased our knowledge of the way in which individual names have developed since their adoption as inherited surnames hundreds of years ago. Members of the Guild, either singly or in groups, collect not only as many specimens of particular surnames as possible, but also as much information on individuals, including their genetic connections, as the surname's rarity will allow. Over 2,600 sources available for so doing are contained in B. W. Christmas (1991). The steps in this present book are more limited in ambition, being confined to the history of the surnames themselves, but it is perhaps worth mentioning here that County Record Offices sometimes maintain extensive card indexes for different surnames, and that individual counties are the subject of a series of books by Stuart Raymond which indicate the existence of published sources available to genealogists and family historians.

Needless to say, one of my aims is to encourage others to follow in, and improve on the results of, my footsteps, to discover something of the history of some of the tens of thousands of surnames in England (and thereby something of the history of those who inherited or married into them), and to experiment with sources and techniques which have not been exploited for this book. Lasker (1983) reported over 32,000 different names in just the first quarter year's marriages indexes of 1975 (England and Wales only), so there is plenty of scope for the surname detective to be involved in some original research. Your local Family History Society (addresses from the local library, from the Federation of Family History Societies at the Benson Room, Birmingham & Midland Institute, Margaret Street, Birmingham B3 3BS, or the back of their six monthly *Family History News & Digest*) would be delighted to receive the fruits of your investigations so that others might benefit from it. The steps described in this book would provide a good basis for project work by such societies.

In 1956 the antiquarian, Marc Fitch, established the fund bearing his name for the support of projects in biography, genealogy and other research. He had been a long-time collector of historical instances of his own surname, so it was fitting that his generosity established the Marc Fitch Readership in the History of English Surnames at the University of Leicester, where he had been given an honorary D.Litt. A major outcome has been the English Surnames Series, whose volumes try to trace the early history of surnames in individual counties through a very detailed examination of local records, combined with a knowledge of philology and archaic languages. Although only five volumes have been published to date, the series is already revealing major variations in the way surnames developed in different parts of the country.

One volume, that for Lancashire, provides me with answers to the question I started with. Prestwich appeared as a surname early in the Middle Ages, close to the place which was already so named. Some of Mr Prestwich's genes had thus enjoyed a net movement of no more than a few hundred yards in six hundred years! A central purpose of this book will be the discovery of just how typical he was.

Part 1

The modern distribution of surnames

Introduction

The universe, it is said, started with the Big Bang; English surnames were more subject to Continuous Creation. When astrophysicists examine radiation from outside the solar system, they are looking back to the remnants of virtually a single point in time, from which everything has followed. The surname detective is also dealing with what are, for most historians, comparatively long periods of time, but the form and distribution of modern names is the result of an erratic evolution and slow acquisition of inherited surnames as well as migration, each of which has varied in different centuries and in different parts of the country. An electron is an electron is an electron – but a Jagger might be a Jager, a Jaegar, a Jaggard ...

We start with the present and the familiar by asking the apparently simple question 'What is the modern distribution of individual surnames?' The purpose of answering such a question is twofold – to establish a baseline of information about each name so that, in Parts 2 and 3, we can observe how that distribution has evolved, and to identify patterns of distribution as unique to each name as a fingerprint to a person so that the causes of those patterns can be sought. No two surnames have the same pattern, and we are each a part, however small, of one pattern or another. We will first discuss ways to analyse the available data, and then apply those methods to a variety of surnames.

Sources of information

We look in vain for a source of information about surnames which has been compiled for the expressed purpose of assessing their dis-

tribution. No publicly available source gives a list of all persons who
exist nowadays in the UK – the nearest fitting that description (but
closed to the public) are the decennial censuses, the Social Security
Central Register at Newcastle upon Tyne, and the National Health
Service Central Register at Southport. None is complete – the
former excludes, for example, offspring for whom child benefit has
not been claimed, and those who are able to avoid paying National
Insurance contributions; the latter might exclude some immigrants,
and especially anyone who does not register with an NHS doctor.
The census comes as near to perfect as we are ever likely to achieve,
but is not released for public inspection for one hundred years.
Modern electoral registers, now computerised, can be presented in
alphabetical order of name instead of street, but many areas still
refuse to make that sequence available to the public under the
cloak of the Data Protection Act; but even if all *were* made available, the physical difficulty for a surname detective to get access to
so many separate areas would probably make it impossible to use
on a national scale. (For geographically small areas, however, this
source might be very useful.) For all the above, see Rogers (1986).

The annual electoral register has the great advantage of being
presented as a snapshot in time on a 'qualifying date' (theoretically,
though not in practice, 10 October). For some surnames, the job of
extraction from electoral registers and phone books has already
been accomplished by an American firm called Halbert's Family
Heritage which sells the product – a list of names and addresses of
all known examples of a particular surname. The result, however,
cannot be transposed into the maps found later in Part 1 as they
are not based on boundaries coterminous with phone book areas
but on modern counties. Unlike the census, however, there are
significant omissions from electoral registers – up to 14 per cent in
normal times, according to the Office of Population Censuses and
Surveys' own estimates (Todd and Dodd, 1982), but perhaps more
since the introduction of the community charge in 1989 (Scotland)
and 1990 (England and Wales).

Given the above difficulties, I have no qualms about turning
instead to phone books as an alternative source for discovering how
surnames are currently distributed. They are not without their
problems, as we shall see, but for convenience they cannot be bet-
tered, and it is believed they now contain more householders (over
80 per cent) than the electoral register anyway. The full set is nor-

mally available in public libraries, though a branch library might have a set which is less up to date than those found in the local authority's central library, and they do not all stock the directory for the Republic of Ireland. David Hey (1993, pp. 53-8) gives some useful examples of the localisation of surnames identified through this source, while pointing out some of its inherent difficulties.

Counting phone book entries

Counting the number of people who have a phone is apparently very simple. If you seek accuracy, however, that simplicity is deceptive, and complete accuracy is unattainable. In order to assess the effectiveness of phone books in providing the data for studying the modern distribution of surnames, the following problems need to be recognised.

- Phone books are not issued simultaneously. Instead of providing a national snapshot of those on the phone, publication of the books is staggered over a period of time – perhaps up to two years in some cases. This means that a person moving from one area to another might appear in both or in neither, though of course the overwhelming majority will be in only one.
- Boundaries between directory areas are not constant; new areas are created from time to time, with the result that whole sections of the community may be found in a new book while they also remain in the old one, and overlapping areas have now been quite common for over twenty years. At the time of writing, for example, I am in the current North East Manchester directory (September 1991) and also in the newly created High Peak directory (August 1992). Individuals have the right to ask to appear in more than one book, for business or social reasons. Thus, Bishop Tucker, for example, appears in books 336 (Cambridge) and 337 (King's Lynn). Lasker and Mascie-Taylor did not use certain phone books in the London area for this reason and, in asking members of the Guild of One Name Studies to submit data on surnames, requested that such entries be counted in one area only. The difficulties in carrying out this request are so great that many of the resulting maps are believed by the authors to be slightly flawed. Unless the surname is very rare, however, it is

hard to believe that failure to eliminate second entries will have a significant effect, especially in the Banwell system described below. The use of CD-ROM (see below) would effectively overcome this problem for rarer names.

- Modern practices of cohabitation without marriage, and of marriage without change of bride's surname, have an unknown and unknowable effect of numbers, but you have to decide whether 'Mrs H. L. Smith' – probably but by no means certainly a widow – should be counted as a true Smith for the purpose of this exercise. Almost certainly she was not born a Smith; on the other hand, her presence implies that there had at least been a male Smith in that household. It is also possible that there are young male Smiths at that address. I suspect that the purist might wish to ignore all females, but in the calculations which follow, they have been included.

- Sometimes, more than one person with the same surname is shown as having the same phone number, evidently sharing the same premises. If only initials are given, this might refer to man and wife, or to two brothers (common still among farmers, for example). The former raises once again the problem raised in the last paragraph.

- Some people have more than one phone. In the case of solicitors, for example, it is normal for the business and domestic premises to be separate, and when both appear in the same book, one can be discounted. However, what if the solicitor lives in another directory area, or if that second address is occupied by someone with the same initials? Occasionally, one resident will have two phone numbers at the same address. In the 223 phone book for Northampton, M. Rogers even had two phone numbers on two different exchanges for the same address! (Note also that new phone companies, such as Mercury, have their numbers in the BT directories.)

BT issues the whole country's phone books on CD-ROM, so that you can see, at the touch of a key, the addresses of all 47 Ullathornes, for example, currently on the phone. However, few libraries take the trouble to hire the disk, and there is a 200 instance upper limit to the number of subscribers who can be shown at a single call; it is also copyrighted and subject to the Data Protection Act, out of date copies being returned and destroyed.

Merely counting the number of phones, or rather phone numbers, without having regard for the persons concerned, may lead to errors which vary in number considerably from one surname to another. A list for any surname could contain that surname as part of a firm. The A. E. Tinkler School of Motoring in Brighton has no domestic counterpart in the rest of the list, so you could count that as one entry; but A. E. Tinkler might live in an adjoining directory area, and only the keenest surname detective would go to the trouble of checking every area for that eventuality. Even then, he or she might be ex-Directory, an increasingly numerous category, or indeed might have died thirty years ago. For this book, arbitrarily, a sole A. E. Tinkler, whether '& Co' or not, has been included, but 'Tinkler & Co' has not been.

It should be added that anyone using phone books as a source for surname study is alarmed at the growing army of people who now choose to be 'ex-Directory'. Unlike ninety years ago, when the phone numbers were given in the books but without names attached, there is now no indication of how many are involved, though it is hoped that new electronic systems of tracing would give more confidence to those unfortunate enough to have been pestered in the past. Once again, however, the means of analysing all but the rarest names, described below, can eliminate the problem, on the understanding that there is no correlation between a particular surname and being ex-Directory.

Another decision, which might be of some significance in the case of the rarer names, is whether to count the occasional entry which is only a surname, without initials or indication of occupation. However, if you decide on a blanket ban on all firms, on the grounds that the domestic user is never resident there, you would be equally incorrect. There are many such instances, particularly shops such as newsagents, where the proprietor(s) live on the premises and have one number for both business and domestic purposes. Bold typeface in the directory is a hint that the firm does not have a domestic element at that address, but once again it is not foolproof. BT has begun to separate business and residential numbers in directories, starting with London, Birmingham, Bath & Swindon, Bristol & Weston-super-Mare, and Gloucester, greatly facilitating the count.

It should be said that some surnames are so common that the odd problem such as those above disappears into the crowd. In these

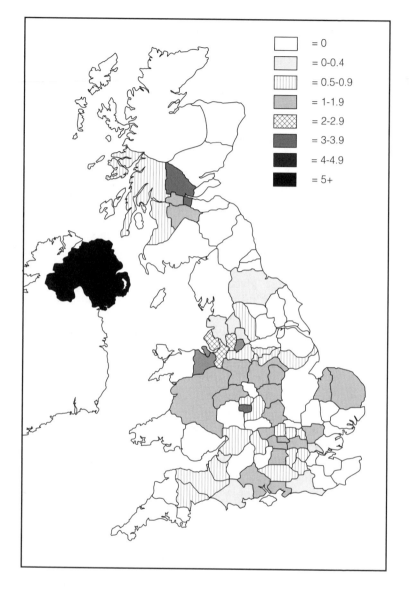

1.1a, b   Cully (224) *above*   **Culley** (806) *right*
Slight variations in the spelling of a name can show major differences in
distribution. (See page 22 for explanation of the key.)

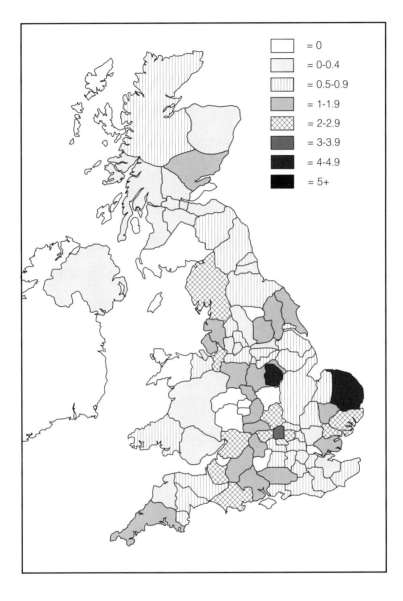

	= 0
	= 0-0.4
	= 0.5-0.9
	= 1-1.9
	= 2-2.9
	= 3-3.9
	= 4-4.9
	= 5+

cases, you may care to adopt a means of assessing the totals (as I have done with Smith, rather than counting them individually). Needless to say, you should build in some means of checking your assessments, by sampling for example, otherwise the exercise might prove to be a waste of time because of its inherent inaccuracy.

Finally, there is the thorny question of variations in the spelling of most names. I can think of few surnames for which such variations cannot be found, a fact which very considerably raises the total number of surnames in the UK. The Registrar-General's Annual Report for 1856, reprinted in part in *Local Population Studies* (Spring 1992), says that 'Until a comparatively recent period, an entire disregard of uniformity and precision in the mode of spelling family names prevailed, even amongst the educated classes, and many family Bibles and writings might be adduced as evidence that this was apparently less the result of carelessness than of affectation or design. While the sound was in a great measure preserved, the number of different surnames become greatly multiplied, by these slight orthographical variations, as well as by other corruptions ...' Such developments continue even in today's bureaucratic society, though not nearly so often as in former times.

Not all these earlier variations have developed into modern, inherited names, but a surprisingly large number have. The 'standardisation' of the spelling of names, largely but by no means entirely in the first half of the nineteenth century, resulted in a hardening up of the variation then in use by individuals (though the majority were illiterate) rather than by national consensus.

In some ways, this need not be a problem. Brown(e), Cuff(e), Foot(e), Kemp(e), or Wild(e) are easily recognised and accepted as different ways of spelling the same name, though curiosity may be aroused as to whether there are geographical differences between them (see, for example, Map 1.1). However, such 'trivial' differences may cause significant problems in a large number of cases. For example, following the name Tinker in most phone books (where there is no Tinkerbell café) is the surname Tinkler. Are these variations of the same name, and if so of which one? Whitfield and Whitefield might be different places, but each seems to have given rise to both as surnames. What of the addition of the letter 's' in so many names (Weaver-Weavers; Wood-Woods; and so on); are they from the same root?

The above examples are only too easy to find during your phone book search. However, there are many other variations which are not so obvious, but which nevertheless need to be identified if your exploration of a surname is to be as complete, and your conclusions as valid, as possible. Reference to Reaney and Wilson (1991) will quickly indicate an extraordinary variety of forms in which an apparently simple surname can appear, and their list is by no means complete. Genealogical works abound with horror stories such as Willis being spelled in eight different ways (Willis and Tatchell, 1984), or Dixon in thirty-seven different ways (Mander, 1984), though many of these forms are now archaic.

There is no guarantee that the variations will adjoin each other when placed in the strictly alphabetical order of a phone book – indeed, it is almost certain that they will not. Haworth, Howarth, Howard, Heyworth, Heyward and Hayworth might all be related genetically, but will be found widely separated in the phone books. Accordingly, considerable imagination will be needed in order to ensure that all possible variations are included. One of my former students, tracing the name Orrell which comes from the place near Wigan, identified variations which were then separately plotted on a map, and some interesting differences noted, suggesting that the name was more likely to be changed the further away from the original place the individuals lived. There are Orrills, largely though not entirely in Leicester, Orrellses in Shrewsbury, Orriells in Leeds, and even (recognising that well-known northern technique of adding a capital H to a word in order to demonstrate a touch of class), Horrells in Birmingham. This is a theme to which we shall return later.

How can you tell if you have located all possible surviving variations? Well, you cannot, nor can you be absolutely certain that the variations you have found are from the same root. The best you can do is to use maximum ingenuity and the surname dictionaries which will point to a few of the less obvious ones. Who would have thought that Blake is a variation of Black, for example, Camp of Kemp, Woosnam of Wolstenholme? To add to your other problems, authorities may differ as to whether they *are* from the same derivation. Weekley suggested that Bunyan and Benyon were derived from the same Welsh AbEnion, and Morgan and Morgan (1985, p. 93) appear to support that as a possible derivation; Reaney, however, (1967, 1991) avers that Bunyan is quite different, being either a nickname or an occupational name; neither writer refers to the numerous Bennions. Indeed, there are so many possible variations of this name that I have been able to draw no conclusions about it using the techniques which follow, and wish I hadn't included it in the list of 100 names in the first place!

Presentation of data

Once you have finished a count, the simplest form of presentation of the data is to prepare a map of the UK (most conveniently by template, or by tracing from an atlas), and to place one dot on the map for each domestic phone attributable to a particular surname. Map 1.2a is the simplest form of 'dot' map, giving a rough indication of distribution. It is useful to get into the habit of captioning each map with the surname concerned, the total number of those entries in the phone books, and the approximate dates. (Unless otherwise stated, all maps in Part 1 are derived from directories dated between 1984 and 1986.) Notice, incidentally, that it *is* for the whole of the UK – some of the results which follow might be significantly changed if we had confined the search to England and Wales.

Map 1.2 is feasible, however, only because of the relative rarity of the surname concerned. (I have found Spruce in only one book about surnames – Kneen (1937) believed that it meant Prussian.) For somewhat more numerous names, one dot, or different sizes of dots, for every five/ten/twenty phones has to be used, the number being adaptable for convenience. As a general rule, use the smallest reduction possible which allows different areas to be distinguished, and (of course) the largest map! This is the basis on which Lasker and Mascie-Taylor (whose principal interests are genetic rather than genealogical or social) produced their *Atlas of British Surnames* (1990), giving maps for the distribution of over 150 names (listed in Appendix 2), largely rare, and many supplied by members of the Guild of One Name Studies. A series of dots indicate the number of instances in each area in three bands – 1–4, 5–9 and 10+. Another way to represent the same data, whether on an individual or a proportional basis, is to work out for each area its percentage share of the total number of phones to a surname, and to shade the area accordingly.

One hundred of the commonest surnames were mapped by

Lasker (1985, also listed in Appendix 2); incidentally, the fifty most common surnames in England and Wales in the middle of the last century were listed by the Registrar General in his 16th annual report, 1856. The maps themselves are on the same basis, dots and varying sizes of squares representing the actual number of domestic phones counted, but each dot is accompanied by graphs showing, on east-west and north-south axes, the degree to which those numbers vary from what would have been a random distribution.

If you simply want to know, and to represent, where people of a particular surname now live, Maps 1.2a and b are perfectly acceptable, and easily constructed from data available to the general public. It is normally to be expected that there will be concentrations in the main urban areas (which have their own phone books, of course) and along retirement coasts. If you are lucky, you will find a significant number away from towns and cities (e.g. Map 1.2b), and this might be an early clue to the geographical origin of the name. Local areas may therefore prove just as interesting as the national maps. This exercise is useful not just for surname study, but also for identifying potential customers (locations of businesses) or distribution of ethnic groups which may remain identifiable through retention of distinctive surnames.

Often, however, the most numerous concentrations are living within urban areas which scarcely existed there when surnames became inherited. More significantly, the total population of the urban areas is large, almost by definition, so that we should expect a higher number of all surnames in towns, especially in London, and in those parts of the country which have proved popular places for retirement. The phone books of the major cities, in any case, cover very few rural areas, so their surname distribution has obviously been affected in two ways – not only has there been a massive inmigration over the last couple of centuries (much longer in the case of London); the effect is to submerge the surnames of the original inhabitants of the town under a sea of 'strangers', as they were once called.

So far, we still do not know how (or indeed whether) the current numerical distribution of an individual surname differs from that of the population at large. In trying to discover this, we hit two major problems. Phone directory areas do not correspond to any administrative boundary, BT (and the old Post Office) being a law unto itself for the convenience and efficiency of delivering the technical

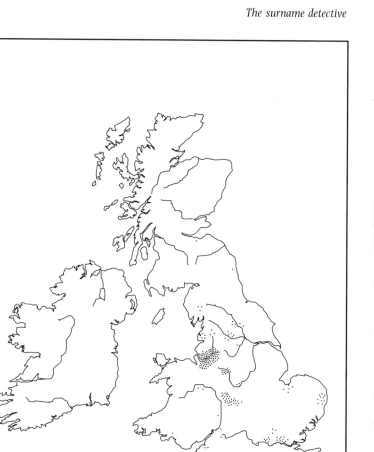

1.2a, b   Spruce
An example of a rare name which can show interesting concentrations
outside urban areas. Phone books can give local as well as area distributions.

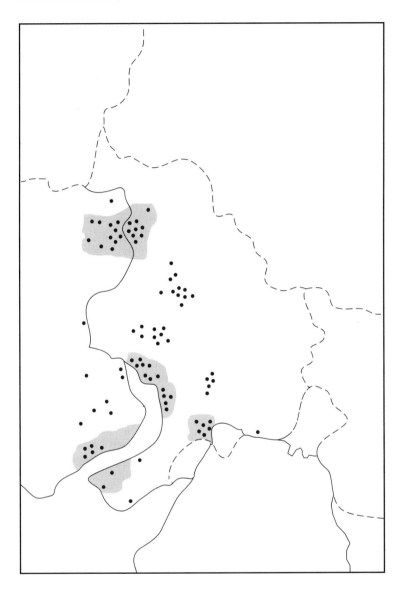

service. We may feign surprise that such a degree of irrational plan-
ning across departments has been allowed to happen with no
thought given to the consequent inconvenience to the surname
detective; but BT will be found to be distinctly unhelpful when it
comes to providing certain information such as the known population in its different areas. Suffice it to say that the largest area is
about fifty times more populous than the smallest. Maps such as
1.2, therefore, will be expected to skew concentrations to the areas
with the largest populations, and it is not at all surprising that the
maps for the less rare names in Lasker and Mascie-Taylor's atlas
begin to emphasise urban areas.

Secondly, even if we knew the information about population of
each area, a further problem occurs. Because BT does not publish
the statistics, we do not know how many people are ex-Directory,
though over 80 per cent of householders have a phone. However,
it is generally believed that areas with a high proportion of poorer
families, such as Liverpool, and those with a large student population, have fewer phones per head of population than elsewhere
(Rogers, 1986). There are major variations across social class as
well as area, 50 per cent more professionals than unskilled manual
heads of household having a phone.

We therefore need a way of ironing out differences in population
density and overlapping areas so that the true proportions of those
names can be revealed. Luckily, there is a relatively simple way of
bypassing both of these problems at the same time, by counting all
phone book entries and using the result as the total population in
each area. This is the basis of a method proposed by Donald Brett
(Brett, 1985). As life is too short to count the actual number of
phones, a rough estimate can be obtained by counting the number
of pages containing individual entries, though obviously the preface
and pages taken by advertisements have to be ignored. (For some
reason which is unclear, his estimates are consistently lower than
mine, though if the difference is evenly spread this makes little difference to the results. The number of phones increased rapidly
during the 1980s, and this might account for some of the discrepancy: the number of Spruces on the phone has risen from the 165
shown in Map 1.2a to over 400 in twenty years.) Brett himself goes
further by ascribing an average of 350 domestic phones on each
page, but prefers to use a quick-measure 'column-inch' guide. If
you try the former method, do not forget to add 33 per cent to the

number for those areas (such as London and Birmingham) which have four columns to the page instead of the normal three. The method is rough and ready – it ignores the fact that the proportion of non-domestic to domestic phones will vary from area to area, but it is nevertheless the most convenient basis for the calculations which follow.

The aim is to obtain a figure for each surname within a specified directory area which will indicate how far it is above or below the number which you would expect from an even distribution. Donald Brett calculates the fraction of the total for each name within each phone book, takes the largest proportion in the country, and converts all the others as percentages of that. One of my former students, Eric Banwell of Wells in Somerset, has proposed an alternative formula in order to reach a figure for the density of a surname irrespective of the size of the population of that area. For the mathematically minded, the formula used is:

$$c = \frac{\dfrac{a}{\Sigma a}}{\dfrac{b}{\Sigma b}}$$

where a is the number of instances of a particular surname being studied in that book, b is the number of pages in each book, and c is the required figure for that surname's comparative density.

For those who, like me, are regrettably deficient in maths, the following 'easy steps' of the process might be more useful.

1. Count the number of domestic instances of the surname you are studying in each book ('a' above).

2. Find the grand total of 1. in all areas (Σ a).

3. Divide the number in each book by the grand total (i.e. divide 1. by 2.) The resulting figures should vary from 0.000 to over 0.050.

4. Count the number of pages of entries in each book ('b' in the formula above).

5. Find the grand total of 4. in all areas (Σ b).

6. Divide the number of pages in each area in turn by that grand total. The resulting figure for each area should vary between 0.000 and about 0.050.

7. For each area, divide the figure obtained in 3. by the figure obtained in 6 ('c').

The result ('c') will vary from 0.0 in areas which have no instances of that surname, through 0.5 (in areas where you find only half the number of surnames compared with the figure you would expect if they were spread evenly throughout the population), 1.0 (average), 2.0 (twice the number expected from a random distribution), 3.0 (three times) and so on.

Thus, both Brett and Banwell eliminate many of the problems identified earlier – the consequences of varying sizes of area, varying population densities, and overlapping areas, leaving only the degree to which the surname is over- or under-represented in each. In the Banwell method, if a surname was spread evenly throughout the population, each area would have a final figure of 1.0. The degree to which this is not the case is a product of the history of that particular surname and might therefore tell us something about it – perhaps the nature or location of its origin, and its subsequent geographical mobility. Separating these two is a major challenge, and might prove impossible to assess in some cases.

All that remains is how to represent the final figure visually. Attractive maps can be drawn indicating the final figures positioned in each area concerned, and drawing isobars connecting each level of density, or percentage banding, the levels being decided arbitrarily (see Map 1.3). The result has an attractive, not to say dramatic, visual impact, though the preparation of each map can be rather time consuming. An alternative method of presentation requires access to the BT area divisions. Any library which houses a complete collection of phone books should also have a map showing the boundary of each area. This map can be copied, and each area shaded according to its level suggested in 7. above.

These maps are not without their drawbacks. Large geographical areas such as the Highlands and Islands cannot be subdivided to enable us to see whether a surname is concentrated in specific areas or scattered evenly throughout the area. For example, in Map

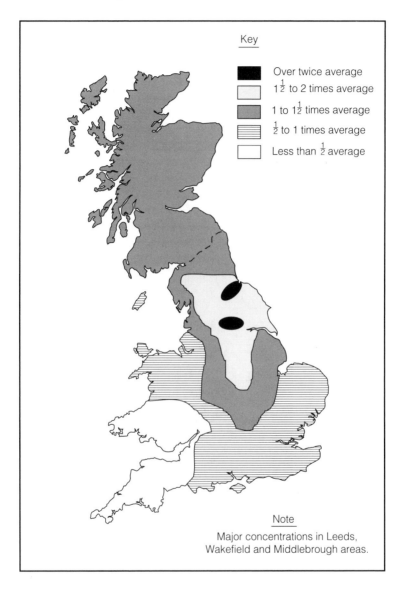

Key

■ Over twice average

▨ 1$\frac{1}{2}$ to 2 times average

▨ 1 to 1$\frac{1}{2}$ times average

▤ $\frac{1}{2}$ to 1 times average

□ Less than $\frac{1}{2}$ average

Note

Major concentrations in Leeds,
Wakefield and Middlebrough areas.

1.3 Walker (based on over 50,000 telephone directory entries)
Eric Banwell's isobar maps can reveal meaningful distributions for the commonest names. (Reproduced by kind permission of Eric Banwell).

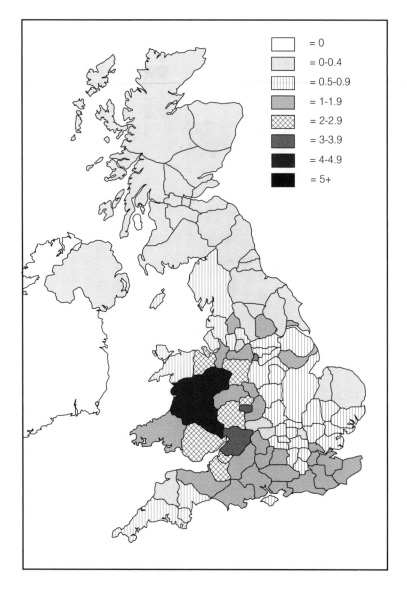

1.4   Weaver (4,137)
Maps might help to choose between different theories for the origin of individual names – Weaver is either occupational or a Cheshire locative.

1.4, Weavers are not really spread evenly over Shrewsbury and Mid-Wales, though the map itself is useful for pinpointing the need for a local map along the lines of Map 1.2b to discover just that. The maps can also be fairly meaningless if there are so few examples of a surname that they can be represented by the method in Maps 1.2a and b – one dot per phone. There might also be a tendency to give a false impression when relatively few examples are found in an area whose population is itself very small.

This raises the question of the minimum number of grand total instances below which a Banwell map is not worth constructing. The most accurate answer is also the most unhelpful: that a minimum of, say 500, still leaves some maps below that level quite useful, and some maps above the level misleading. Map 1.5, for example, suggests a high concentration of the surname Drinkwater in the Isle of Man; but that effect is quite legitimately produced by only nine instances of the name. Drinkwater has been variously described, e.g. by McKinley (1990, p. 162), Weekley (1916, p. 252), as a nickname in origin for a drunkard, a landlord, or someone too poor to buy beer; it has also been considered a corruption of Derwentwater. The map suggests that a placename origin is not so far-fetched, but not in Cumbria. Kneen (1937, p. 102) disarmingly suggests that the meaning is 'self-explanatory', but does reveal that the family had migrated to the Isle of Man in the early nineteenth century.

Try to construct a map for Merryweather: the incidental movement of a few individuals a couple of generations ago could have caused gaps of 0.0 or concentrations of over 5.0. In other words, the fewer the instances of a surname, the less a Banwell map is likely to tell you about its history, and the more you will find wide variations in final figures across adjoining areas.

The presentation arising from the calculation based on this formula is very revealing, but it creates another problem. The original aim was to see whether the current distribution of surnames can be seen in any way as an echo, however faint, of their origin, and whether it can reveal anything about the migration of people over long periods of time. The purpose and effect of the Banwell maps, however, is to hide the latter by converting the number of surname holders to a proportion of the total population. Thus if, say, Cartwrights moved *in normal numbers* from Staffordshire into the main Lancashire and midlands conurbations with the rest of the

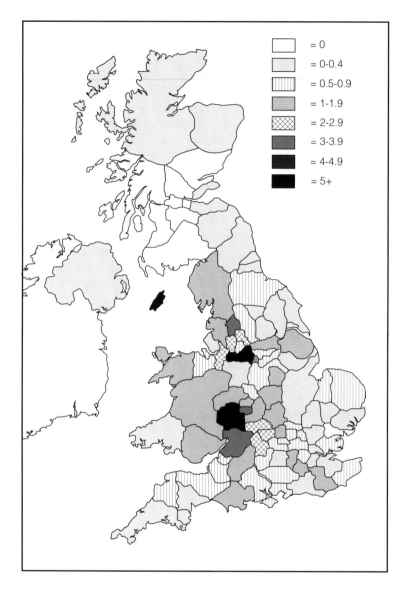

	= 0
	= 0-0.4
	= 0.5-0.9
	= 1-1.9
	= 2-2.9
	= 3-3.9
	= 4-4.9
	= 5+

1.5 Drinkwater (1,332)

Concentration of Drinkwater in the Isle of Man, though not elsewhere, is probably a statistical aberration.

population, the Banwell map would not reveal that movement.

To summarise, Banwell may tell us something about origins, but a Spruce map must be developed to reveal likely patterns of movement – not one map, of course, but a series, spread over time. As we have seen, however, the normal Spruce map (one dot for each phone) breaks down when they are too numerous, and the use of different symbols to represent multiples is not easily converted by the eye into comparative densities. There are two ways of doing so – either by a direct scaling down of numbers combined with the use of more levels of shading in order to cater for the vast range in those numbers; or shading to show the *proportion* of total instances of a surname in each area (the calculation already made in step 3. on page 21 above). The latter may be more convenient, but will not permit comparison of the densities of *different* surnames, of course. The former discourages direct comparison with the Banwell map for the same surname.

In the event, however, the differences between Spruce and Banwell are obvious only for the commonest of names. With the exception of London, which normally has up to 5 per cent or more of the instances of any surname, the great centres of population do not have the massively distorting effect which common sense would suggest. Take Darlington, for example (Map 1.6). Normally there is a difference of no more than one degree of shading for the same area in the two types of map. However, in the case of names which, in origin, were fairly evenly spread across the country, we clearly perceive movement into the large urban areas (see the maps for Chapman and Smith in Lasker, 1985, for example).

The conclusion seems inescapable. The expansion of large towns since the eighteenth century has been achieved by increases in the reproductive rate of their citizens, by immigration from abroad, and/or by migration over *relatively short distances* from the British countryside – not from one end of the country to another. This is why Smith reveals urbanisation: the name was common enough everywhere so that an expanding town was never far away. But Fullers stay in the south-east and Tuckers stay in the south-west, on the whole – they have not been attracted in large numbers to the industrial north or midlands.

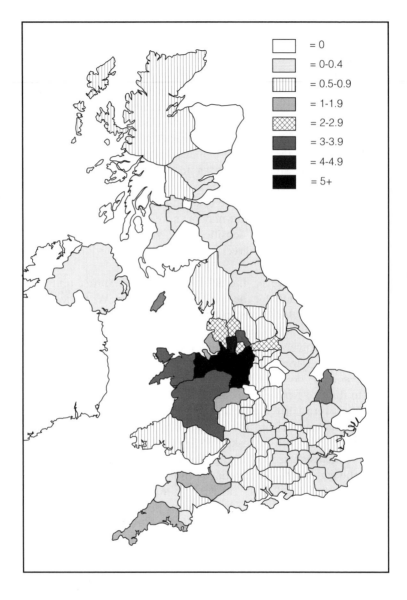

1.6   Darlington (1,250)
Darlington shows no connection between surname and placename.

Subjects for investigation

We now turn to my choice of subjects for research, which are designed to be merely a 'taster' for the tens of thousands of surnames which you might care to investigate. I had thought of taking them entirely at random, or based on my own friends and relatives, or (as has been done before by, for example, Weekley, 1914, pp. 2-5) from the names of members of famous cricket or football teams, and so on. What I have done is to choose 100 surnames which fall into specific, illustrative categories (spiced, for me at least, with a few in which I had a personal interest). Additionally, Eric Banwell has kindly given me the results of several of his own researches, and I have been given access to a number of others at various times – I am very grateful to the authors concerned.

One of my criteria for inclusion in the list was that the names should have relatively few alternative spellings, and were identified by a combination of advice from Reaney and Wilson (1991) and common sense, with which I am not particularly well endowed. To research so many names has been very time consuming, and I was not prepared to extend that much further by having to search for many variations of the same name within the 103 phone books concerned. Even so, some names refused to conform to my requirement, and if I were to be studying only a handful of names, I would not try to exclude them – the distribution of variations can cast some interesting light on their history, as already suggested. (I started out with Shields, but abandoned that surname as a hopeless task, as it quickly had to incorporate Sheilds, Shiels, Shiells, etc.).

The categories from which the hundred surnames in Appendix 4 were drawn were as follows:

- Names which are based on the name of a specific place ('locative' names, supposedly more common in certain parts of the country such as the north of England and Cornwall; see Appendix 1).
- Names which are based on a type of area such as a marsh or a hill; (toponymics, supposedly more common in the south-east, especially Sussex).
- Names which are based on occupations (many of which will end with ...er, though this can be as misleading as it is incomplete).
- Different names which arise from the same occupation.

- Names which are based on nicknames.
- Names which are based on personal (i.e. Christian, or first) names.
- Names which are of relatively recent origin through immigration into the UK.
- Names which have been subject to major migrations within the UK.
- Names whose origins are in dispute, or not known.
- Names which are either very common or very rare.
- Names in which I have a personal interest and therefore curiosity.

We started this quest with three major sources of information easily available to all – surname dictionaries, gazetteers and phone books. The last have now been used as the basis for two kinds of maps, which show where surnames are currently distributed in relation either to area (e.g. Map 1.2) or to other people (Map 1.3). What we now need to explore is how much these maps might tell us about the history of each name, especially in the light of the problems listed pp. 9–10. The two kinds of maps give rise to different sorts of questions.

The number of instances of a surname

Why should there be more instances of one locative surname than another, even allowing for multiple examples of that place name in the gazetteers? Is it true that the larger the place, the fewer examples of the surname? (How few are called Rochdale, yet how many are called Butterworth, Chadwick, Clegg, Hamer, Wardle, Whitworth, all places within Rochdale parish?) How few are called London, Birmingham, Manchester, Cardiff, Edinburgh, Swansea, Sheffield ... ? Why do some places seem to give rise to no surnames – e.g. Purston in Northamptonshire and the West Riding of Yorkshire? (Or have all the Purstons died out, short of enough Y-chromosomes to maintain a critical mass?) Why should there be more called Webb than Weaver if they mean the same thing? If shoemaking was an important trade, why are so few called Shoemaker, or Cordwainer? (Shoesmith, it turns out, was a man who made horseshoes.) Why are there almost twice as many called East as there are called South, twice as many Norths as Easts, and twice as many Wests as Easts, Norths and Souths added together? (Were there originally over ten times as many Wests as Souths, have Wests been ten times more prolific, or are there more places called West?) And why, oh why are there so many Smiths?

The geographical distribution of a surname

Obviously, all names will be affected by the uneven distribution of the total population, and by patterns of mobility which have driven people for economic or social betterment, or a place in the sun, for hundreds of years. Given that, how far does the present pattern of distribution of, for example, Pollard (meaning bald) or Redhead, reflect medieval location of those physical characteristics? Are Jaggers in the north midlands now because that is where all Jaggers originated or simply because jaggers were called by other names in different parts of the country? Alternatively, is this merely a regional variation of Jaggard, a diminutive, or 'hypochoristic' of Jack? Are variations in spelling likely to be found where the name is common, or where it is very rare? Were people given a place-name because they lived in it, or because they had once lived there?

There are one or two general issues which override many of these questions. How far has the numerical or geographical history of a surname been determined by the number of sons who survived to marry and generate more? Are even major differences in the number of instances or in regional distributions merely the result of the vagaries of the Y-chromosome, so that they have little relationship now to the origin of the name? Secondly, is there a way of approximating a person's likely number of descendants over hundreds of years? Sturges and Haggett (1987) suggest figures which would allow several hundred descendants over the few centuries since medieval times, and a cursory examination of what is known about completed family size during that period would lead me to believe their estimates to be quite modest.

Surnames and migration

The evidence suggests that, on balance and only on balance, the current distribution of surnames is neither random nor remote from their place of origin and, as the remainder of Part 1 is based on that premise, it is worth spending some time looking at that evidence. Locative names are often thought to provide the best, though by no means the only, basis for examining how far migration rather than origin has played a significant contribution to that distribution. If there can be established a link between the place and where people of that surname now live, then by choosing places of which there is only one example in the country we can establish the likelihood of using the placename as a litmus test of migration, especially as it seems well established that such surnames became inherited up to a couple of centuries earlier than others and therefore have had much more time to move.

Of all categories of surname, those based on a placename are the most numerous, though not all will be easily recognised as such, and the proportion seems to vary from one part of the country to another – there are very few in Wales, for example, but large numbers in the north of England. To P. H. Reaney, this association between name and origin was so obvious that he omitted to include most examples in his *Dictionary of British Surnames* even though he had collected the relevant data (this omission has now been made good in the 1991 posthumous edition). However, it would be equally perverse to suggest that the origin of locative surnames correlates so well with their present distribution that we should exclude them from a list of subjects for research.

As a measure of mobility, however, they cannot be equalled if, as is believed, the point of origin of the family was in the place concerned. If you are in any doubt as to the possibility of a name being a placename, I can thoroughly recommend the Ordnance Survey Gazetteer of Great Britain and the census index of placenames which can be found in large public libraries. The former is far more complete than any other gazetteer. (A combination of the latter and Reaney's dictionary judiciously placed on my knee suggested an origin for most queries on my local radio phone-in series.)

I took an interest in Sladen when one of my sons married a Sue Sladen from Milford Haven in South Wales. She had been told that it was a Lancashire name, but the gazetteers did not include it; yet it is clearly locative, because of the suffix ...den. The phone distribution of Sladen and its variants (Sladden, Sladin, Sladdin) suggests three possible areas of origin – Bradford, the adjoining north-east Manchester, and Nottingham (Map 1.7a). A closer examination of the three areas along the lines on p. 17 suggests investigating north-east Manchester, where the numbers are excessive compared with those of the normal population (Map 1.7b). Enquiries among those who know the area of Rochdale well show Sladen as a tiny, uninhabited area just outside Littleborough between the roads to Todmorden and Halifax. It seems likely, therefore, that Sladdin is a trans-Pennine variation, and that the Nottinghamshire Sladens are descended from an earlier migration – we shall try to see in Part 2 how to test that theory. Meanwhile reference to ESS4 shows that McKinley had identified this as yet another Rochdale township to generate a surname, as it must have been inhabited during the Middle Ages.

Also among my 100 names, the meaning of Pinchbeck was far from clear, but it is a civil parish near Spalding in Lincolnshire. (The old, proper names of counties have been used in this book for convenience, as well as to remember their passing with much sorrow.) Map 1.8a shows the location of 196 Pinchbecks (and variants) on the phone, together with Pinchbeck itself. Purslow (with a sole variant Pursloe), chosen as a desperate bid to please my eponymous editor, is a placename, and a substantial number are seen to be living very near, if not in, the place concerned (Map 1.8b). John Titterton (1990) demonstrates how the method can be used to pinpoint the origin of a placename which has indeed totally disappeared – or changed so radically that the origin is uncertain. Furthermore, there is a tendency for the sons of migrants to return to where their fathers had come from (Lasker, 1985). Lasker and Kaplan (1983) showed that locative names are 90 per cent more likely to be near their point of origin than randomly scattered.

Eric Banwell's own investigations included his own name, of course, which is a place, together with Binning, Duckett, Durston, Ham, Laver, Mapstone, Pitman and Tutton, all of which show a remarkable concentration in their areas of origin, and all on the eastern side of the Bristol Channel.

However, I would not like to give the impression that all placenames are now surrounded by a penumbra of their equivalent surnames, even when such exist. Some, indeed, seem to have become totally divorced from their origin. Darlington is a startling case in point (see Map 1.6). There are so few Darlingtons living in County Durham, and so many in Cheshire, Shropshire and Staffordshire, that I am tempted to think that it did not originate in the north-east. There is no other place called Darlington in the country, nor

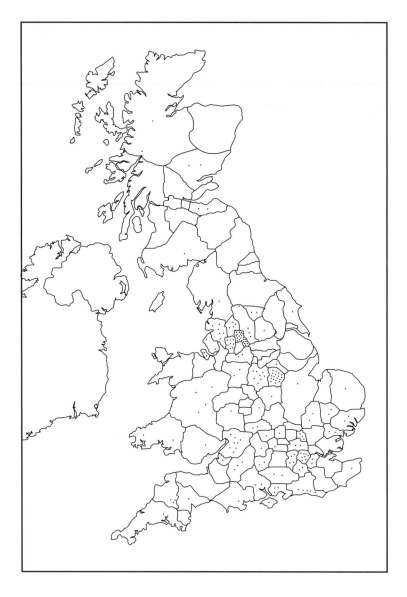

1.7a, b   Sladen
With ...den as a suffix, this is clearly a placename – but where did it originate?

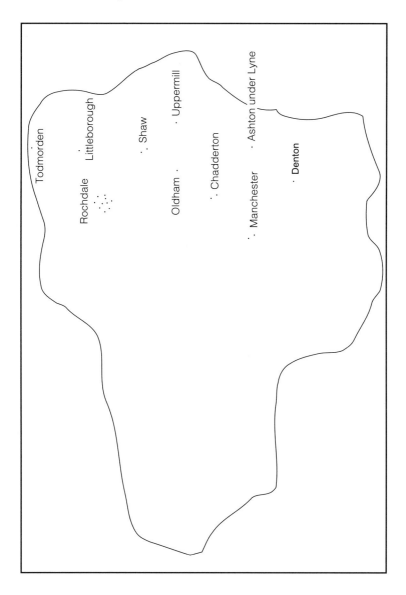

1.8a, b   Pinchbeck *above*   **Purslow** *right*
The relationship between a locative (placename) surname and the place itself is not always straightforward.

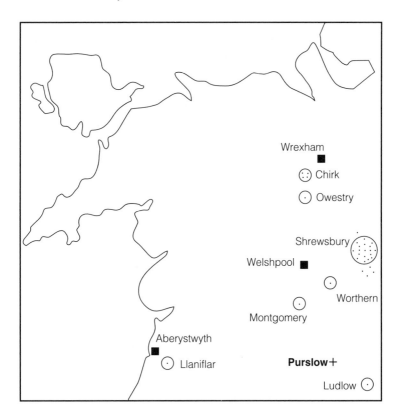

is there an Arlington, which might have acquired a d' (e.g. through a John de Arlington) within the counties concerned. There are, however, many lost places which now survive only in the form of surnames so we will leave a large question mark over Darlington, and refer it forward to Parts 2 and 3 for solution. Cheshire also seems to have attracted a large number of Washingtons.

Lasker has asserted that 'place-name surnames generally arose when individuals moved away from the place and these moves would more often have been to distant places in the case of town and city dwellers than for villages' (Lasker, 1985, p. 68). We will need to examine the first of Lasker's assertions in Part 3, but the second, which sounds eminently plausible, needs future investigation. Similarly, Morgan and Morgan (1985) found that 'The place name is used most often when a person or family moves to another district; there is then a very strong motivation to attach the place-name of origin to the person's name. If the move takes place in an English-speaking neighbourhood, there is a good chance (in the early or formative period) that the place-name will become a surname'. Reaney is more liberal, believing that they derived from 'where the man held land, or the place from which he had come, or where he actually lived' (*Dictionary*, 1976 ed., p. xv), giving emphasis to the second specifically in the case of people living in early medieval London.

It is interesting to note McKinley's assertion (1990, p. 201) that locative surnames were most common among the landholding classes, and we shall return later to discuss the relationship between surnames and social class. The earliest of the inherited locative surnames certainly seem to be associated with the inheritance of estates by primogeniture, with examples of junior males inheriting neither estate nor surname. Darlington is by no means the only locative name to be dispersed far from its point of origin, though they appear to be a minority. McKinley (1990, pp. 30, 66–70) identifies a number based on 'a series of towns along the mediaeval Great North Road', a finding which was replicated recently by Alan Crosby (1993) in Lancashire.

Another type of test to be applied in order to see how far surnames have travelled from their points of origin exploits the fact that some names of physical features or occupations were also region-specific. Probably the best-known example comes from the woollen industry in which the process of trampling the cloth in a trough, to thicken and whiten it, was called fulling in the south-east, tucking in the south-west, and walking in the west midlands, north, and in Scotland, a point on which all authorities seem to agree. According to McKinley (1990, p. 143) 'traces of the original state of affairs have not entirely disappeared' from current surname distributions, and the evidence of Maps 1.3, 1.9 and 1.10 suggests that this is an understatement. The initial concentration has certainly dispersed, but the regions of origin still seem very plain indeed. (For other versions of these particular name maps, see Brett (1985); for Fuller and Walker, see Ecclestone (1989); for Walker see also Lasker (1985). Appendix 2 indicates the location of published distribution maps for other surnames.)

Other occupations are region-specific not because of the use of different words to describe the same job, but because of the nature of the local economy. Ashburner is suggested by Addison (1978) as a Sussex name, associated with the ironmaking industry, but the current distribution would indicate that only Bedfordshire now has any significant concentration in the south of England, whereas the Lake District (which also had a thriving iron industry during the Middle Ages), abounds with them. Perhaps we can investigate the earlier history of the name in Parts 2 and 3 to see if Addison was correct, but Weekley adds to the confusion by suggesting (1916, p. 226 n. 1) that it can also be abbreviated to Ashburn.

Redhead, unlike Whitehead, has not been subject to alternative interpretation as to origin – all writers agree that it is a nickname referring to colour of hair. Unlike almost all other surnames, however, Redhead suggests that a double check on migration should be possible. Just as the surname has been inherited, so has the red hair and, although we might expect some differences in distribution allowing for transmission by married women *nées* Redhead, it would cast considerable doubt on the above account of the slow dispersal of surnames if people with red hair and people called Redhead were found in radically different places.

Map 1.11 indeed suggests at first glance some major differences. However, people in Wales would not have been called 'Redhead' even if they had red hair – not only is the proportion of nickname surnames very low; there is no Welsh word for red-headed, the closest being Gough (which *is* found as a surname in the west of England also; Morgan and Morgan, 1985, pp. 71–3, give a number of alternative spellings). Similarly in Ireland and Scotland, it is very

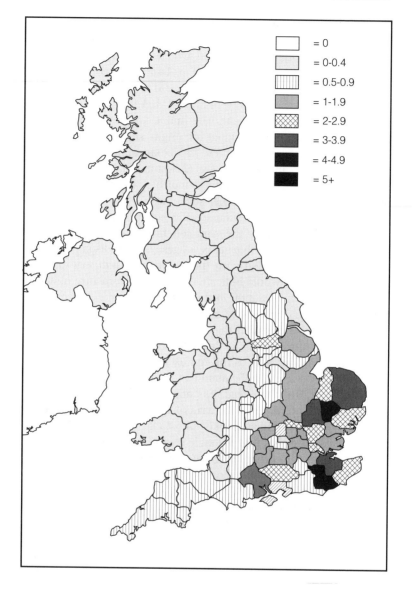

1.9, 1.10 Fuller (6,853) *above*   **Tucker** (7,924) *right*
Two words for the same industrial process used in different parts of the
country; Walker (see Map 1.3) is another.

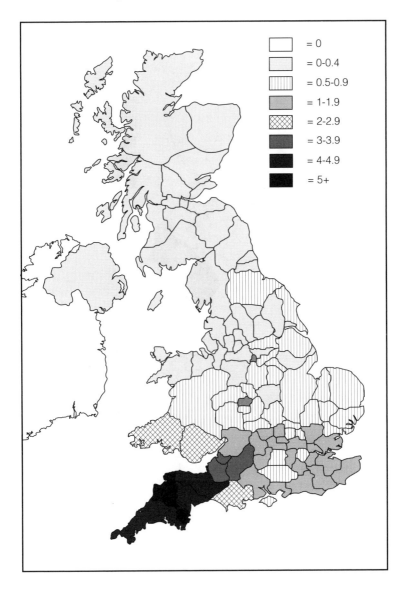

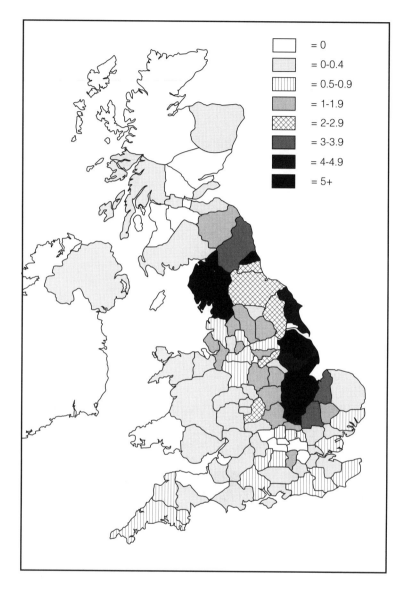

1.11   Redhead (889)

Redhead is still most commonly found where there are redheaded people, with possible racial implications.

unlikely that the word Redhead would have been given to a person with red hair – in Ireland, it might have been Flanagan, Flannery, or Flynn, though Redhead itself can be found in thirteenth-century Scotland. To apply the genetic comparison, therefore, it is safe to use only England, and a remarkably strong correlation then becomes apparent, with people called Redhead, and people with red hair, being commoner to the north-east of Watling Street (a line from Chester to London) where there were Danish and Norwegian settlements centuries before the Conquest. (There is a reported prejudice against 'red-haired Danes' in Cornwall, but it is thought that the immediate genetic origin of the immigrants concerned was Irish; see Thomas, 1973.) Support for a correlation with the distribution of people with red hair comes from Beddoe (1885) who mapped the birthplaces of 13,800 deserters from the armed forces whose descriptions were issued in 'Hue and Cry' between 1870 and 1885. Analysis showed the east and north to have above average numbers of those with red hair.

So far, then, we have uncovered no hard and fast rules about the relocation of surnames over the last five to seven hundred years from their points of origin. It does seem, however, that on the basis of the examples so far the modern epicentre of a locative name, which was given to only a few families, perhaps only to one, and which might have been subject to individual whim or misfortune many generations ago, can still be found close to its own place-name *or may now be removed far from it*, especially towards the urban centres – look how the Pinchbecks have gradually moved north and west, so there are three times more of them in Hull than in mid-Lincolnshire nowadays. On the other hand, names which derive from physical characteristics, from a dialect, or from occupations, which were themselves localised and adopted by a large number of families, have been much more resistant to change. Whim and misfortune does not affect them all, or even the majority. The dispersal of the name may be clearly visible, yet at the same time, the geographical area of origin is unmistakable.

P. H. Reaney criticised Guppy (see below, p. 101) for assuming that the distribution of names when he was writing in the late nineteenth century was still a reflection of their points of origin. How much worse a century later, if he is correct. (My four sons are now living in Bedford, Leeds, Pennsylvania and Swindon!) However, it appears that, if the above examples (which are acknowledged to be few enough, indeed) are typical in the relationship between their origins and modern distribution, we might have reached a conclusion which can be used as the basis for asking questions about other surnames whose origins are by no means as clear. The rashness of such a suggestion is all the more startling when we remember our normal impression of migration over long periods, especially since the industrial revolution two centuries ago. During the nineteenth century, the proportion of people living in urban areas changed from about three in ten to about eight in ten, the balance shifting by mid-century, and the extent of movement implied by that change does not seem consonant with the suggestion of extraordinary conservatism coming from the surname maps. What seems to have happened is that whereas the total number of moves has been very great indeed, their average length has not been great – even nowadays, let alone a couple of centuries ago, the average distance moved by individuals already living in England and Wales is under ten miles.

As Mascie-Taylor and Lasker (1985) conclude from their study of the 84 commonest names found in the first quarter's marriage indexes for 1975 in England and Wales (165,510 persons), 'the present heterogeneity of distributions of common surnames indicates the slow rate of their diffusion since many of them originated as much as seven hundred years ago but still display distinctive geographical patterns'. Each surname is distributed in a unique pattern – and the commoner the surname, the *more* likely it is that it can reveal the nature of its origin. I am very conscious that this offers an alternative perspective to that of David Hey who believed that 'counting common surnames such as Turner or Walker will not prove a worthwhile exercise' (1993, p. 53) and must try later to explain why this difference of view has emerged.

Some guidelines on the interpretation of surname maps

Before proceeding into the unknown, it may be useful to summarise the way in which a combination of hard evidence and common sense might help to interpret maps which are going to represent a wide variety of interesting and mysterious surnames. The first two have already emerged during the discussion of earlier maps.

- It will not be surprising to find that, if there are relatively few instances of surnames, say under 1,000 in the UK, there will be quite dramatic differences in level of shading across *adjoining* geographical areas, as it needs only a small number of families to make a disproportionate impact on the final figure for each – very obvious, for example, is the absence of Garlicks in Harrogate, Darlingtons in Burton-on-Trent and Nottingham, or Spicers from north Devon.

- Locative and rarer surnames are more likely than others to have drifted away from their original source, though many are still surprisingly close to it. Paul Hair (1976) found this with the family of Luggers in Herefordshire, which disappeared about a hundred years ago despite surviving there for at least five hundred years. Dearnleys had disappeared from Rochdale by the sixteenth century (only to reappear over four hundred years later); Ullathornes left the Lake District in the Middle Ages, moving via Yorkshire to London and to Manchester (Ullathorne, 1992, researched by one of David Hey's students.)

- It occasionally needs only one person to trigger a difference in shading level, even with the commoner surnames. Unless divided in a major way across the country (e.g. Rogers or Smith), your eye should try to ignore the difference of one level and concentrate on differences of two or more levels.

- The purpose of moving from a Spruce to a Banwell map is to remove the inevitable magnetic effect of the large populations in urban areas; if surnames remain represented at high levels in large cities, it is either because their meaning is associated with the life of a medieval town rather than the countryside, or, more likely, because the name is of relatively recent origin in the UK, through immigration. It is notable that the maps in Lasker (1985) for Kaur, Mistry and Patel all show how families of relatively recent immigrants are located in the major cities; and even Cohen, which has been here many times longer, still shows the same characteristic, with mainly doctors and solicitors venturing first out of the urban areas.

- Hopes to identify the area of origin of certain nicknames might be dashed by the 'Little John' syndrome, and use of fauna and flora which are not necessarily local at the point of origin.

- If there are no areas showing more than twice the national aver-

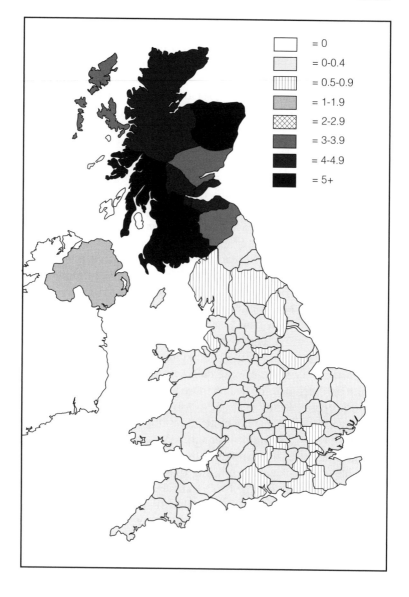

1.12a, b   Murdoch (3,169) *above*   **Murdock** (453) *right*
Another slight spelling variation which suggests two quite distinct origins.

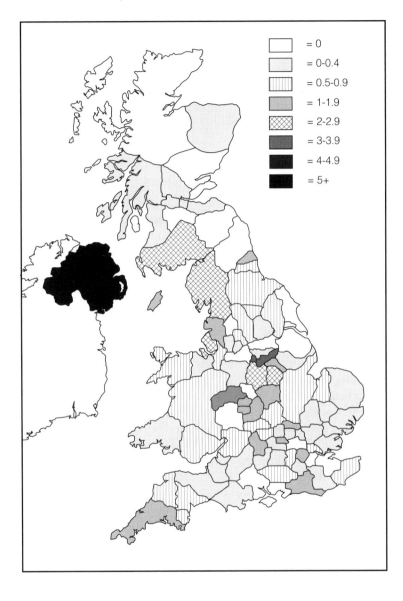

age or more, the name must have been generated over a wide
area, and by a large number of families (see, for example, Map
1.25).

• Conversely, if there are a large number of areas (i.e. say, more
than half) at level 0, the name must be rare and have few points
of origin whereas the number of areas showing maximum levels
is dependent on the number of levels chosen for presentation purposes.

Surname variations

How should variations in spelling be interpreted? Is there any significance, either regional or etymological, in the fact that almost all
names can and do appear in different forms? The orthodox
genealogical answer will be that such variations arose at random
when most people before the mid-nineteenth century could not
read or write, and there is ample evidence that, among those who
could, the same person could use different spellings of the name
even on the same page of writing. Alas, even my own great-great-
grandfather brought shame to the family by signing his will and
testament 'Rodgers', but I suppose deathbed could be adduced as a
mitigating circumstance.

Normally, spelling in documents before the twentieth century
was the result of how *other people* thought a name should be
spelled, rather than formal agreement or individual whim. This
explanation, however, tends to be self-cancelling, as the next
person to use the name might spell it differently again. In any case,
the name Murdoch/Murdock alone gives sufficient encouragement
to treat all variations as potentially worth tracking, especially if
instances of each are in significant numbers. I had assumed Murdock to be a Sassenach corruption of Murdoch, but Map 1.12b
clearly suggests the Irish origin of the latter spelling, and the only
corruption of either, evident from the phone books, is Murduck
which appears nine times, no further north than Hemel Hempstead.

There is no doubt that rare enough names which left their original area were subject to sometimes significant variations. Reaney
(OES, pp. 44–5) gives many ways in which common elements of
placenames have changed over time. Although most of the Orrell
family kept to the original spelling, places remote from Wigan are

seen to use variations which have become fixed in certain small areas. In the case of commoner names, which would have been familiar to scribes all over the country, the explanation of strangeness of name will not hold, for it appears that the variations themselves have taken over as the normal way of spelling over very wide geographical areas.

The simplest variation of all, reflecting normal spelling before the nineteenth century, is the addition of the letter 'e'. In some cases, such as Kemp(e), this is now a relatively rare variation, and you will find it in only ones and twos (up to eight in south-west phone districts) across the country; in other cases, conversely, such as Jolliff(e), the additional 'e' has taken over to such an extent that Jolliffs are overrun except in Leeds, Oxford and the extreme south-west. There are names, however, such as Foot(e) or Cull(e)y (Map 1.1) in which both versions vie with each other on more or less equal terms.

Foote has ramified far more than Foot in the east of Scotland and around Blackburn, though total figures suggest that a mere popularity of spelling in the first century of industrialisation is sufficient to account for the differences. In the case of Cully/Culley, however, although the words sound the same, the extra 'e' in the middle of the word rather than at the end has to be of potential significance because the suffix ...ley often (though not always) denotes a place. Sure enough, there seems to be a major difference in the ways in which these two surnames were created, both geographically and etymologically (see Map 1.1). Knowing one Culley descended from an Irish family, however, I think it may be that others have had their name anglicised, but this would not account for so many. Perhaps Culley is itself a variation of Colley (or Collie). Lasker and Mascie-Taylor (1990) provide a number of contrasting maps for different spellings of the same surname (Atwell/Attwell/Attewell, Cuff/Cuffe, Crabb/Crabbe, Keats/Keates) and, provided there are a significant number of instances, there are obvious similarities in the overall patterns even though there are different emphases.

Rodgers and Rogers once again appear to reflect early alternatives of spelling the same name, the added 'd' infection having a severe grip in south-west Scotland and south Yorkshire, and is generally more common north of a line from East Anglia to Liverpool Bay. About 10 per cent of areas indicate the same level, and no area has over the 1.0 level for both variations. Bear in mind, how-

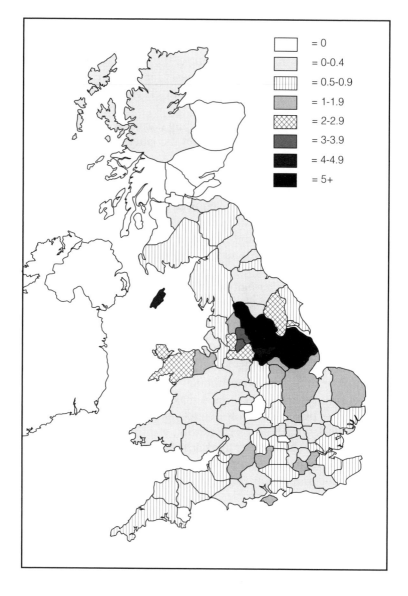

1.13a, b   Tinker (693) *above*   **Tinkler** (729) *right*
The Tinkler/Tinker 'sandwich' – but definitely a northern name.

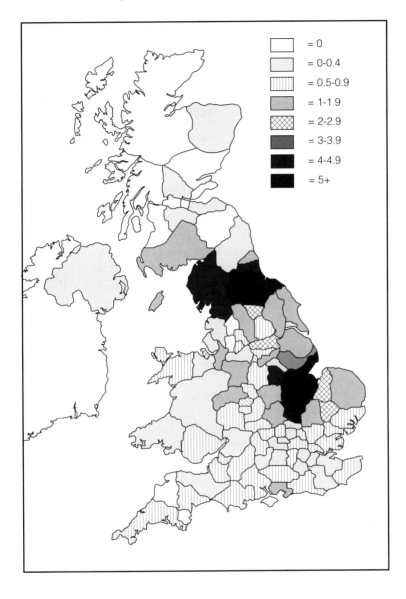

ever, that Rodgers provides only 20 per cent of all Ro(d)gers. Additionally, as Morgan and Morgan (1985) point out, the absence of
the sound for the Rogers' 'g' in Welsh led to many being called
Rosser or even Prosser (ap Roger).

With Tinker and Tinkler, we add a new dimension to the problem, and it is thanks to P. H. Reaney that we can accept them as
basically the same name. Reaney rightly criticised Bardsley for
believing that the name Tinker was confined to the south of England, and in turn the maps (Map 1.13) question Reaney's own
implication that Tinker was not 'characteristically northern' like
Tinkler. In this case, the two words *sound* slightly different (a very
important factor in judging variations from an age of illiteracy),
and have slightly different meanings, both referring to the occupation of utensil mender, one directly, the other through the noise
made by the bell announcing his presence. It is unclear why all the
areas having more than twice the average are confined between
East Anglia, North Wales and Scotland, but the regional 'sand-
wiching' of Tinker is very marked. Applying our guidelines to these
names suggests that they were not of pinpoint origin and that,
although there are relatively few examples of each one, their distribution has not shifted dramatically over the centuries. In the
light of what was said about variations being created at a distance,
we will also examine in Part 3 whether all were tinkers in origin.
Two questions may be referred to Part 2 or even to Part 3 –
whether the medieval working conditions of tinkers were not con-
ducive to marriage and raising children, resulting in a common
occupation having few surname holders; and whether the same
occupation gave rise to other surnames in the south and in Scotland.

Only one step further is the use of different, though vaguely similar, names for the same occupation, and by this time we should not
be surprised to find regional variations, almost on the
Fuller/Tucker/Walker intensity. Maps 1.4 and 1.14–16 show the
distribution of Weaver, Webb, Webber and Webster. Webb and
Webster appear to divide the whole country between them,
whereas the far less common Weaver and Webber have a more limited regional concentration. Reaney offers a possible explanation for
the former, as it might have derived from Weaver Hall in Cheshire
(where he might also have noted the River Weaver, on which some
of my own ancestors earned their living) and the town of Weaver-

ham. If indeed Weaver is a locative name drifting southwards, against the normal trend towards Lancashire from that part of the country, we would expect a preponderance of Weavers in the towns of BT areas 303 (Shrewsbury, Hereford and mid-Wales) and 226 (Stoke-on-Trent). McKinley also notes that, originally, Webber and Weaver were 'both much rarer names, with only scattered examples of both' (1990, p. 144). (See also Addison (1978, p. 17 and OES, p. 356) for these four names.)

The lesson concerning variations of surnames over all, then, is to treat them as potentially interesting at minimum, and significant in many cases which are hard to predict in advance. Even if there are a mere handful of instances, it will repay making a note of their number and plotting their location.

Country and county surnames

Immigrants to England have commonly been accorded surnames associated with their former country, and we might expect those names still to be found in largest numbers where the newcomers settled. Ireland, Scot(t), Welsh/Welch need to be investigated, as their patterns are not necessarily similar to each other. I chose French, which turned out to be certainly more common in parts of the UK closest to the country of origin, though Kneen (1937) offers the somewhat startling opinion that the name really means one who lived near ash trees; and Dutch(man) which was also the result of very early waves of migration. Reaney even hints at a difference between Dutch (weavers) and Dutchman (also brickmakers from Flanders). Dutch has concentrated in major ports – London, Liverpool and Glasgow in particular, though the total numbers are small, and recent enough to question whether these were the original 'routes in'.

So, what of England or English? Is this a name given to Englishmen who have migrated to other parts of the British Isles? (And, incidentally, do we have here yet another surname variation?) Weekley was of the opinion that they have quite a different origin, believing that English (with variation Inglis) is a Scottish name, whereas England was based on a place (a meadow by a stream) or even a person called Ing. (Weekley, 1914, pp. 96, 98) The maps (1.17a and b) clearly suggest that both were names given *in*

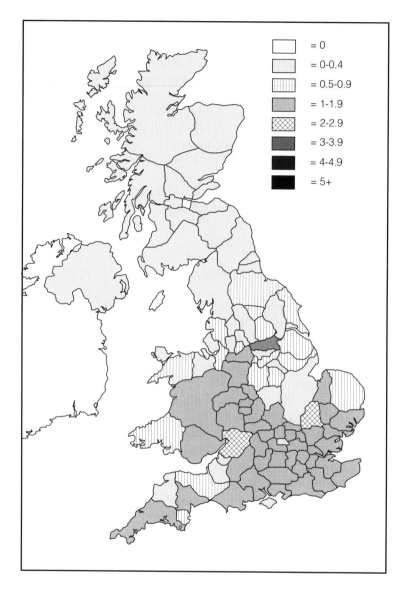

1.14, 1.15, 1.16   Webb (19,996) *above*   **Webber** (4,504) *right*
Webster (13,225) *p. 56*
Distinctly different geographical emphases to these three names for the
same occupation.

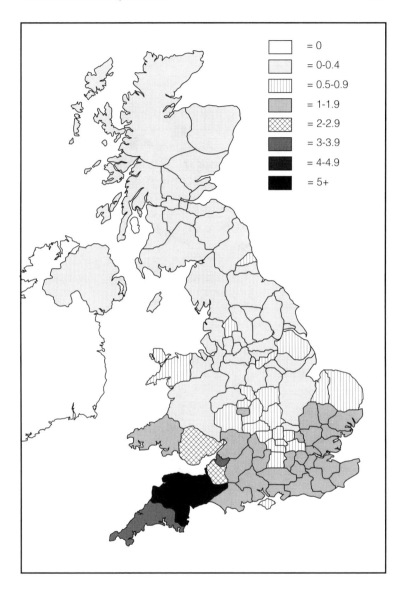

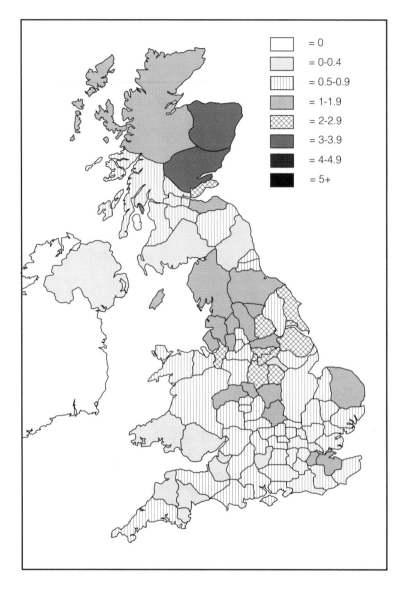

England – though perhaps Inglis should have been investigated as a Scottish version. We seem to have different regional emphases, England being popular in the south-west and Yorkshire, English in the south-east and north-east. Reaney clearly had difficulty explaining why anyone would acquire such a surname in their own country, toying with generation on the Celtic fringes rather than going far back to pre-medieval Angles. Neither theory would explain their present distribution which, given the numbers concerned, are unlikely to be far from their area of origin if our guidelines for interpretation are correct.

A similar mystery surrounds North, South, East and West as surnames, but here the modern maps help to narrow down the possibilities. The difference in the number of instances has already been noted, and Reaney suggests a standard alternative explanation for all four – either a 'man from' that direction, or a 'man dwelling in' that direction. He also reminds us that we may need a fuller picture by researching a wide variety of names with similar origins – Easterby, Norton, Southern and Weston, for example. The maps (Maps 1.18–21) reveal other surprises, but seem to favour the 'man dwelling in' explanation. All four names are associated with the area south-east of a line from the Humber to Lands End, and all have particularly high concentrations in Lincolnshire where, it need hardly be said, few men can have migrated from the east! (See OES (pp. 54–5) for a large range of variations on the 'points of the compass' theme.)

As it seems unlikely that there has been a major redistribution of the main concentrations in the last few centuries, it would appear that, in the south and east of England, it was common practice to call a man by the direction of his dwelling place from the village centre. The large discrepancy in numbers defies explanation, but then so does the even more mysterious absence of Townhead as a surname in contrast to the common Town(s)end (observed by Dr J. H. Smith).

County names need far more exploration than I have been able to give. Many appear to be absent as surnames – Bedfordshire, Sussex, Yorkshire, for example – whereas others – Derbyshire, Devonshire, Hampshire – are found quite frequently. It will be interesting to discover if many have died out. As with country names, it does not seem sensible that a man should be given it while still living in that county, but eminently appropriate if he had

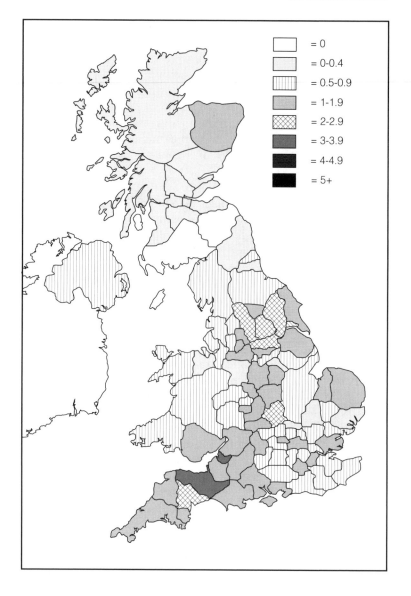

1.17a, b   England (3,387) *above*   **English** (3,466) *right*
Both England and English appear to be names originating well inside England, not at its borders, with both names particularly popular in East Anglia.

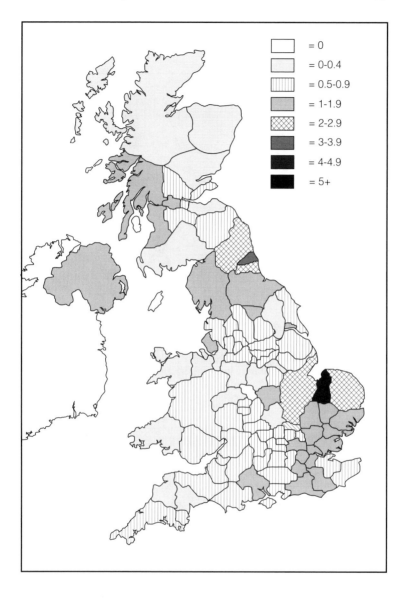

	= 0
	= 0-0.4
	= 0.5-0.9
	= 1-1.9
	= 2-2.9
	= 3-3.9
	= 4-4.9
	= 5+

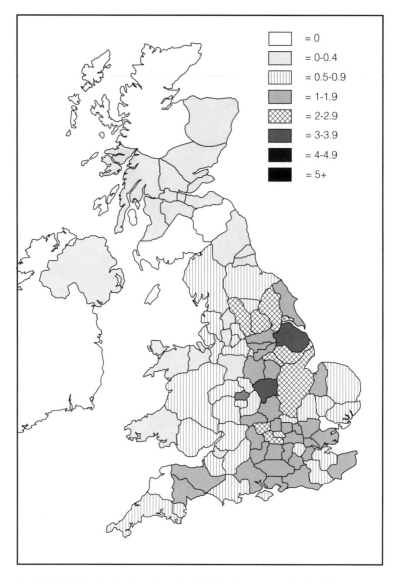

1.18, 1.19, 1.20, 1.21   North (4,886) *above*   **South** (1,392) *right*
East (2,443) *p. 62*   **West** (15,388) *p. 63*
All appear to be based on which part of a village their medieval ancestors
inhabited, rather than which part of the country; but why should West be
by far the most popular?

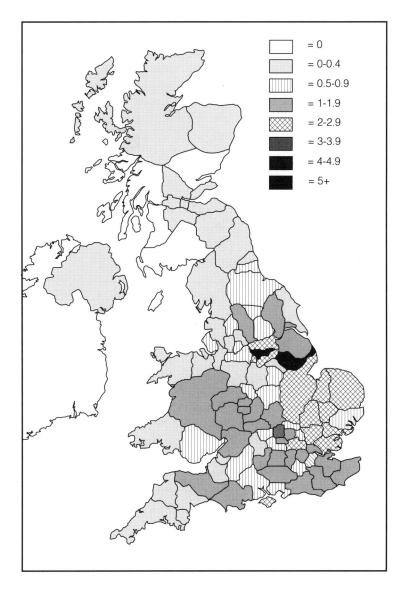

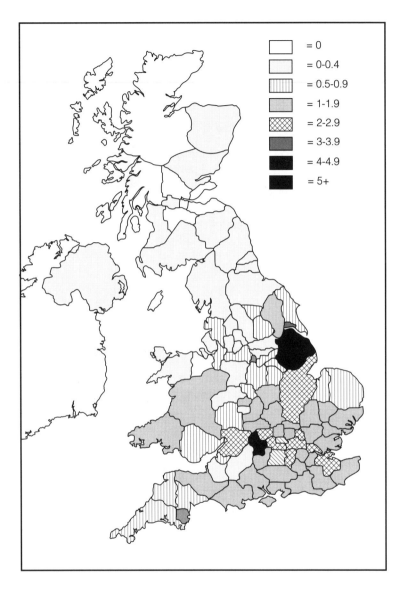

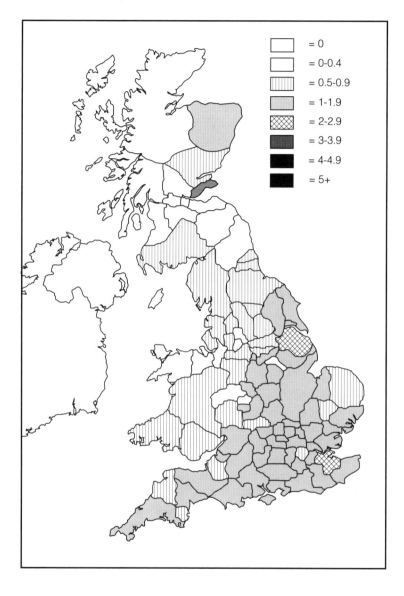

moved from that county when he acquired a surname. Movement across county boundaries was common enough in medieval times, and we should therefore expect greatest concentrations of a county name in areas immediately adjacent. Lancashire as a surname is much rarer than Lancaster, a dot map indicating highest concentrations in Manchester (near the border, but the surname is commoner to the north of the city), in Derbyshire, Nottinghamshire, and south Yorkshire. Lasker and Mascie-Taylor (1990) mapped 1,803 Derbyshires; at least 60 per cent were found to be in adjoining Lancashire. Kent, however, while fanning out nicely from the south-east, seems to be most popular at the greatest distances of the above-average levels – East Anglia, Lincolnshire, Oxfordshire, and the south-west – rather than in London as I would have expected; Kneen (1937) found evidence of the name in the Isle of Man as early as the sixteenth century, and Black (1965) says they were in Scotland in the twelfth! Although McKinley (1981) does not list it as a Lancashire name, Professor Dolley concluded from his study of names in the Isle of Man (1983) that it probably originated from the river in that county.

Where experts disagree ...

As we have already seen, there are many surnames whose origins and etymologies are in doubt, either because a writer has identified more than one possible source which could have produced the same end result, or (more rarely) when different writers plump for different interpretations of a name, often delighting in disproving someone else's theory. We should remember that it is always possible that one surname *has had* different origins; but can the surname maps drawn up from modern phone books help to support competing claims about what happened several hundred years ago, perhaps by casting doubt on one theory rather than proving another?

Death has been the subject of much speculation, partly because of fascination that such a word should be a surname at all, and partly because of the wide variety of forms in which it appears – among them, De'ath, De'Ath, Deathe, De'athe, De'Athe, D'Eath(e), DeAth, Deeth, and so on. The presence of the apostrophe has been regarded as an affectation, to remove the suggestion of death, but its origin is possibly from Ath in Belgium, an occupational name or nickname associated with death, or even a maker of fuel or tinder (Reaney, 1967, pp. 11–12, and 1976). Bardsley (1901b, p. 2) thought it came from 'some little, and now forgotten, spot' in Cambridgeshire. Mapping the name leaves little doubt that, even with relatively few examples, there is a concentration of the name in East Anglia, from south-east Essex to Norwich and Peterborough. This area satisfies the requirements of both main theories: it has received several waves of immigrants from that part of the continent, and has in consequence several pockets of very interesting names – Ong, for example, which is further complicated by the even more recent influx of Chinese names into the London area; but according to Reaney death (pronounced dethe as most of those with the surname do) is a middle English word used in East Anglia.

Nightingale is supposedly a nickname given to one who had a remarkable singing voice. Ewen (1938, pp. 87–9) was sceptical about it being a nickname (as he was with most nicknames), despite equivalent names in France and Germany, and suggested various places in Huntingdonshire and Wales as points of origin. Ewen, it should be noted, was one of the writers singled out by McKinley for 'laying on one side' (1990, p. 207). However, the name is found, with many variations, in greater than average concentrations north of a line from Birmingham to East Anglia, being particularly numerous in and around Bolton. These are not places with which one would automatically associate the songbird – indeed, nesting sites of the nightingale are south-east of a line from the Humber, through Bristol to south Devon, so either nesting habits of the species have changed radically in the last six hundred years or (improbably) the nickname was given well away from where the bird was found. They nested further north into the East Riding of Yorkshire, where there were Nightingales over six hundred years ago, earlier this century (Sharrock, 1976, pp. 352–3, 462). The only other obvious alternative is the unthinkable – that there has been a mass migration of people called Nightingale away from the south to the midlands and north-west. This will have to be investigated in Part 2, for the direction of such mobility is one commonly understood consequence of the industrial revolution. Another theory – that it is a corruption of Nigel – certainly accords with early spelling variations, but Nigel has never been a popular name in the north-west. Perhaps Ewen was right after all!

Oliphant, with its variant Olivant, has had a wonderful variety of explanations – from the Christian name Oliver; from elephant, as suggested by Bardsley (1901) and Kneen (1937), the use of animals almost as nicknames being not uncommon; from one bearing an olive branch, or peacemaker; or from an inn sign. Such a name is ripe for investigation, and its current distribution makes plain its *area* of origin – somewhere within England north of the Lake district, or, more likely, Scotland. Once again, variations are more likely to occur far from the commonest locations, 76 of the 86 Olivants and similar names being south of the Lakes, and account for the relatively high density in Lincolnshire. It is not a placename, nor would we be likely to encounter so many elephantine (or pacifist?) Scots over such a wide area.

Pipe is a surname which might be based on a place, or be in origin a different type of name altogether – a corruption of the occupational Piper, or from a baptismal name (Bardsley, 1901). There are places called Pipe in Herefordshire and Staffordshire, and we can compare its distribution with that of Piper. Mapping suggests that the latter place is the more credible, though we should remember the propensity of rare locative names to move across the country over several centuries. Another version of the name – Pipes – has another distribution altogether, being largely concentrated in York, Hull, Nottingham, Derby and Burton on Trent. The addition of the letter 's' to names other than Christian names is something of a puzzle, to which we need to return later.

Quick(e), according to Bardsley (1901b) and Weekley (1914), is a nickname, but Reaney suggests a variety of placenames which, on the basis of examples from the early Middle Ages, could be the point of origin – Cowick in Devon, Quick Mere in Saddleworth, a lost place called Quick in Prescot, to which might be added Kequick south-west of Warrington. The map, however, seems to favour only one of these places, the slightly pronounced emphasis around Merseyside being matched by similar levels along the south coast, and dwarfed by ten times more individual Quicks in the south-west peninsula. Local maps might home in on certain rural areas in each case, perhaps giving Prescot a fighting chance of sharing the honours. We must see if the name returns back to the place as we regress in time, however; as we shall see, a nickname like Lightfoot can also be skewed geographically.

Setter is agreed by all authorities to be an occupational name, but what was being set is in dispute. A setter might have been an arrowsmith, a silkmaker, or a stonemason (in the sense of a brick setter/layer). In this case, we have an almost endangered species, with only 113 in the UK phone books. They are distributed very largely in the south-west, Torbay in particular, Bristol, and London. It is evident that Setters is a variation, as almost half of the 26 in the country are also in the Torbay area, though a further nine are in the West Riding of Yorkshire. These dispersed nuclei suggest two main areas of origin, but the West Riding could easily be accounted for by a hypothetical, genetically successful migration in Victorian times. An arrowsmith seems unlikely, as they seem remote from the naturally concomitant Fletcher (Map 1.22), and whereas Reaney and others note examples in London (silk weavers) and York (brick setters) in the Middle Ages, there seems no way yet to explain the high concentrations around Torbay and the south-west.

Spring has been surmised as deriving from a physical attribute or ability, from the season, and from geographical phenomena. Other seasons have indeed been used as surnames, even the rare Autumn (one Robert Autumne was living in Cromwell, Nottinghamshire during the Civil War, and Nancy, daughter of Harry and Alice Autumn, died of consumption in Manchester on 10 October 1789). Springs are relatively few in number, so are likely to have moved over time, but if so, they seem to have avoided major urban areas except Bristol. Reaney (1976) says that there seems to be 'no evidence for a topographical origin' for Spring. This is not surprising – the Abstractions Ground Water Department of the National Rivers Authority advises that there is probably nowhere in this country more than two kilometres away from a natural spring, even after our industrial society has removed so many.

Waugh is found extensively along a line fifty miles on either side of the Scottish border, but according to Reaney the earlier theory that the wall itself generated the name cannot be substantiated. He preferred the meaning 'foreigner', from a word given by Anglians to Strathclyde Celts. The map favours Reaney's interpretation, as a placename would not be as likely to have spread so uniformly across the country. Bardsley (1901b) was happy to classify it as a Scottish name because he was thus able to exclude it from his *Dictionary of English and Welsh Surnames*! I just hope that the name Warr, much more common further south, is not a variant I should have mapped!

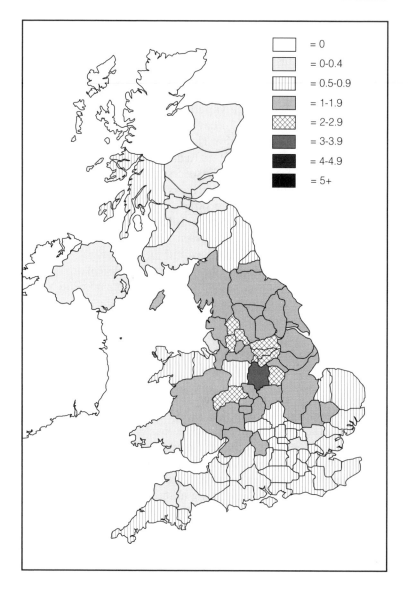

1.22   Fletcher (16,404)
A fletcher was a bow maker. Was the north of England more belligerent in medieval times?

Winder has had a number of different explanations. According to Reaney, they were probably winders of wool; McKinley points out, however, that Winder is a placename in the Lake District and in the West Riding of Yorkshire, and also found the name derived from a winding street in Sussex (1990, pp. 3-4). Bardsley (1901b) had no doubt that it was locative and quoted several examples of possible placename origins in the north of England which he knew best. The present holders are certainly concentrated in the north-west, especially in Barnsley, Blackburn and Cumbria, suggesting the placename origin has the strongest claim; Part 2 will show whether the distribution regresses back to those places.

Except for Death and Spring, maps showing the modern distribution of the above nine problematic surnames have thrown some light, admittedly through a somewhat opaque lens, on questions raised by earlier writers on surnames, and we should therefore at this stage consider the technique to be *prima facie* a legitimate tool for the solution of such problems. We must recognise, however, that it might raise as many questions as it solves, and we must reserve judgement until Part 2 or even Part 3 on how effective a tool it has been.

Problems, problems ...

Anyway, enough of other people's problems – I've too many of my own. An exercise which started out as an attempt to examine how far names can be used as genetic markers over time in order to assess the strength, timing and direction of migration has rapidly developed in several other directions, and we have been sidetracked into the meaning of names, the significance of spelling variations, and arguments between other writers. Perhaps we can now return to basics for a moment, and ask how much the phone books can tell us anything about the extent to which people have moved, even though they clearly cannot reveal much about the timing of such movement.

There are many names whose origins are not in doubt, including a very significant group from Scotland. Given a large enough number of instances (that is, much larger than the rare, locative surnames whose distribution has been at the mercy of decisions by relatively few individuals), can we come to any conclusions about the scale, distance, and direction of Scottish migration into the rest of the United Kingdom?

Clearly, the number of people migrating will be related to the total population having that surname, and of course we cannot tell how many were originally called, say, Black, Dempster, or Murdoch. What we can measure, however, is the number still remaining in Scotland in contrast to the numbers in other parts of England, Wales and Northern Ireland. The pattern of the three names, chosen at random, is remarkably similar. They are all Lowland names on the whole, and their present distribution suggests that approximately half may be, or may be descended from, migrants south. In all three cases, a significant number are found in Northern Ireland, but few in Wales; there is some suggestion of a concentration in the north – Cumbria to Newcastle – and in the home counties, but on the whole the migrants have spread remarkably evenly across England. Black, incidentally, is a good example of how different authorities can interpret the same name, McKinley believing that it refers to someone with a black or swarthy face, Weekley thinking that it comes from Middle English 'blac', meaning to bleach or whiten!

A notional figure of some 40–60 per cent of 'Scots' now being found elsewhere within the UK, to say nothing of international migration, does not necessarily mean that half of all Scots have left Scotland. Some examples of the three names may be found so early in England that they may not be so completely 'Scottish' as might be believed. Reaney says that the name Murdoch had been brought into Yorkshire by Norwegians from Ireland before 1066! More significantly, the proportion of *men* migrating (carrying the surname with them) may well have been much higher than the proportion of females, resulting in a greater reproduction rate *for the same surname* outside Scotland.

Once again, a picture is emerging of surname distribution akin to the spread of ink in water – after a certain length of time, much of the ink has dispersed to wherever tiny currents have taken it, but much is still located fairly close to where it first appeared. With most toponymics, the significance of this proposition is negligible – there are so many places which could have given rise to Hill, Marsh or Wood that their modern distribution probably conveys little of their origin. McKinley says that they are most common in south-eastern counties. On the other hand, names based on topographical features, or synonyms for those features, which are relatively localised might betray an original cause for their present non-random location.

Clay (Map 1.23) figures most prominently as a surname across central England, from Cardigan Bay and Liverpool Bay to Humberside and the Wash, being especially strong in the east around Nottinghamshire. Superficial deposits of boulder clay are exactly in areas where the surname is *not* common – Scotland, northern England, from Newcastle to Hereford, and East Anglia south to London. However, clay as a type of heavy soil, used for many products (pottery, for example) in the Middle Ages, extends from Weston-super-Mare north-east to the Humber, with extensions further east to the Wash, where the surname is most common.

Heaths (Map 1.24) lie in a semicircle from Humberside through to the west midlands (especially Stoke-on-Trent) and to the south-east counties. However, rolling hills where heather grows are not found in these areas, though there are a few stretches to the north-west of Birmingham, and in East Anglia; equally problematic is the absence of Heaths in areas where there *is* heath – across the south coast from Southampton to Bodmin Moor, and in the Pennines. (Because of the peculiarities of Welsh surnames, we should not expect Heath to have been generated among the Welsh hills.)

We have already noticed that some occupational names also have a non-random distribution relating to the use of those different words for the same job in different parts of the country (Fuller, Tucker, Walker), or to regional concentrations of those occupations (Ashburner). Occupational names are among the commonest in Britain, and a rather large-scale operation is often needed in order to collect the data. Clearly the more numerous the holders of a surname, the more likely it is to be polygenic – that is, having arisen in many different places. In no case discovered, however, is a name evenly distributed among the population, though Smith comes close to it. A century ago, Guppy believed that Smith was more common in the west of the country than in the east; modern researchers, having greater access to data on a large scale, find the name more common in the east (Lasker, 1985). Map 1.25a and b shows Smith to be a name close to average in a very large percentage of areas – nevertheless, all those with more than average are in the east. We should think of Smith as the 'background noise' of the surname world, whose slight geographical perturba-

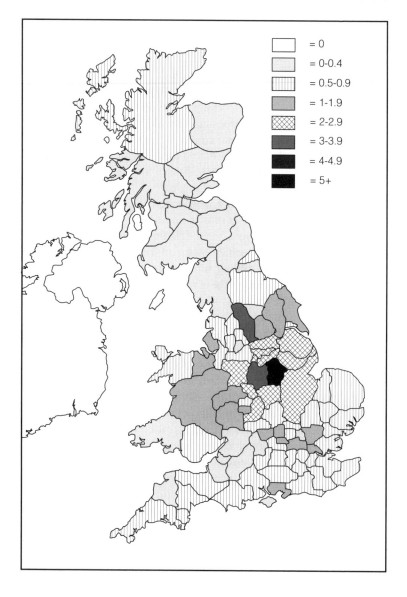

1.23 Clay (3,031)
Clay is concentrated where it exists in rock (as opposed to boulder) form.

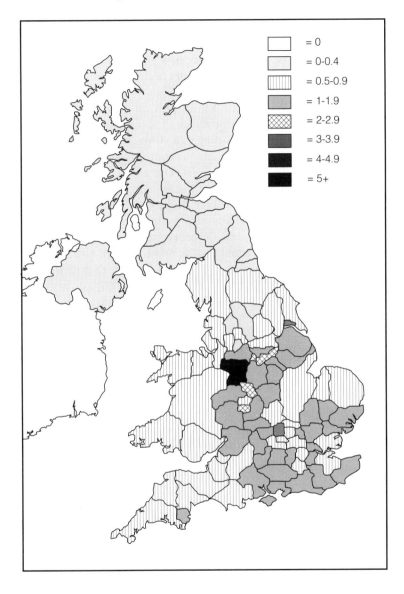

1.24   Heath (7,810)
Heath is a toponymic whose current distribution suggests that it was generated by families in several parts of England.

tions are of very long-term significance. This very fine echo of the early evolution of the creation of surnames may be explained only as a consequence of there having been a greater population in the east during the Middle Ages – we will check that out in Part 3.

Indeed, each occupational name among my chosen 100 offers an intriguing puzzle to account for its present concentration. Both Fletcher (Map 1.22, an arrow-maker, but originally a maker of feathering for arrows) and Stringer (a stringer of bows) might be expected to be found in the same parts of the country, as indeed they are – but why are they clustered between the Lake District and the south midlands, with very few indeed along the south coast? Is the high concentration of Bacon from south Yorkshire to East Anglia, especially around Derbyshire, a remnant of the distribution of medieval pig-farming? Did Carpenters originate largely where most shipbuilding was carried on – across the south coast and the Bristol Channel, especially as the name is French in origin? Were carpenters further north called Wright, an Old English word, as Black (1946) suggests? The distribution map in Lasker (1985) supports such a view, though the latitude graph suggests that it did not extend as far as Scotland. What did Packers pack? Whatever it was, they appear to have done it across the south coast from Torbay and Bristol to Kent. If Spicers were grocers (according to Reaney), why are so few found north of Birmingham? Why are Trinders (probably braiders) largely found south of the midlands, as are local officials such as Alderman and Constable?

There are concentrations of some occupations further north, but at this stage we can only surmise whether they are accurate echoes of a medieval past and, if they are, why they have a peculiar pattern. Barkers (tanners) are located in the north midlands and Yorkshire, but in this case they are balanced by Tanners themselves who are found largely south of the midlands; Cartwrights stretch across central England and Wales, being particularly common in Stoke and the west midlands; while Stalkers (as in deerstalkers) are further north still, and are considered by Black (1946) to have a Scottish name.

Distinctive patterns which characterise each name in the locative and occupational series are also to be found in those which originated as nicknames. In most cases, we can probably no longer tell whether such names had more than random original significance, even if they are correctly identified as such (Whitehead, for example, is a placename). Are we really to believe that more people were so fleet of foot in the north-west of England that the Lightfoots still predominate in that area? Perhaps, however, the name was given only when its recipients were very rare in the population, or when they were really cursed with opposite attributes! Perhaps it is a simple case that those who could run fast were given other names in different parts of the country – Speedy or Swift, for example – though Lightfoot is known in Ireland during the Middle Ages. In Wales, nicknames were common, but they were rarely adopted as inherited surnames.

Non-random distribution of other nicknames is often even harder to explain. Wiseman might have been an appropriate (or ironic) nickname anywhere in Britain; but it is not, being common only between London and the Wash, and in the north of Scotland, and is numerous enough to reflect its areas of origin. Black (1946) found them in Moray and Angus as early as the thirteenth century. Perhaps, if I had considered all synonyms together – Wise, Wyse, Wisdom and so on – nicknames associated with wisdom (or idiocy) would be more evenly spread. Counsell, Fox and Smart might be added to such a list, though they have a slightly different tone, and Quick might be a place or a physical attribute also. Fox is concentrated on Yorkshire and Lincolnshire, where there are more than average numbers of Wisemans.

Merryweather is most common in the north-east, from Lincolnshire to Middlesbrough, though one could hardly suppose that this is the result of any accurate description of local meteorological phenomena. Their total numbers, however, and the great disparity across adjoining areas, suggest that the present distribution of rare names should not be assumed to be a useful basis for guessing their origins, for the incidental migration of only a few persons as late as the industrial revolution might have significantly reflected their geographical history. We must not be surprised, therefore, if Merryweather has quite a different disposition when we return to the name in previous centuries during Part 2.

Wagstaff(e)s are numerous enough to suggest multiple points of origin and therefore suggest a more certain basis for assessing where it arose – but why should that be across the midlands? McKinley (1990, p. 165) suggests that it was a nickname for an

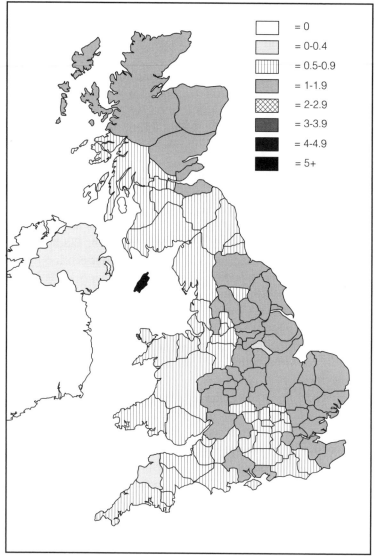

1.25a, b   Smith (213,123) *above*
Smith is quite evenly spread – but why is it more popular in the east of
England? (Its popularity in the Isle of Man might be another statistical
aberration, resulting from the small population of the island.) When surnames are represented as a percentage of the whole (*right*), ignoring total
population, London and the main urban centres tend to predominate.

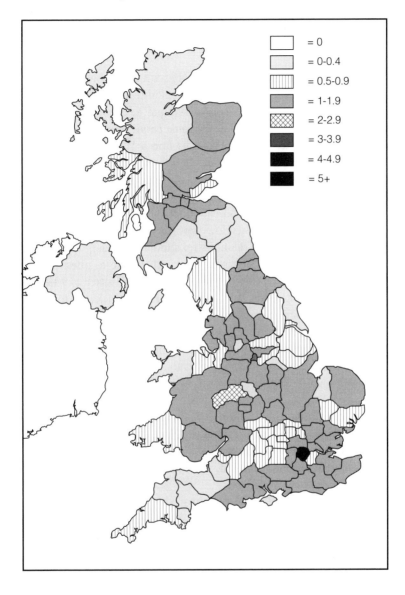

officer of the peace, like Shakespeare – i.e. a parish constable. Wagstaffe and Shakespeare are also discussed by Reaney (OES, pp. 285–7, 292).

Similar problems occur with surnames which are based on Christian names. I have long been of the opinion that a logical sequence of events has been for, e.g., son of William to become Williamson which in turn was abbreviated *by some people* to Williams', finally becoming Williams. Thus, a Williams and a Williamson might be genetically related to each other. If this is correct, Williams and Williamson should be treated as one name, as should Johns and Johnson, Harris and Harrison, and so on. Another consequence is that the number of Watts will be reduced if the number of Watsons is increased, and vice versa. However, the normally accepted origin for 's' is genitive, so this relationship should not exist.

Maps produced by others have now caused me to question this theory. Among the hundred names mapped in Lasker (1985), all eleven ending with 'son' (Anderson, Harrison, Jackson, Johnson, Pearson, Robinson, Simpson, Thompson, Watson, Wilkinson and Wilson) are shown to have a strong northern bias. I do not understand why people in the north should have been less inclined to abbreviate their names, but interestingly, the graph for Harris is the reverse image of that for Harrison, as predicted by the theory. But why should those names ending with 'son' be more common in the north of England than in the south? Reaney suggests (1976, p. xix) that the bias was already evident by the end of the Middle Ages, and was associated partly with a Scandinavian influence and partly with the comparatively late adoption of hereditary surnames in the north of England.

I'm sure you are all anxious to hear about Rogers and Rogerson. Again, the maps seem to contradict my theory. Rogerson is relatively rare (having a below average concentration everywhere) south of a line going through Stoke-on-Trent and Hull; it is very popular across the north of England, and especially in south-west Scotland. The distribution of Rogers, on the other hand, bears little relationship to this picture, being much more common in the south. Experts seem to disagree on the origin of names which are basically another name with 's' added, and we must return to this problem in Part 3.

Of course, Christian name surnames are never evenly distributed, any more than any other type of surname, the rarer ones having a pronounced geographical skew, with Wales having the strongest tradition of patronymics long before they became inherited. Moxon (son of Mog, or Margaret), for example, has a high concentration in Yorkshire, and it is no coincidence that the well-known first class cricketer plays for that county.

Incidentally, Tyson is also strongly associated with the north of England, from Lincolnshire to the Lake District. Weekley believed it to originate as Dyson, meaning the son of Dionisius, but according to Reaney Tyson is from a word meaning a firebrand, so should be considered a nickname – an appropriate name for one of the fastest opening bowlers England has produced. There are also many placenames in Britain ending with 'son' – Abson, and two places called Nelson; McKinley (1990, p. 116) gives several other examples.

In summary, therefore, it seems that, of all the names which we have investigated so far, only one category may be giving a misleading impression of where they originated – those having so few examples in the phone books (say significantly under 500) that the mobility of the family over the centuries might have been subject to the random whims of relatively few individuals. Unfortunately, and ironically, these include the locatives, the very surnames whose geographical origins are well enough known already as the placenames from which they derive. Even when the locative names seem more numerous than this, their inheritance at periods earlier than the time when most other surnames became inherited means that medieval migration could have had a significant effect on their present location, as we saw in the case of Darlington.

In all other cases, it seems likely that, despite the dispersal of half the name holders or more, their present distribution is an echo of their origin, an echo which is still audible enough to allow for a reasonably researched guess about their earlier history. The reason for the original distribution is often far from clear, however.

That proposition must now be put to the test in order to see whether, as predicted, the modern day dispersion and the effects of the industrial revolution are reversed over the centuries, but still concentrated on their present centres of gravity. Have they remained in more or less their present geographical position, or have they moved unpredictably from different parts of the country? If the latter, then so far we've been wasting our time!

Part 2

The distribution of surnames since the Middle Ages

Introduction

The principal emphasis in Part 1 was on the representation and interpretation of the distribution of surnames in modern times, using over 80 per cent of households which happen to be on the phone. The resulting maps are static, there being no attempt to incorporate changes over time to that distribution. In Part 2, the emphasis will shift so that we can also seek out those changes in order to put the results from Part 1 into a three-dimensional context, not only seeing the expansion (or contraction) in numbers of individuals bearing particular surnames, but to see whether it is possible to estimate the degree to which surnames, and therefore the individuals who had them, have been subject to geographical mobility. We also need to test the theories propounded in Part 1 about the relationship between modern whereabouts of surnames and their origins – in particular, the suggestion that there has been relatively little movement in the epicentres of the commonest names, but random, unpredictable movement among the rarest.

In Part 2, we will briefly examine the advantages and limitations of a range of sources which are available for this purpose covering the last five hundred years, with a few illustrative examples showing how they can be used. Those sources are taken regressively back in time until we reach a period in the seventeenth century when it becomes possible once again, using published sources, to approach a national picture for surname distribution in England. For the intervening centuries, until the 1881 census index is published, the surname detective is advised to concentrate on a much more limited geographical area. There is certainly nothing compiled nationally before 1837 which matches the records of civil registration or the census, though there are 'censuses' earlier than 1841.

Some are individual local copies of the 1801–1831 period when no national census *showing names* survives. Others have been taken for a variety of purposes from as early as 1522 (in Coventry) and have been listed by Gibson and Medlycott (1992); see also Gibson and Creaton (1992) and Chapman (1991). However, among these early censuses, the only one which covers a major part of a whole county is that for Westmorland in 1787, published in 1992; normally they do not extend beyond the boundary of an individual parish.

Since Guppy (1890), few writers on names have explored the changes which have taken place during the long period of time we are now entering: for the most part, they have been interested in the original derivation of surnames and, to a far lesser extent, their current distribution. (Bardsley, 1901b, is perhaps an exception.) However, we may be able to seek the guidance of two other groups who *have* investigated change from a slightly different perspective. Those who have researched the history of individual names, particularly members of the Guild of One Name Studies, have mapped the locations of as many holders as possible of the particular surname in which they are interested, and some, such as Prideaux (1989) or Ullathorne (1992), have written up their findings. Take care to note, in such 'family histories' as they are categorised by booksellers and librarians, whether a book is about selected branches of the family or about all who hold the name – only the latter will be of significant help to the surname detective.

Secondly, there has been a widespread academic interest in migration, summarised in Rogers and Smith (1991, pp. 122–6). Much of this has been inspired by studies of Victorian censuses which provide place of birth, and by the writings of Peter Laslett in the 1960s which destroyed the myth of a static society in preindustrial England by identifying a turnover of about one third in parish lists of surnames every ten years or so. A wide variety of sources, far wider than that presented in this book, has been tapped in this quest – constables' accounts in the early seventeenth century were used by J. R. Kent in her study of Irish and Scottish migration into the Midlands, to take but one example. The results of this research can form a useful backdrop and contrast to the surname investigations which may be undertaken.

People migrate – change residence – to get away from something ('location avoidance') or to attain something ('location selection'). The causes of each have changed over the centuries, but the fundamentals still apply. Until and including the early eighteenth century, some location avoidance was in order to escape from areas of food shortages in which, despite some continuing arguments among historians about the actual causes of death, famine conditions were certainly present in England, and in the nineteenth century in Ireland. By then, location avoidance had also prompted the development of suburbia, particularly after railways facilitated short-distance commuting into those industrial centres which had apparently become obnoxious as dwelling areas. After the First World War, such opportunities were extended to working-class families by slum clearance schemes.

Location avoidance has had little effect on surnames because the distances and numbers concerned have been relatively small. Location selection, on the other hand, has lured people over great distances, for there is less choice about the place concerned. London's pavements of gold, or the retirement delights of Blackpool and Bournemouth, are not on everyone's doorstep. The latter is, of course, a relatively modern phenomenon, though retirement to the home of an adult offspring is a subject all too little studied. Most location selection has been for 'betterment', and the root of that betterment is an increase in income.

A very considerable body of evidence has been accumulated about preindustrial as well as industrial migration, and a similar picture emerges no matter which researcher, which geographical area, or which time period is involved. Until this century, migration started relatively early in life as adolescents, both boys and girls, moved out of the family home into domestic, agricultural or, later, industrial service. Selection was determined not only by the location of work but also by the presence of relatives who were prepared to support them – as gene followed gene, so surname often followed surname across the country. Labourers were taken on for twelve months at a time at the annual hiring fairs, changing agricultural employer with a frequency almost as high as urban workers changed employer or dwelling, always seeking to maximise their income.

The scale of this movement has been vast, a gross generalisation suggesting that 5–10 per cent changed residence every year, a generalisation which hides migration 'hot spots' in the towns, or cold spots such as Myddle in Shropshire. Pioneering studies showed that, even as early as the seventeenth century, as far apart as

Devonshire and Nottinghamshire, up to half the inhabitants of villages had moved out within a decade. The research of Dr Colin Pooley at Lancaster University is based on 1,800 individual histories in Lancashire and Cheshire from 1750 to 1950, and family historians have been invited to contribute data from their own families towards this project. Similarly, the social change project of Dr Ken Prandy and Dr Wendy Bottero in the University of Cambridge will capitalise on the vast resources of the trees compiled by genealogists over many years.

We must now examine the suggestion in Part 1 that, however many *people* moved, the *average distance* moved was quite small.

Sources of information on migration

Phone books

To gather this information, of course, we require the equivalent of phone books on a national scale every ten years or so – certainly every generation, which we will assume to be a period of about thirty years – but it will come as no surprise to anyone that such a series does not exist.

The phone system itself started in 1879, being privately owned until 1912 when the National Telephone company was nationalised. However, phone books from before the Second World War are of little value to the surname detective because of the relatively small numbers they contain. In 1935, one book of 1,158 pages covered the whole of Lancashire, the Isle of Man, Westmorland, Cumberland, Northumberland, Durham, Yorkshire, and parts of Lincolnshire. This same area was covered by 10,828 pages in the mid-1980s, and included a far greater proportion of domestic users. Earlier, the position is even more inadequate for our purpose. Chester, North Wales and Stoke-on-Trent generated only 90 pages in 1927, 1,465 in the mid-1980s. At the beginning of the twentieth century, the whole of the British Isles was contained in the equivalent of under 500 pages.

This is not to say that phone directories from the first half of the twentieth century do not have their uses. If you are investigating a common name, an overall trend might be observable. The absence of Darlingtons in the north-east, for example, and their presence in the east midlands, is clear even on a reduced constituency; but the absence of a rare name such as Vamplew, which is currently located almost entirely in the area of Barnsley, might simply mean that no one of that name was on the phone, rather than that no one lived there in the 1930s. The directories are more convenient than electoral registers in so far as they cover a much wider geographical area; on the other hand, they are much more difficult to locate, as almost all are consigned to the dustbin when replacements are issued.

British Telecom has an Archives and Historical Information Centre at 2–4 Temple Avenue, London EC4Y 0HL which is open to the public. In addition to a considerable amount of other historical data relating to the service, it holds an almost complete set of telephone directories from 1879 when the first publicly available system was introduced in Great Britain.

Happily, before the twentieth century, there are plenty of other sources which are available to replace, and even improve on, phone books as a source of information about where named people lived. Those sources are of two kinds, which have radically different problems of access, of completeness, and interpretation. The simpler are lists of individuals, collected for a wide variety of purposes, who were all alive at a particular time – lists of taxpayers, lists of petitioners, lists of communicants, and best known of all the censuses which have tried to list everyone of all ages alive on one night every ten years. We may describe such records as 'snapshots' of the population, or part thereof.

The second type of source is more like a moving film; each still, or unit of information, is of little significance in itself, but when combined over time they reveal a changing story which can be followed over hundreds of years. The representation of such records as birth certificates or burial registers into a two-dimensional picture is by no means straightforward, but the results should repay the effort, and those interested in the rarer names at a level too detailed for consideration here can even see the movement of every molecule in the flow of their family's history.

The census and methods of analysis

The decennial census is by far the most complete source for the distribution of surnames, offering the address of everyone living in Great Britain every ten years (1939 instead of 1941) since and including 1841. Since the Registrar-General has to keep the original returns confidential for one hundred years, those which are currently available to the general public are 1841 to 1891 inclusive. At that point, they are transferred to the Public Record Office (PRO), the next being scheduled for release at the start of the year 2002.

By far the most convenient way to start investigating surnames over a hundred years ago will be through the census of 1881, not because it is radically different from any of the others available, but because of the massive effort involving the PRO and a large number of organisations affiliated to the Federation of Family History Societies, to prepare full indexes in a way which reorganises most of the data in the original returns into alphabetical order of surnames. Computerisation of the transcripts is being undertaken by the Church of Latter Day Saints in Salt Lake City. The project covers the 30 million people in England, Wales, Scotland, the Channel Islands and the Isle of Man. The bulk of the work of transcription has been undertaken by over five thousand volunteers, and has been organised in such a way that errors inevitably resulting from the use of so large a taskforce have been minimised. With the approval of HMSO and the PRO which holds the copyright, paper copies of the entire census have been distributed to these volunteers, whose transcriptions are checked and double checked before they are finally entered on to the LDS computer.

For each county, the index is available in four different forms, but it is mainly the surname index which directly concerns the surname detective; in addition, the same material is also available arranged by birthplace, by census place, and as a direct reproduction of the original enumeration. To all intents and purposes, 100 per cent of the whole population is thus being made accessible for 1881, in contrast with some 85 per cent of householders a hundred years later.

Eventually, when the entire project has been completed county by county, the whole country will be issued by surname, and by birthplace, both then available as standard sources for short- and long-term migration studies in Great Britain.

Until that happy day, we have the benefit of a steadily increasing number of fiches which can be used to pinpoint surname distribution towards the end of the nineteenth century – that is, if you can find the fiches! A main condition of being allowed to reproduce

the census in this form is a restriction on the number of organisations which are permitted to hold copies – no individual is allowed
to buy them.

When each county has been completed, the output is made available to LDS Family History Centres (listed in your local phone
book), and to those Family History Societies which have con-
tributed to the transcription – they allow their members free access,
charging at cost only for photocopies of specific pages. (See p. 6
above for details of how to locate your nearest Family History
Society.) The fiches are also sold to libraries and to universities. The
index, produced in the form of a microfiche, gives name, age, sex,
relationship to the head of the household, marital status, area of
residence, occupation, place of birth, and the name of the head of
the household.

Naturally, counties with the smaller populations are the earliest
to become available on this scheme; as this book goes to press, the
fiches have been issued for Anglesey, Bedfordshire, Brecknockshire,
Cambridgeshire, Cardiganshire, Carmarthenshire, Cornwall, Den-
bighshire, Devonshire, Dorset, Flintshire, Gloucestershire, Herefordshire, Hertfordshire, Huntingdonshire, Isle of Man, Leicestershire,
Merioneth, Montgomeryshire, Oxfordshire, Pembrokeshire, Radnor-
shire, Rutland, Shropshire, Somerset, Suffolk and Wiltshire. (Other
counties have been completely transcribed, but remain to be
entered on to the main computer.) We can use this currently available selection, albeit unrepresentative geographically and industri-
ally, to see whether a hundred years have produced significant
changes in those areas. In doing so, we should bear in mind the
possibility, however remote, that there is a non-random relationship between those who are not on the phone, and particular types
of surname.

Using the indexes is a pleasure after the peculiarities of most of
the other sources; entries are very easy to count, being in groups
of three with fifty-one entries on each numbered page. However,
unlike those in the International Genealogical Index, by which the
LDS is best known in family history circles, the names are arranged
strictly by alphabetical order according to how they were spelled in
the original census returns, so a number of sections must be
inspected for variations of the same name.

The PRO also sells microfilm copies of each census in its keeping,
and copies are normally available in public libraries, the whole

country being available in local libraries of the Church of Latter Day Saints (for details of local library holdings, see Gibson (1988)). To the surname detective, however, this is rather like winning the pools when there are twenty score draws on the coupon, for each library normally has copies only of its own local area(s). On grounds of cost alone, using this source through individual purchase on a national scale seems impossible. In any case, this particular form of coinage is virtually worthless, because it would take a lifetime for anyone to go through the census returns themselves in order to extract and count specific surnames, even if they *were* all available.

Luckily there is a partial solution to the problem of wide access to Victorian censuses other than that of 1881, a solution which applies particularly to that of 1851 a generation earlier. For many years, volunteers in Family History Societies have also been publishing surname indexes to their own areas; 1851 has been targeted as the earliest of those most useful to genealogists (as it gives birthplaces and exact ages), though some societies, such as Nottinghamshire, have indexed 1861 to 1891 also.

Few, if any, public libraries will have made a collection of these indexes from other parts of the country, but those of such organisations as the Society of Genealogists (in London), the Institute of Heraldic and Genealogical Studies (in Canterbury), and the PRO itself should have complete sets, and many local societies have a reciprocal exchange agreement so that they receive copies of indexes issued by others.

When you are using these (and any other) indexes, you should be aware of the following problems.

• Some indexes give the page numbers concerned, others inform how many instances of a surname, if more than one, appear on each page. (This discrepancy is one of the reasons why genealogists welcomed the opportunity for centralised co-ordination of the 1881 project.) When you are relying on the index instead of the original document, this discrepancy can cause havoc with your statistics, and make it impossible to determine the number of persons on a page. Furthermore, 'page' here refers to folio number, stamped on to the census itself, which are really *leaves* with two pages. This makes the whole exercise less effective than the phone book technique, for although those equally will not provide the total numbers of surname holders living at one address, the defect in most census indexes is compounded by the well-researched fact that the chances of having people of the same surname living close to each other (and therefore likely to be on the same folio) are considerably higher than random (Lasker suggests by a figure of 1,500 per cent). Recognition of this defect enables a consequent statistical flaw to be avoided – numbers from one type of index should never be compared or amalgamated with those from the other, as a single page reference can be disguising in the first more instances than a page entry specifying ten instances in the other. The only safe thing to do in the circumstances is to count the page references, not the individuals.

- Some indexes collect together different spellings of the same surname, others do not. You might have to repeat the exercise involving surname variations suggested in Part 1.
- Indexing 1851 (and to a much greater extent the other censuses) is an ongoing exercise. Counties vary in the extent to which the job has been completed. Furthermore, the published indexes are not necessarily for adjoining areas.
- In order to achieve progress as rapidly as possible, indexes have been published in quite large numbers, particularly for the urban areas. In order to complete a surname search for the City of Manchester in 1851, for example, you would have to amalgamate the contents of eleven volumes.
- Census returns for a few areas have not survived, or are now illegible.
- Until the 1881 census index is complete, it seems extremely unlikely that anyone in the foreseeable future will go to the trouble to check even the published indexes, let alone the unpublished portions, of other returns.

It will be noted that we are now proposing to count surnames on a county, rather than a BT or country, basis. *This enforced transfer of potential source material from national to county level is of some significance, and should not be greeted with dismay.* For one thing, it is inevitable that the further back in time we go, we need to find a way of overcoming the problem of comparison with more modern, national results rather than throwing in the towel. At the same

time, an increasing number of researchers will find that the surnames in which they are interested are becoming more and more
associated with specific counties (if not parts of counties) until,
when we go back far enough, only the commonest surnames will
have an extensive geographical spread.

As the statistical data about surnames is researched increasingly
on a county, rather than a country, basis, several questions arise.

Which counties should be researched? Clearly, the answer will
depend on your knowledge of the later distribution of the names
concerned, and the accessibility of the indexes to you personally,
but as many as physically possible should be the aim.

*Until the 1881 census is complete, can the Banwell formula be used to
compare one county with another?* No. The problem is that Banwell
shows the number of times above average *for the whole country.* If
the whole country, or at least a substantial part thereof, is still not
available we need a different basis for arriving at a figure, as suggested below, because the 'missing' counties might contain significantly high or low numbers of the surname you are investigating,
and you will find that, with only a relatively few counties available,
the number of times above or below average for each can become
greatly distorted compared with the late twentieth-century results.
Furthermore, if the basis for the surname count via published
indexes in one county has been different from that in another, they
should not be collated anyway.

How, then, will the comparative county figures be calculated? Very
simply – divide the number of instances of a surname, multiplied
by 100 for convenience, by either the total population in that area,
or the total number of entries in the source you are using. Counties which, for whatever reason, have yielded no data should be
ignored, and blanked out on the resulting maps; any which *has*
been searched but no examples of your surname(s) found should be
treated as a zero as in the case of phone books.

*How can county data be compared with phone book results when bound-
aries do not coincide?* Exact boundaries have to be ignored for this
purpose. What you will be looking for are overall and regional

trends, and common sense (with one eye on the district figures) must dictate when to accept that a moderate return for a whole county can be masking relatively small 'hot spots' where a surname might be common. For example, almost all the Ashburners in Lancashire were confined to the extreme north of the county in what would now be called Cumbria.

What should be the county equivalent of the number of phone book pages used in the Banwell systems? (i.e. 4. on p. 21 above) One of two possibilities, so long as you use the same for each area being collated. It might be the total population, as given in the volumes which were published a year or two after the census concerned, or the total number of page (folio) references in the index. (For convenience, the population figures for the 1881 census, which will give a more accurate result, are given in Appendix 3.) Being much smaller, the latter will give an absolute result much closer to that of the phone book process, but the cut-off points for different shading will have to be adjusted to suit the final range of numbers. It also frees you from dependence on county total populations which are available only from 1801.

Having collected data from a census, we are again faced with the question of how best to present the evidence in graphic form in order to facilitate drawing conclusions. The population has doubled in the last hundred years, so it may be possible to produce more 'Spruce' type maps for the earlier period; however, in 1881 we are looking at *all* the people, so the number of individuals concerned remains large. The purists could, of course, count only the 'breeding pairs' in 1881, but the task of doing so with a popular surname would be considerable. Other solutions include expressing the number of instances of a surname as a proportion of the total population of an area, a technique which could be used for phone books and for sources in periods earlier than the censuses, and is certainly useful when by no means all the counties are available.

Results from the 1881 census so far   There can be little doubt that, given time, 1881 will become the pivotal point for surname detectives for a generation to come. It will be the only point available at which the exact location of all bearers of any surname in England and Wales will be easily accessible. Data from earlier or later, less adequate, sources will be compared with the baseline of 1881. Meanwhile, however, we can only wait for the curtain to go up on this spectacular show by viewing the dress rehearsal in relatively small scenes, but the sixteen English counties published at the time of writing already yield some tentative conclusions.

Surnames which are common enough to make up a significant proportion of the total population appear to be displaying distribution characteristics similar to those revealed in phone books over a century later. The bench-mark obviously has to be Smith. Of every ten thousand people in 1881, Smiths provided 191 in Bedfordshire, 166 in Cambridgeshire, 35 in Cornwall, 57 in Devon, 95 in Gloucestershire, 150 in Herefordshire, 173 in Hertfordshire, 195 in Huntingdonshire, 319 in Leicestershire, 231 in Rutland, 86 in Shropshire, 93 in Somerset, 215 in Suffolk, and 165 in Wiltshire – far fewer in Wales, and only 11 in the Isle of Man, figures which suggest that Guppy was wrong even in his own time in ascribing a greater number in the west of the country.

Sixty per cent of all the Fullers in the first sixteen counties published are found in Cambridgeshire and Suffolk, and 75 per cent of all the Tuckers are in Cornwall, Devon and Somerset. Strikingly reminiscent of a century later, the north-west already shows a preponderance of those called Cartwright, Darlington, Purslow, Tasker and Weaver; Cambridgeshire and Rutland: Bacon, Chapman, Constable, Death, England, Moxon, Nightingale, Redhead, South, Spicer, Spring, Tinkler and Wiseman; Cornwall: Foot(e), Kent, Piper, Quick and Webber.

There are some discrepancies – but they seem to include only the rarer names. There are pockets of Box, Duncalf and Garlick in Cornwall (virtually the only examples in the six counties). Negatives are harder to spot, of course, but the absence of Nightingale from the Isle of Man, Setter from Cornwall, and Winder from Cambridgeshire is striking. This seems to support the contention in Part 1 that the rarer names are more prone to erratic changes in distribution over time.

Finally, there are many areas which today have a few examples of a surname where none existed a century ago. The first six counties published offer not a single instance of Culpepper, Culverhouse, Dutch(man), Edrich, Faber, Hatter, Lancashire, Linter, Maudling, Merryweather, Prevost, Restell, Setter, Spindler, Stalker, Summerscale, Tinker or Trinder. In short, there has been some permeation of these names into new areas, but only on a very small scale.

The meagre evidence from 1881, therefore, suggests that the amount of internal migration within England in the last hundred years has been much less than is normally imagined – if many have moved, they have not moved far, and although the data are not yet forthcoming, common sense would suggest that much of that movement has occurred since the Second World War with the advent of an enlarged higher education system which has drawn its clients away from their home area just before their average age of marriage and family generation. The proposed expansion of higher education will increase that fluidity – but only if students are encouraged to study away from their home town.

Civil registration records

The general public has the right of access to all the indexes of births, marriages and deaths in England and Wales since 1 July 1837. Most of these indexes are issued on a three-monthly basis, though some are annual. They are held in St Catherine's House, 10 Kingsway, London WC2B 6JB, but microfilm (and, increasingly, microfiche) copies have been purchased by a number of centres, libraries and Record Offices, as listed in Gibson (1993). Again, there are various problems associated with using these copies of the indexes.

- Not all years are available in all centres, particularly as the years after 1912 are more expensive to buy.
- Public demand for access to these indexes, especially from geneal- ogists, is very considerable. Some centres have a booking system, but in others there is a risk of turning up only to find all the microfilm readers in use. You should ring the centre concerned in advance of your proposed visit.
- The indexes provide a name and a reference number (plus the maiden name of the mother after 1 July 1911, the spouse's sur- name at marriage after 1912, and the age at death after 1866). The reference numbers are to registration districts, many of which are not instantly recognisable – how many of us know the whereabouts of Glendale, West Ward, or Wrayton for example? Furthermore, there were significant changes to names and boundaries in 1852 and 1974. Maps showing these districts are

available from the Institute of Heraldic and Genealogical Studies,
Northgate, Canterbury. The period before 1852 usefully coin-
cides with the earliest available censuses a generation before
1881, a time before railways greatly facilitated migration.
- Virtually all births, marriages and deaths are included except for
a period up to the middle of the nineteenth century, during
which researchers have discovered omissions – perhaps as high
as 10 per cent in the registration of births.

The record of vital events is a moving target. Although Mascie-
Taylor, Boyce and Brush (in Lasker, 1985) based their maps of the
ninety-four commonest surnames on the marriage indexes of the
first three months of 1974, most surname research involves the
extraction of all entries of a particular surname over a long period
of time, perhaps 1837 to the present day. The immediate product
is, against each surname chosen, a long list of forenames, registration districts, and dates, and the graphic representation of this data
is by no means straightforward. You could, of course, simply count
the total over whatever period you have chosen, and carry out a
process similar to the one which resulted in the phone book maps.
The longer the period chosen, the less desirable this solution is,
because it eliminates the great advantage of this source over any
other discussed so far – its ability to reveal changes in location over
time.

The simplest way to solve the problem is to select relatively short
periods – say, every five years – and to draw a separate summary
map for each. The actual length might depend on the rarity of the
surname involved, but for the very common names not much geographical movement is going to be detectable anyway, and for the
rarest, the maps are scarcely worth drawing because the movement
can easily be seen in the lists themselves.

You still have to decide whether to map births, marriages or
deaths, though no doubt the keenest surname detectives will
attempt all three. There are, of course, problems with each. In the
case of births, do you count all entries, all male entries, or simply
parents as what the geneticists call 'breeding pairs'? (This ignores
the very substantial proportion of births in modern times, over 50
per cent in some areas, which are now illegitimate, for which the
same child will appear twice in the indexes before 1 April 1969 if
the father's name appears on the entry.) The last is not recom-

mended except for the rare names as it is impossible to distinguish between such pairs before the mother's maiden name is supplied in the indexes from 1911. Marriage is often in the bride's parish, so the location of a male name holder in these indexes might be misleading. However, G. W. Lasker judges that this is not a serious problem because of the small sex difference in the locations of surname holders, and the minor disadvantage is outweighed 'because the population sampled by marriage records is the adult breeding population of interest in human population genetics' (Lasker, 1985, p. 90).

The death registers were probably more complete than births in the nineteenth century, though up to 1 in 600 had no surname because they were unidentified. However, death did not necessarily occur near to where people lived, and they are therefore the least favoured of the three indexes to use as the basis of surname mapping.

Maps 2.1a–d are based on data extracted from a list compiled by J. H. Sagar lodged in the library of the Manchester & Lancashire Family History Society, and used with his kind permission. In view of the difficulties explained above, male marriages were chosen for investigation as the line of least resistance to demonstrate the likeliest areas of family formation which would illustrate surname movement over a 130-year period. Notice that these are 'Spruce' maps of sorts, but we are collating all events over a ten-year period so it is just possible for the same person to appear twice on the same map (in the event of a second marriage following close on the heels of an earlier one during that decade).

The total numbers of marriages for the periods were 86 (1841–50), 124 (1881–90), 167 (1921–30) and 122 (1961–70). Because this is a relatively uncommon name, geographical movement becomes very clear using this method. In the 1840s, almost half the marriages (46 per cent) took place in Burnley or Blackburn, and 77 per cent were in Lancashire, with a small overspill into Yorkshire. There was little difference forty years later (45 per cent in Burnley or Blackburn, 65 per cent in Lancashire). By the 1920s, these had fallen to 35 per cent and 63 per cent respectively. The biggest change took place in the last period, as the figure fell to 5 per cent and 36 per cent, though the former can be explained to a large extent by changes in the boundaries of, and the creation of new, registration districts. (By the time of this post-war period,

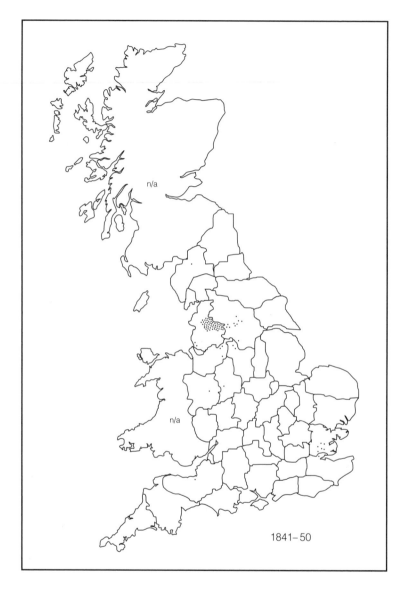

n/a

n/a

1841–50

2.1a–d   Sagar *above, right, p. 98, p. 99*
Sager/Sagar marriage maps reveal the slow dispersal of the surname over
a century and a half.

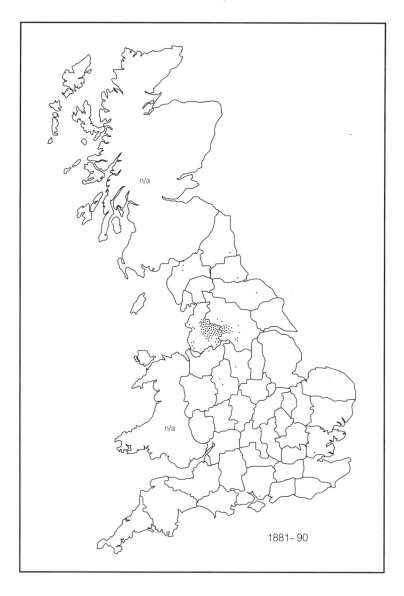

n/a

n/a

1881–90

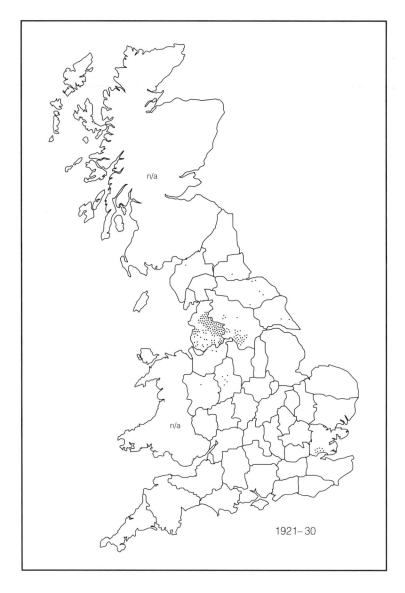

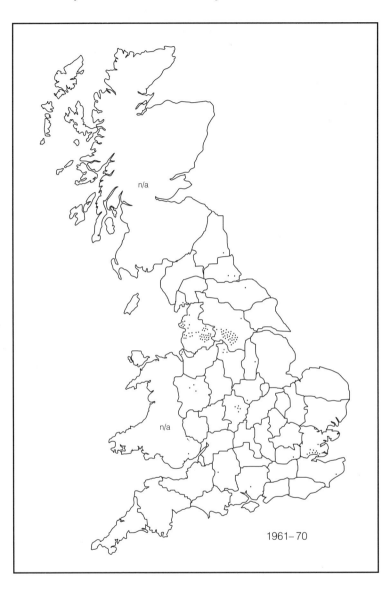

n/a

n/a

1961-70

all areas may also be slightly affected by a number of immigrants using this surname.) More significant is the rise in the absolute numbers in other areas, especially in the West Riding of Yorkshire. There are much smaller increases in the west midlands and London.

The maps do not tell us, of course, whether the increases in Leeds, Bradford and Sheffield were the result of successful breeding of male children in those areas, or of migration from Lancashire. For that, you would need the family trees themselves, though following unusual forenames and surnames from birth to marriage might give a more accessible indication.

There is no suggestion that this particular migration is 'typical' in direction. A lot of research needs to be undertaken before any conclusions can be drawn for the twentieth century using this method. (Eventually, figures will be obtainable from censuses until the birthplace question was dropped in 1961 but there are plenty of studies available for migration in the nineteenth century using this source.) What may be more typical is the relatively small degree of change in the distribution of this surname over the period covered. However inexplicable it may be for Lancastrians to take flight into Yorkshire, that distance is not great anyway – indeed, Burnley is next to the West Riding frontier, so it is much closer to Yorkshire than it is to most other places in Lancashire.

Some relief for puzzled Lancastrians may be achieved through a Banwell map for Sagar (and its minor variant Sager) in the 1980s. BT's Blackburn phone area (which includes Burnley, Clitheroe, and adjacent areas listed separately as registration districts) remains the surname's centre, having almost as many phones as any three other areas added together. The whole of West Yorkshire has almost as many, which supports the male marriage map as a credible, as well as an easy means of identifying surname distribution using General Register Office indexes.

This study of admittedly only one surname supports the general contention of Part 1 that such movement has been relatively small over long periods. It also suggests that an effect of tracking certain surnames back in time is to find them not only fewer in number (in line with the general size of the country's population – in 1841, England had under fifteen million inhabitants) but also more concentrated in place. We do not know whether the same effect would be evident if all the several variations of the name Sagar had been followed – that might have revealed that the nickname (it means 'sea-spear' according to Reaney) also ramified in other parts of the country.

Directories

Before we travel further back in time, the more astute of the tyros might find themselves wondering why so little has been said about the principal source used by that pioneer of surname detectives, H. B. Guppy. Variously known as county, town, Post Office, or Kelly's directories, they have been produced in numbers since the latter half of the eighteenth century, and were published regularly throughout the nineteenth and twentieth centuries. They were originally commercial, intended for anyone seeking customers for their goods, but they have also been used for many other purposes including, I suspect, a primitive form of creditworthiness by banks. Nineteenth-century directories normally included detailed maps of the area, but these have largely been pilfered by those who have seen more profit in having them framed and sold separately.

There are several reasons why the use of directories is no longer advocated for basic surname distribution exercises. Most important is the number of individuals within them, which is very small compared with the census (which was unavailable to Guppy) or with civil registration indexes. They are rarely for an area larger than a county, and those which did cover more were even more deficient in the proportion of the population found within them. Only those for the larger towns, published almost annually by the way, normally have a section in which names are presented in alphabetical order, and I have never seen a county directory indexed. The county directories list individuals place by place, so you might have to look at a hundred or more lists of names in order to extract data for the whole area.

The availability of directories is usually very good in Record Offices or larger libraries, but normally only for an area within the normal topographical orbit of the library's main interests. There are some very large collections in the Copyright Libraries (which nevertheless have only about half of all those published), the Society of Genealogists, the Institute of Historical Research, the Guildhall Library, all in London, and some major metropolitan libraries such as Manchester.

However, if you want to study the surnames of individuals with specific occupations, directories remain an excellent source, provided you are interested in the sort of occupation which they normally contain – farmers but not farm labourers – for neither of the main sources for the nineteenth century have occupations indexed. Some directories, indeed, are for specific trades or professions. Guppy used them for this reason, because he wished to identify the surnames of farmers whom he believed to be the least mobile in society; their surnames would thus reveal most about the 'homes of family names'. Directories are also useful when used in conjunction with other sources. For example, if we have detected from the civil registration indexes geographical migration from Burnley to Leeds among the Sagar family, we could consult the West Riding or Leeds directories to pick up the easiest clues as to why they moved – very often, such movement was for occupational reasons.

Discovering which directories are known to exist is now much easier than in Guppy's time, for there are three guides (Norton, 1950; Goss, 1932; and Shaw and Tipper, 1989) as well as occasional county guides which list them and give an indication, albeit incomplete, of where copies might be found. They also have useful introductions to their content. Perhaps we are interested in the occupational, as well as residential, characteristics of those immigrants, or their descendants, who can be recognised as such from their surname – again, directories are an easy guide, though their limitations as listed above must be remembered.

Electoral registers

These have been compiled more or less annually since 1832, with a break from 1940 to 1944. They record those entitled to vote at parliamentary elections, constituency by constituency, and until the 1880s they normally appear in alphabetical order of surname, district by district. This has two consequences – not only do you have to look through a large number of different electoral districts to cover the same county; you also have to look down all surnames starting with the same letter within each district in order to ensure that you have extracted all examples of a surname. (Since 1918, electoral registers have had to be printed in order of street and address.)

From 1832, relatively few people had the right to vote – only men owning property worth more than £10 per annum. This was extended to urban voters in 1867, to all owners of houses, and to lodgers paying £10 per annum, a right given to the countryside in 1884. Once again, therefore, we are dealing with those above the lowest social classes. There was a major reorganisation of constituencies in 1885, before which some MPs represented boroughs, others counties outside the borough boundaries. Before 1886, therefore, some electoral registers cover very large areas of counties, though the boroughs within those areas were not included.

The present location of extant copies of electoral registers is most conveniently found in Gibson and Rogers (1990b); maps showing constituencies before and after 1832 can be found in Gibson and Rogers (1990a).

To take one example, the electoral register for the Northern Division of the County of Wiltshire in 1841 contains the names of 5,241 men – but in each of 210 parishes separately! Nevertheless, it takes a surprisingly short time to seek out a few surnames and, if desired, note the parish of each. From the maps in Part 1, for example, we can follow through such names as Carpenter, Tanner, Trinder or Webb and find them as relatively prevalent a century and a half ago as they are today.

From rural to urban voters: for example, Liverpool in 1849 had 16,854 residents entitled to vote. Most were in the parish itself, but there are separate alphabetical lists for Everton, Kirkdale, Toxteth Park and West Derby. From this register, we can see that there are no Spruce voters, but two called Quick, two Furlongs, a couple of Taskers, and five Ashb(o)urners. The actual distribution within the city is not as significant as over a whole county, of course, unless you are engaged in a particular exercise which might involve, for example, the location of immigrants – but for that, the census is a far better source. Not only does that provide everyone's place of birth; it includes the great majority of immigrants who are notably absent from lists of those entitled to vote, especially before 1867.

Land Tax assessments

The tax on land ran continuously from the 1690s to 1949, but for most of that time its records are of little use, either because they have survived in very small numbers for the first ninety years, or because there are far better sources after the 1830s. Between 1780 and 1832, however, the Land Tax assessments were compiled annually and have been preserved among the Quarter Sessions papers in County Record Offices as evidence for the right to vote during that period. Until 1780, the few surviving returns are often simply lists of names, but for the next half century, owners, occupiers, and sums assessed are clearly specified. By definition, therefore, sub-tenants, lodgers, and servants are excluded, and often, especially in urban areas, a row of houses will be represented as simply 'John Smith and others'. For the whereabouts of all known Land Tax assessments, see Gibson and Mills (1984).

Tracing surnames across a whole county using these documents is time consuming. The only county known to have published a complete set of assessments is East Sussex (only for 1785), so the only way to extract the information is to spend some considerable time in a Record Office concerned going through the records of every parish in turn. Sometimes, they are stored in order of place, so ordering a whole batch is relatively easy; in other places, they have been stored in order of date, which will considerably extend the time needed to bring up the documents requested.

Poll books

Voting at regular Parliamentary elections was open until 1872 when the Secret Ballot Act introduced the system which we all take for granted. For almost two hundred years, the voting decisions of individual members of the electorate were not only declared in public – the record of how individuals had cast their vote was also published so that anyone could know which candidate they had voted for. In so doing, the entrepreneurs producing the books converted the original manuscript entries, written in chronological order of voting, into alphabetical order of surname (often arranged by capital letter only, however) in order to facilitate finding individuals. Residence and sometimes occupation are also provided. The present location of all known surviving poll books in Great Britain can be found in Gibson and Rogers (1990a).

Potentially, therefore, the whole country's electorate could be accessible every seven years at minimum long before the introduction of electoral registers in 1832, as well as continuing long after it. The counties (excluding boroughs) were regarded as single constituencies before 1832, even though they were represented by

more than one MP, and should have preserved such a record from
1696. Counting the total is done for you, of course, though it
should be remembered that in county constituencies each elector
had two votes.

However, the following problems should be taken into account
when using this method of research.

- Many constituencies were uncontested at each general election,
  so no poll was taken.
- Counties (and to a much lesser extent boroughs) varied in the
  number of pre-1832 poll books which were published, or which
  have survived, the west of the country (Cornwall, Devon, Dorset,
  Somerset, Gloucestershire, Cheshire, Lancashire, Westmorland,
  Cumberland and the whole of Wales and Scotland) being particularly poor. Oddly, though legislation compelled the recording
  of borough votes only as late as 1834, their earlier poll books
  have on the whole survived better than those for counties.
- The franchise was even more limited before 1832 than afterwards. Freehold land or tenements worth £2 per annum (and,
  after 1780, payment of the Land Tax) gave the right to vote in
  counties – there was no standard in boroughs, where custom
  prevailed. Thus, the limitation on numbers was made worse,
  from a surname point of view, by yet another record which is
  biased according to social class.
- Not all electors actually voted when an election was held; nevertheless, non-voters are often listed.
- Occasionally, only those voting for one particular candidate were
  listed. See Sims (1984) for bibliographical details.

For anyone researching the surname history of individual counties, therefore, poll books may be far more useful than relying on
them for a national coverage. Northumberland, for example, has an
excellent sequence of publications for the eighteenth and early
nineteenth century as several were republished with later polls. The
number of voters rose from 1,960 in 1722 to only 2,336 in 1826,
and the degree of continuity shown in their names in this admittedly rural constituency, over a century which saw the start of the
industrial revolution, is remarkable. Out of the 100 names which
form the core of this book, 81 were not found in any of the five
polls taken between these dates, and a further twelve were represented by only one example. It is clear that names were more

highly localised than they are today, but that names predicted from
Part 1 to have a strong presence in the north-east – Baxter, English, Redhead, Turnbull and Waugh – were indeed already there in
strength. Once again, there is strong evidence for continuity over
long periods of time.

Registers of baptism, marriage and burial

By far the most important source of information about these 'vital
events' before the introduction of civil registration on 1 July 1837
is the recording of religious ceremonies which, in the case of the
Church of England, has had a continuous history from the sixteenth century to the present day. Surviving registers in Wales,
Scotland, and indeed many in England tend to start somewhat
later. Anglican records of these events are called 'parish registers';
those of other denominations should be called 'non-parochial' registers. The many Protestant denominations are collectively known
as 'non-conformist registers', though this term is often used to
embrace Roman Catholics, Jews and others. The overwhelming
majority of people who lived in England before 1837 were Anglican, the proportion being greater the further back in time until the
Reformation of the sixteenth century. The numbers of non-Angli-
cans increased rapidly from the latter half of the eighteenth century.

They are not a complete record of birth, marriage and death as
the civil registers purport to be, and there are many reasons for
their deficiencies.

- Many registers have been lost, especially those before the seventeenth century.
- Baptisms, weddings and funerals have never been compulsory.
- Individual clergymen have varied in the assiduousness with
  which they have made and kept a permanent record of the
  events.
- Attendance was by denominational preference, which had a
  marked geographical bias.
- There were few laws governing the keeping and preserving of
  non-parochial registers.

As these registers have been so important to historians with widely
different interests for well over a century, their preservation and

accessibility have long been a matter of concern. Laws now govern the physical conditions in which the older parish registers are allowed to remain in churches, and most have been centralised into Diocesan Record Offices which are effectively the same institutions as City or County Record Offices in most areas. The majority of pre-1837 non-parochial registers were handed over to the Registrar-General in the nineteenth century for safe keeping and official recognition, and are now available to the public via microfilm or microfiche copies. A large number, particularly Anglican, have been published, certain counties having had societies devoted to this exercise – Bedfordshire, Cornwall, Cumberland, Devonshire, Lancashire, Shropshire, Staffordshire, Westmorland and Yorkshire are well served in this regard. Elsewhere, publication has been spasmodic, though there are good series of marriage registers in print for some counties.

Access to some form of index to any but the smallest registers is essential for the surname historian. By their very nature, they are voluminous, yet they cover only a small geographical area, so an unacceptably large amount of time would be necessary to extract the data required. I once presented a paper to the Lancashire Parish Register Society estimating how long it would take to publish all pre-1837 Anglican registers for the county at the then current rate of one volume a year (each covering some 7,500 entries) – we had worked on this task for a hundred years, but it would take the Society a further 550 years to complete!

Normally, each published volume is indexed, though there are some annoying exceptions, including the Phillimore marriage series. What we really need, however, is an index (county by county if not country by country) which will amalgamate all the data in separate publications. The idea of so doing is quite old – Hitching (1910) started a series of such indexes for the whole of England showing that in the year 1601, the surname Kent, for example, could already be found in Gloucestershire, Hertfordshire, Norfolk, Suffolk and Yorkshire.

That early attempt is now dwarfed by the International Genealogical Index (IGI) produced on microfiche and CD-ROM by the Church of Latter Day Saints (the Mormons) and sold to any interested party at a relatively modest cost. The full set is normally available in the larger FHS libraries, and public libraries commonly have the fiches for adjoining counties (see Gibson (1993) for their location). The IGI is not an index to every entry in every register of course; it should cover all but the most recently published and all those non-parochial volumes deposited in the PRO. It also includes a large number of register entries which have never been published or indexed before. Transferring data into the index is an ongoing task, but the whole set is reissued about once every four years. See Ecclestone (1989) for problems associated with using the IGI for analysing surname distribution, and for statistics of the 1988 edition.

The coverage is uneven across different counties and different time periods – some idea can be gleaned from an article in the Genealogists' Magazine (Vol. 21, No. 3, September 1983), which showed that Cumberland, Derbyshire, the City of London, Monmouthshire, Warwickshire and Worcestershire had been particularly well served at that time, whereas Berkshire, Cambridgeshire, Cheshire, Dorset, Herefordshire, Huntingdonshire, Norfolk, Northamptonshire, Rutland and Somerset were the worst. (Since then, of course, the incorporation of numbers of events in all counties has significantly increased, with a total of over fifty-six million entries in the 1992 edition for England.)

Thus, the IGI is more useful for periods earlier than the one we are presently considering, when a greater proportion have been published, and a greater proportion are in the Anglican registers. It also merges together variations of the same surname, and disentangling them in order to study the development of such variations would be a major, time consuming exercise. Given those provisos, we should be able to use the IGI in a way similar to the civil registration indexes, with the added advantages that for England (not Wales or Scotland) they are conveniently divided on a county basis already, and that places as well as names and dates are included, thus facilitating the pinpointing of families down to an individual parish.

Once again, we are faced with a problem of which section of the index to use, though in this case there is no counterpart of the death indexes – the IGI contains almost entirely baptisms and marriages. I would include all entries for the purposes of surname distribution, though marriages only might be more appropriate, according to your purpose. The same person might well appear as a baptism and later as a bride or groom, and many children baptised will die without having children; but these problems should affect all surnames equally, so the problems become self-cancelling when we are trying to estimate not total numbers of individuals but rough percentages in each area.

A seventeenth-century surname scan

We now reach back to a time when lists of some considerable importance to the surname detective become available once again. None is yet published complete on a national scale but, with the important proviso that they were produced at different times, it will be shown that *collectively* they can provide a very significant overview of the distribution of surnames in England during the seventeenth century. They are also to be used for comparison with the results of the extraction of names from the IGI.

From Appendix 3, you will see that there are two lists in particular which contribute to this attempt at a national coverage, plus a number of others whose publication can be used in order to fill an otherwise 'missing' county; the chart also indicates gaps in that accessibility which I hope can be filled in the not too distant future. A large number *are* available in manuscript or microfilm form, of course, but they are normally unindexed. See Gibson and Dell (1994) for a useful list of these early seventeenth-century sources.

The Protestation, 1641/2   All males over the age of 18 years were required to sign this petition immediately prior to the Civil War, pledging loyalty to the King and also to Parliament, naming Catholics as the common enemy. The names of those refusing to sign should have been added, and it is evident that occasionally some aged 16 to 18 and/or women were included. The resulting manuscripts, now in the House of Lords Record Office, take the form of long lists of names in sequence of individual parish.

Contributions for Distressed Protestants in Ireland, 1642   Both Royalists and Parliamentarians gave enthusiastically to relieve Protestants in Ireland following a massacre by Catholics; local officers collected gifts of cash from everyone in their parish, noting names and sums given. Returns are in the PRO. On the whole they are not as full as the Protestation, which was taken at the same time in many places, but there seem to be more names than in the Hearth

Tax (see below). Because it was a free gift, the sums should not be taken as a measure of wealth in the same way that a tax was supposed to be. See *Genealogists' Magazine* 21.9; returns for Buckinghamshire and East Sussex have been printed.

The Free and Voluntary Present, 1661   A Parliament relieved to see Charles II restored voted him a 'free and voluntary' gift in the first effective year of his reign in order to give tangible financial support in his straightened circumstances. Relatively few have been published, and the number contributing was, naturally, often much smaller than the normal, involuntary, taxation which followed. The returns are in the Public Record Office, and have been listed by Gibson (1990).

The Hearth Tax, 1662–74   At six-monthly intervals for most of these thirteen years, each house was assessed for a tax of one shilling payable for each fireplace. Often, though incorrectly, called the chimney tax, its collection necessitated invasion of homes by the collectors. In consequence one of the most unpopular taxes, it nevertheless left a legacy of assessment and payment documents which are very useful to many different historical interests. The returns are in the form of lists of names, the number of hearths shown against each occupier and those who were exempt for reasons specified in the legislation. Sometimes those who were exempt were omitted, and some names are now illegible – but we have in the Hearth Tax a very useful source of surname distribution, as the vast majority of householders appear to be named. Original returns are in the PRO, and are listed by Gibson (1990). The Hearth Tax is the commonest of all these seventeenth-century records to have been published, and others are available locally on microfilm.

There are in addition a number of other sources which have been used in the survey which follows merely to fill gaps in areas where the Protestation or Hearth Tax has not been published, but which, of course, could be used to supplement much more detailed studies of local areas, and the minute changes within them.

The Poll Tax, literally a tax on a head, each adult having to pay a fixed rate except for higher graduations for the richer elements of society. The tax was levied in 1660, 1667, 1678, 1689, 1691, 1694 and 1697, but relatively few survive. They are listed in Gibson (1990).

The Militia Assessment, 1663 has been located for Herefordshire only (excluding Hereford itself), and is a county valuation for the financial support of the county militia. It is in the British Museum, and has been published.

The Association Oath, 1695 was a response to a series of Jacobite plots, real and imaginary, during the early 1690s to unseat the newly crowned William III and his wife Mary Stuart. The 'Association' was a fervent affirmation of support for the House of Orange, and was signed by the majority of adult males in the country, as well as some females. Parliament laid down penalties for anyone not subscribing to the oath of allegiance. The surviving records are in the PRO, and are conveniently listed in the *Genealogists' Magazine* for December 1983 (Vol. 21, No. 4). Very few have been published, however.

Muster Books   These are lists of able-bodied men who were identified for call-up to a local militia, should the need arise. A guide to those which exist, including reference to those which have been published, can be found in Gibson and Dell, and Gibson and Medlycott, both published in 1989.

Problems – and how to overcome them

The scan of surnames using the above sources from the seventeenth century will provide a fascinating contrast to that in the late twentieth century, but anyone tempted to follow me along this exploratory trail should be forewarned that there are four major problems which were not encountered in the phone book search, as well as several we have met before.

- Some areas are not available in print, without which facility the relevant data is inaccessible to anyone who cannot read secretary script *and* spend many hours searching the original records in London repositories. So few of these records have been published for Scotland or Wales that the present scan is for England only. Even here, there are serious gaps, as nothing appears to be available, to anything like a county-wide extent, for Berkshire, Cumberland, Hertfordshire, Kent, Middlesex, Northamptonshire, Warwickshire and Worcestershire. The East Riding of Yorkshire is also missing.

If we happen to be interested in surnames which are predominantly distributed in later centuries in those counties which are not available in the seventeenth, however, there may be no option but to tackle the original records, with all the palaeographic problems which that entails. Furthermore, it may be important for the rarer names to notice whether the source concerned is available for the *whole* county. Much of south-east Lancashire is omitted from the published Association Oath roll of 1696, for example, so those Rochdale names referred to in Part 1 are largely underrepresented. (No Nightingales appeared in those parts of Lancashire available for the scan. All the Sladens have disappeared from Nottinghamshire and the West Riding, confirming the suspicion that it originated in Rochdale; a quick glance at the IGI reveals that all pre-1700 Sladen marriages in the county were in Rochdale or Burnley.) London, Norfolk, Oxfordshire and Westmorland are similarly defective.

It is also fair to warn that some of the publications are either not indexed at all (e.g. the Huntingdonshire or Leicestershire Protestation, and the Westmorland Hearth Tax, for example) or are indexed in a way which still leaves a massive amount of searching still to be done. (Instead of saying how many times a surname occurs on a page, the index will merely say whether it is more than once, leaving the surname detective to go through every entry – in the case of a common name like Smith, this may be for the majority of pages – in order to get an accurate total.) In many instances also, the total number of entries in the record is not given, leaving sometimes thousands or even tens of thousands of names to be counted. (See Appendix 3 for suggested totals for each record used in the present scan.)

We should examine the possibility that data for counties missing from the scan could be replaced from other sources, particularly the IGI. All counties have entries from the seventeenth century in the IGI, arranged in alphabetical order of surname, which might be used. There are, however, two difficulties which appear to be insuperable. There seems to be no way of equating a number of entries in a register with numbers found in the Protestation or Hearth Tax. The closest would be to count the number of marriages of males between, say, 1640 and 1670 which might provide a basis for assessing the number of 'breeding pairs'. However, counties vary dramatically in the proportion of all registers whose baptisms and marriages have been incorporated into this index, causing difficulties far worse than that described in Problem 3 below. Furthermore, the 1640s and 1650s (the 'Interregnum') include a period notoriously prone to entries missing from parish registers. The most I believe we can hope for is the roughest indication of whether the surname is present, and if so its extent – but this would be closer to a subjective impression rather than a statistical calculation.

Another way to acquire data for counties unprovided with a major published source is to use indexes of probate records, which are available for many areas for periods as early as the seventeenth century. They too have their disadvantages – they are not a simultaneous snapshot of testators, who in turn are not drawn from a cross-section of society; and, although it is unlikely that the same person will appear more than once, it is probable that certain families will have left a far greater proportion of probate records than others. Nevertheless, in the absence of another source, they can be used to effect, and in the scan, I have used probate indexes for Berkshire (1653–1710). (Accordingly, it may be that results for that county are somewhat more suspect than those for others.) The whereabouts of probates, and which indexes have been published, are most conveniently found in Gibson (1985). For Monmouthshire (not included in earlier or later *English* scans, of course), I have used the unindexed survey of the Duchy of Lancaster Lordships in Wales 1609–1613, with all the problems of allowing for an unknown number of multiple references to the same person.

• A second problem is that we are not presented with sources which have been created simultaneously. Appendix 3 will indicate that several sources have been used to compile the present scan, from as far apart as 1608 (Gloucestershire) to 1696 (Bristol, Lancashire, London). The majority are taken from the Protestation or one of the Hearth Taxes – whenever possible, the former has been preferred to the latter because so many more individuals (up to three times as many) are recorded in it. (Two

families called Kent in 1641 had expanded to nine by 1674 in
the Bassetlaw Hundred of Nottinghamshire, but this is very
exceptional.) Even the Hearth Tax publications may be several
years apart in different counties; but they may be a generation
apart from the earlier Protestation or later Association Oath. As
migration of individuals clearly takes place even between Hearth
Tax returns from the same year, there is potentially a huge
methodological problem in trying to combine data from sources
so many years apart. To take such a cavalier approach in merg-
ing data in similar circumstances for the nineteenth or twentieth
centuries would be unacceptable. However, I do not believe the
problem is nearly as great as appears to the purist on the surface.
The main reason for this conclusion is the fact that those counties most distant in time nevertheless reveal the same overall patterns as would be expected from the middle of the century.
Furthermore, comparison of results from Protestation and
Hearth Tax returns for the same county shows that very little
migration had taken place across county boundaries, despite the
intervening Civil War. Research has already discovered that
mobility was extensive but *over short distances*, though London
can be expected to contain examples of a large number of surnames as it was already attracting so many from the provinces.

- The bases on which the various source documents were compiled were not identical. An important consequence is that more
individuals appear in one than in another, covering the same
area – for example, we have noted that it is not uncommon for
three times as many people to be named in the Protestation as in
the Hearth Tax. For that reason, the former has been used in the
current scan in areas where both are available; but on a Spruce-
type map, using dots for individuals, counties with the Protestation will *misleadingly* appear to have three times as many
examples of a particular surname compared with the same area
if the Hearth Tax had been used. Spruce maps are therefore suspect, using the raw data, without an appropriate massaging
mechanism which eliminates such distortions. The problem is
overcome, of course, if the Banwell technique is used, but that
requires a critical mass of instances in order to be meaningful.

- However, the fourth problem challenges the application of that
technique in the seventeenth century to all but the commonest
surnames. The overall size of the population in the seventeenth

century was very much smaller than anything we are used to, or have been analysing, in later periods. It is generally believed that England and Wales grew from about 5 million people in 1600, only one tenth of its present figure, to about 6 million a century later. As many people now live in Greater Manchester and the west midlands as lived in the whole country at that time.

The total number of individuals in documents from the scanned areas was 616,557 or over 10 per cent of the total population, but as most of these were heads of household, they are considered to be an appropriate sample of the whole. The problem is not one of representativeness but of accommodation to the guidelines established in Part 1 about difficulties encountered when the number of instances of a surname falls below about 500. The Banwell technique is likely to give peculiar results and erratic distributions across boundaries the fewer the instances concerned. We must expect the total instances of each surname to be drastically smaller than three hundred years later, and therefore the number of Spruce-type maps to be far more appropriate. In the seventeenth century, we are helped by the fact that the boundaries, being those of the old counties, are far fewer; nevertheless, there comes a point at which the dot maps, for all their faults, have to be used, and this applies to the great majority of the sample of one hundred, and, I guess, of all surnames then in use.

At the rarest end of the scale the number of individuals with particular surnames is so small that theoretical objections fly out of the window. In a surprisingly large number of cases, so few have been discovered in England that Problem 3 above scarcely matters. It is possible, of course, that those surnames were located only in those areas missing from the scan, especially in the light of the tentative conclusion in Part 1 that the rarer the name, the less likely it is that their present location bears any relationship to their points of origin. The north-east Cheshire Hearth Tax returns have been incompletely published, so I should not have been surprised when I found no Spruces in the scan of that county, for example.

- Variations in spelling take on a far greater significance than in later periods. The problems are greater the further back in time we go, for a number of reasons: standardisation did not begin to take effect until the nineteenth century; many of the records are written by those who could not check other people's spelling of their name; regional and local accents were probably much stronger, putting an evident strain on those scribes who were unused to them; and ill-judged transcription, by some on whose publications we have to rely, is not unknown. In the case of many names, these are easily interpreted – Flecher for Fletcher, for example, which may well carry an echo of the origin of the name. In Devon, Bellamy becomes Ballamy because of local pronunciation. But were the eight people called Window in Bristol really Winders? Were all Devon Tookers really Tuckers? If we are to distinguish between Black and Blake, how do we interpret Blacke, Blac or Blak? In a century when u, v and w are often interchangeable, how can we distinguish between Purslowe and Purslove, two quite different names in origin? What of the sixteen Darlingstones in Cornwall – is this a variation of Darlington or from a totally different origin? Correctly identifying all possible variations is impossible because even 'best guesswork' is ultimately unverifiable.

Results of the seventeenth-century scan

In the light of the above provisos, it is probably safest to start with the commonest names on the list for a preliminary assessment of the probable effect of three centuries on surname distribution, all with well over 500 instances in the seventeenth century, which now show a more marked regional skew. In almost all examples which follow, the distribution already revealed by the Banwell system is confirmed. Barker (Map 2.2a) was more common from the Dee to the Wash and northwards into the North Riding, though with a greater prominence in Norfolk than at present. The name Booth (Map 2.3) was just as marked in a band from Liverpool Bay to the Humber estuary as it is at present with 321 out of 463 examples being found in Lancashire, Cheshire, Derbyshire, Nottinghamshire, Lincolnshire, and the West Riding of Yorkshire. Even within Nottinghamshire, the north-south differential is evident, with 85 per cent of Booths in the Protestation being in the north of the county. Chapman is strong in East Anglia, Lincolnshire and Yorkshire, and already shows that greater-than-average enclave in

Cornwall which is found three centuries later.

The concentration of Fletcher between latitudes through Gloucestershire and Newcastle upon Tyne already existed three hundred years ago, though with a greater emphasis in Oxfordshire than nowadays. The surname Fox, while not unknown anywhere south of Durham, appears in a very broad band from North Wales to the Wash, particularly common in Nottinghamshire. We noticed how Fullers were strongly concentrated in the 1881 census, but that covered only 16 counties; now we can show that over four-fifths of all Fullers in this seventeenth-century scan are found in Norfolk, Suffolk and London.

Rogers (Map 2.4) is clearly seen as a name of the south, with a western bias. The infection of the added, and unnecessary, 'd' had scarcely begun – in the areas where publication distinguishes the two spellings, there were 965 spelled 'Rogers', and 60 only 'Rodgers'. The latter had no bias towards the north-east where they currently predominate. The conclusion seems inescapable (not that anyone could surely wish to escape it) that Rodgers is a relatively modern phenomenon whose significance has little or nothing to do with the origin or distribution of the name; on the other hand, the figures indicate that their market share is growing at an alarming rate.

Smith (Map 2.5) was commoner in the east and in a band across the midlands and down to Gloucestershire – only in one area (Staffordshire) were they more than twice as common as an *average* distribution would have suggested. (Note that we cannot tell where all the Smiths were living because of problems 1 and 3 above.) In the case of this surname, therefore, the underlying trend in its present distribution was already evident three hundred years ago.

Tucker (Map 2.6) is strongly skewed to the south-west, as we saw them in 1881, with three in every five (449 out of a total of 725) being found in Devonshire. Webb (Map 2.8a) is concentrated on an area further north, in Gloucestershire, whereas Webster (Map 2.8b) is between latitudes passing through the Solway and the Wash.

The similarity of pattern across three hundred years shown by all these common names is quite extraordinary, all the more so when it is remembered that the source materials on which the surveys are based are so different from each other. The individual patterns

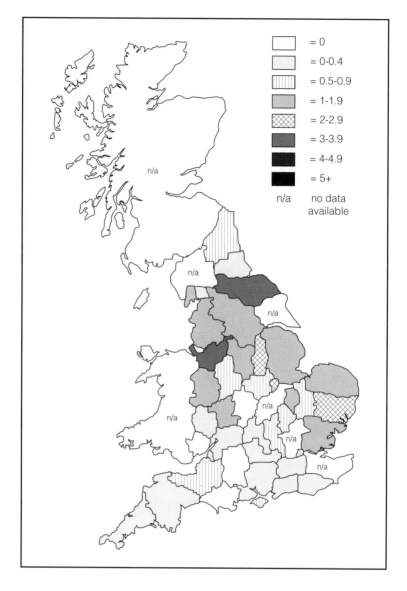

2.2a, b   Barker (1,064) *above*   Tanner (273) *right*
Two words for the same occupation were differentiated geographically
three hundred years ago, just as they are today.

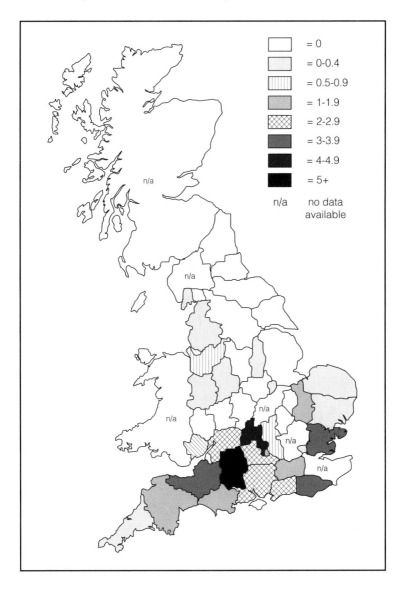

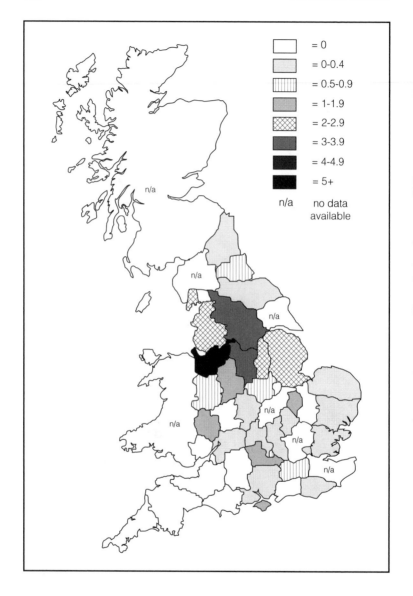

2.3   Booth (463)
Very common in a band from Lancashire and Cheshire to the North Sea –
it is a localised name for a herdsman's shelter.

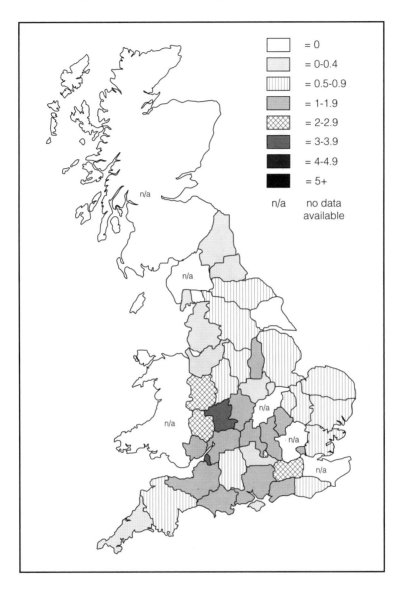

2.4   Ro(d)gers (1,172)

A name biased to the south and west, Rodgers was then rare and very thinly scattered.

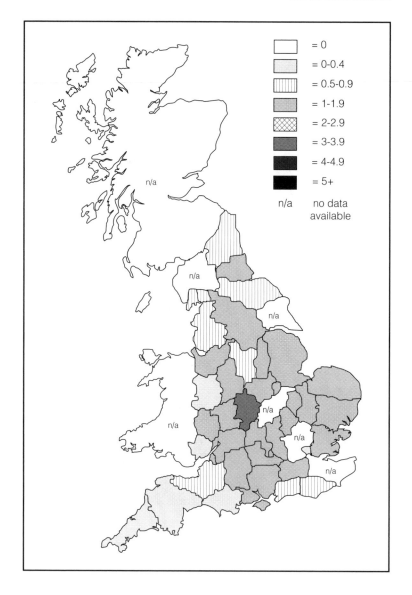

2.5   Smith (7,458)
(See Map 1.25) This commonest of surnames was already rarer in the north, the west, and south-west three hundred years ago.

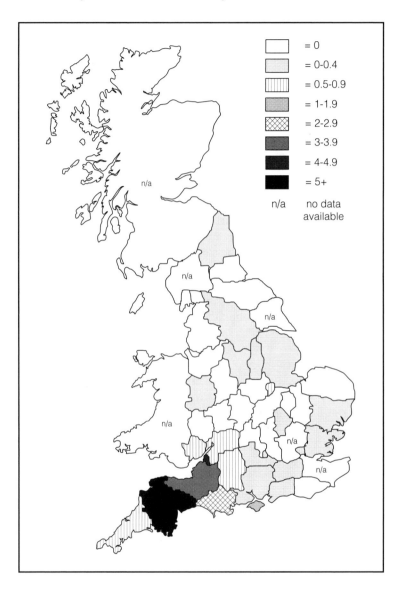

2.6   Tucker (723)

(See Map 1.10) Tucker was almost entirely confined to the south-west three hundred years ago. (Fuller was similarly concentrated in the south-east.)

of common English surnames show remarkable similarities, despite
the chronological distance and the restricted geographical area of
the scan. Once again, it is worth stressing that these are similarities of *proportion in each area, not of the distribution of absolute numbers of individuals.*

*The conclusion seems inescapable, for chance could not give the same
results over so many surnames. The Banwell method, when applied to
phone books in the late twentieth century, provides a fairly accurate pre-
diction of the pattern which would have been found over three centuries
earlier.*

The necessary reconciliation between this evidence of continuity
over three centuries and the undoubted volume of migration
referred to at the start of Part 2 can be found in the average distances involved in these individual movements. Again, all
researchers have revealed the same pattern – that the average was
quite short, the great majority travelling under twenty miles before
the industrial revolution and perhaps thirty miles afterwards. David
Hey (1987, pp. 72–82) in a summary of research into migration,
suggests that part of this limitation after 1660 may be explained by
the Settlement laws (which lasted until well into the twentieth century). Over 80 per cent of people living in Preston as late as 1851
were within thirty miles of their birthplace, with a further 7 per
cent having come from Ireland (Anderson, 1971, pp. 36–41).

The above comparisons across the centuries do not seek to ignore
any major discrepancies which might argue in any significant way
against the general theme of continuity. If the county concerned is
adequately provided with data, the similarities over the three hundred years are striking. The corollary is that, for the English surnames, significant concentrations in the seventeenth century have
not died out; nor have names ramified during three centuries to a
point where they are over twice the expected rate as before. At the
same time, counties which today have several examples of names
associated with other areas were likely to have few or even none in
the seventeenth century. If we take Garlick as an example, its
present concentration in Derbyshire and the West Riding may be
plainly seen by the seventeenth century (Map 2.7), but they had
not yet spread into Lincolnshire, Dorset, Somerset, Sussex, or north
Lancashire where they are not uncommon today.

The name Webster (Map 2.8b) raises the question of Scottish,
Manx and Irish immigrations. If only England is scanned, surely

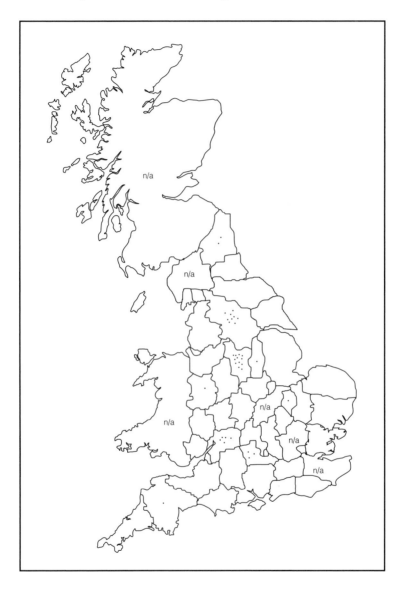

2.7 Garlick
The present concentration of Garlicks in Derbyshire and the West Riding can already be seen in the seventeenth century.

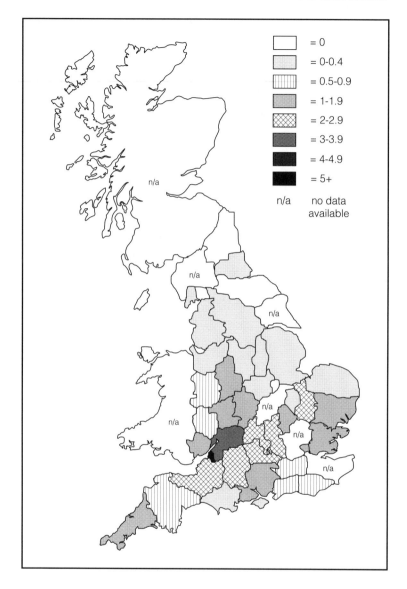

2.8a, b   Webb (1,067) *above*   **Webster** (460) *right*
(See Maps 1.14, 1.16) Webb was a southern name in the seventeenth century, already popular around the Severn estuary; Webster occupied the northern half of the country except for the borders with Scotland.

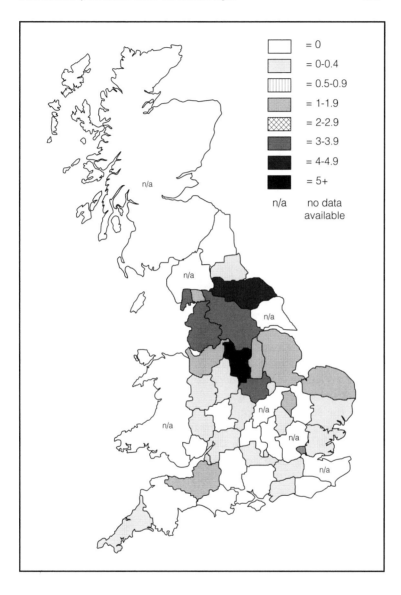

this invalidates any comparison with the phone book exercise? If the name is not English in origin, the criticism is probably correct. We look in vain for Murdoch(k), Oliphant, Shimmin or Stalker; examples of Waugh (not to be confused with Warr) are confined to Northumberland; and there are only eighty-eight called Black in the seventeenth-century scan. Accordingly, using either main method of describing distribution in England might give a very misleading suggestion as to their sources of origin. This, of course, leaves an open question over the study of names which in modern times have strong connections in two countries. Wiseman, for example, has strong connections with Aberdeenshire, but also with Norfolk, Suffolk and Essex where they had a significant presence in the seventeenth century (though nowhere else in England).

There are some discrepancies, however, which we should expect among the rarer names for reasons explained earlier, but which can also be seen in a few with over 500 in the phone books.

The greatest change among the relatively common names may be noticed in the surname Kent (Map 2.9). Whereas today it is found largely in the east, south-east and Cornwall, it was most common in Cheshire and Hampshire in the seventeenth-century scan. This merely adds to the controversy about the nature of its origin, rather than helping to solve it. Turpin, too, appears to have shifted over time – the modern concentration in Cornwall had its counterpart in Dorset a hundred years ago, according to Guppy, but in the seventeenth century they are very common in Devonshire (Map 2.10); similarly, the modern West Riding emphasis appears to have moved north in the intervening three centuries from Lincolnshire and Nottinghamshire. The two names are noticeable because they are so exceptional to the general trend of continuity.

How erratic do results appear if we go below the self-imposed guideline of 500 instances? Bacon was in East Anglia and the north-east midlands, but the former had the greater concentration, unlike the present distribution. Bellamy was far more common in London then than it is now, but otherwise the concentrations in the east midlands and Devon were already marked. The spread of Drinkwater (Map 2.11) on the western side of England from Dorset to Cumbria was evident, though the high concentration in modern times around south Manchester could not have been predicted from the seventeenth-century figures. Foot(e) was largely confined to the counties of Cornwall, Devon and Dorset (77 out of 124) with none north of Nottingham; it is distributed across the south of England, particularly from Dorset westwards, though three centuries ago there was a small pocket in (oddly) Herefordshire greater than today. (Because of the small population, this Herefordshire 'concentration' consisted of only seven families.) Webber, too, is found largely in Devonshire, some in Cornwall, and few elsewhere. It seems that falling below 500 examples begins to increase the likelihood that differences between Stuart and modern distributions will become evident, a finding consonant with the conclusion in Part 1. The break is not dramatic – but the fewer the individuals, the less likely they are to show the same pattern as today. Quite a few Pinchbecks turn up in Suffolk, in addition to the expected grouping in the 'home' county Lincolnshire, and there are some unexpected Lightfoots in Devon. Only a handful of Dutch showed up, on the North Sea coast from the North Riding to London.

Most patterns remain, even among some of the rarer names. Every Ashburner (except one, in Lancaster) was in the Furness district of Lancashire. Even the proportions of people having certain kinds of surname remain fairly constant. Adding together all those with a surname based on the points of the compass (though ignoring the surname Northeast in Devon!), we find that Norths formed 20 per cent in the seventeenth century and 22 per cent in the 1980s; Souths fell from 10 per cent to 6 per cent while Easts did the reverse; and West continues to dominate, with 62 per cent three and a half centuries ago and 64 per cent now. It will come as no surprise, therefore, that the geographical distribution has also changed little.

The overall picture of continuity within original areas (if indeed they *were* original), accompanied by dispersal on the fringes or by migration to considerable distances, can now be used in order to cast more light on some of the problems which were thrown up in Part 1. Of the 115 Quicks showing up in the seventeenth-century scan, 99 were in Devon, and a further six in Cornwall, virtually eliminating other possible origins. Only four Setters have been found, three in Devon forming a genetic base for their present modest presence there in the 1980s.

Another problem left over from Part 1 was whether the surname Blake is a variation of Black (Map 2.12). Although Black is clearly a Scottish name, such variations might be expected to occur some

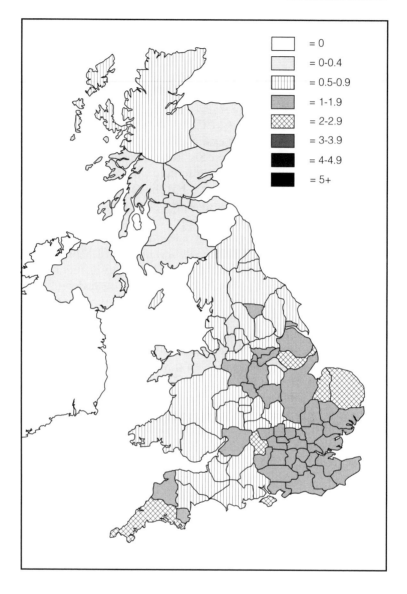

2.9a, b   Kent   20thC. (6,800) *above*   17thC. (528) *right*
Kent shows significant changes over three centuries to an unsual degree.

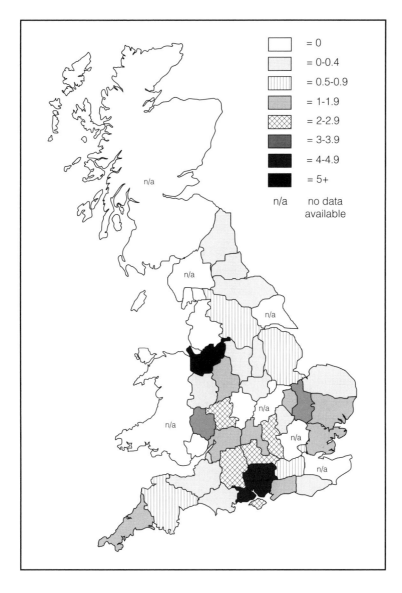

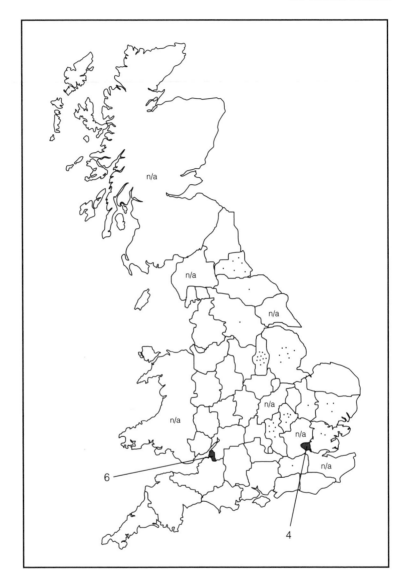

2.10 Turpin
Turpin, another name whose location *has* shifted over time.

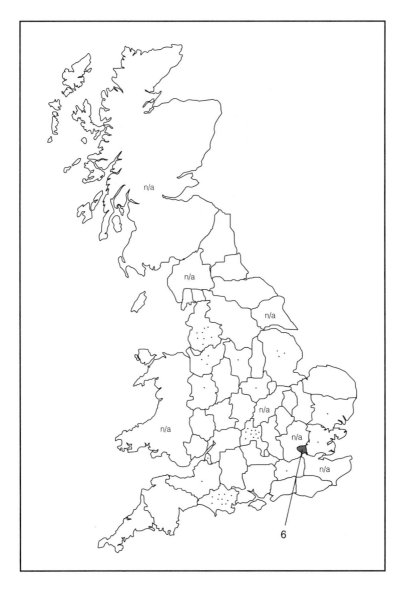

2.11   Drinkwater

Drinkwater (see Map 1.5) hardly seems to have moved in three hundred years.

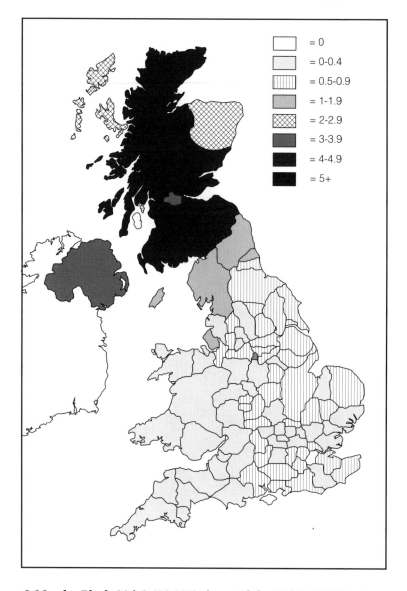

2.12a–d   **Black** 20thC. (12,075) *above*   **Blake** 20thC. (7,838) *right*
          Black 17thC. (88) *p. 136*   **Blake** 17thC. (467) *p. 137*
Are Black and Blake really variations of the same name? The four maps
strongly suggest a Scottish origin for Black, but south-west England for
Blake.

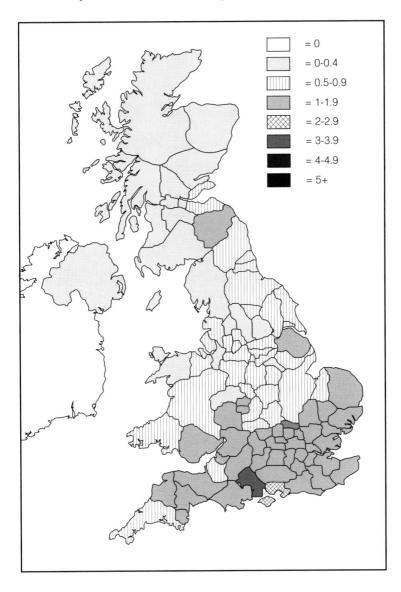

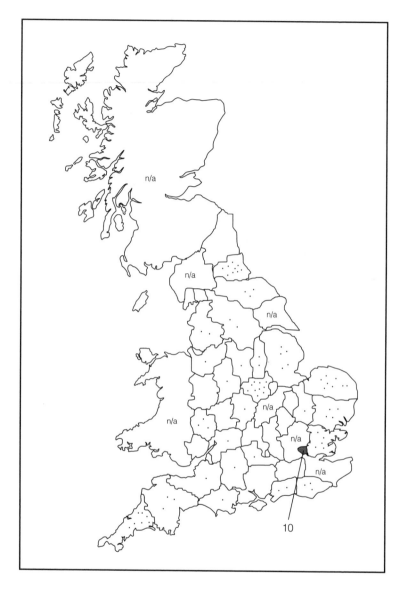

10

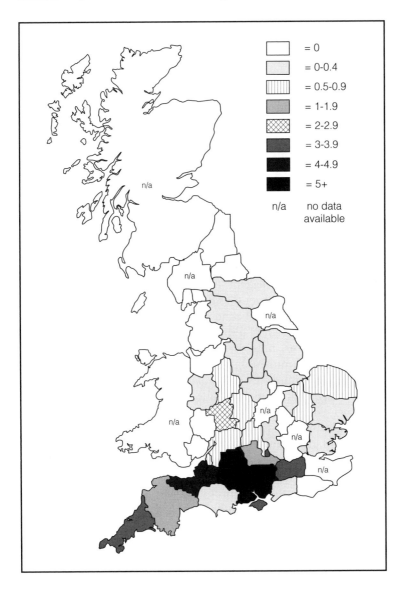

distance from the point of origin, perhaps through differences in accent, or unfamiliarity on the part of scribes. Figures from the seventeenth century suggest, however, that Blake is very much an English name – or at least an English spelling and pronunciation. Only 88 Blacks have been found – ten in London, but no other county having double figures. In contrast, there are 467 Blakes, the name being particularly extensive in Cornwall, Devon, Hampshire and London. This is far too numerous to be a consequence of Scottish migration (which *could* easily account for the number and distribution of Blacks at that time), and requires an explanation rooted in south-west England. The two names are certainly tied in meaning, as the compounds Blakelock, Blacklock, Whitlock and Whitelock suggest.

Winder (Map 2.13) is virtually confined to the north-west of England, where its location in north Lancashire, Westmorland and the West Riding supports the place theory for its origin; there is, however, a significant element in Hampshire. Weaver (Map 2.14) spreads southwards from Cheshire to Gloucestershire, but without that concentration in the north of the area which one would assume to be the sign of a uniquely Cheshire origin.

Many problems, however, cannot yet be solved by the seventeenth-century scan. All but three of the thirty-three examples of Death are found in Essex and Suffolk (one having strayed as far as Staffordshire) but that distribution gives no indication as to its meaning. Similarly, the two occupational names Carpenter and Cartwright, are strongly located in the very counties where we noted them in our own time – the former (Map 2.15) in an inverted horseshoe from Shropshire south to Hampshire and north-east to East Anglia; the latter (Map 2.16) across the north midlands with a heavy concentration in Shropshire and Staffordshire. Why such patterns should be apparently unrelated to the nature and distribution of those occupations remains a mystery.

Several questions left over from Part 1 remain unresolved simply because the common change revealed by going back in time is merely a focusing down of the later distribution. Darlington was located almost entirely in Cheshire three hundred years ago, Pipe being confined to Suffolk, Jagger to the West Riding, and Clay, Heath, Spring, and Spicer similarly conform to a recognisable twentieth-century pattern. Even Tinkers were sandwiched between two layers of Tinklers!

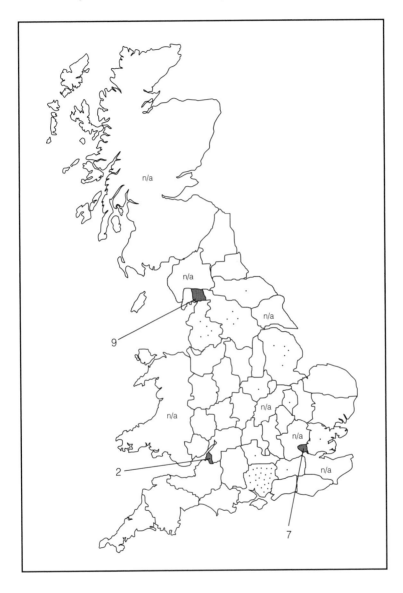

2.13   Winder
The small group in the north-west is to be expected from a placename, but the concentration in Hampshire is unexpected and unexplained.

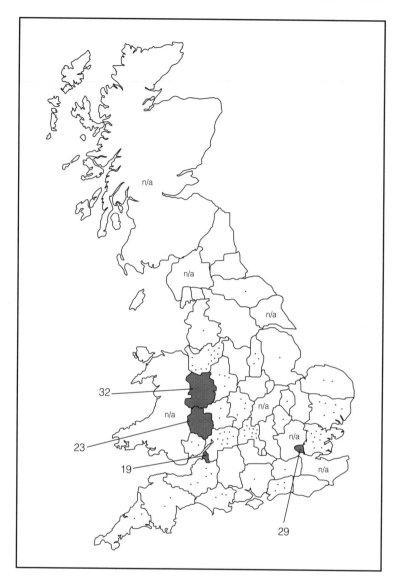

2.14   Weaver

(See Map 1.4) The high figure for London is a reflection of the size of the population, but the concentration in the west seems to indicate its area of origin.

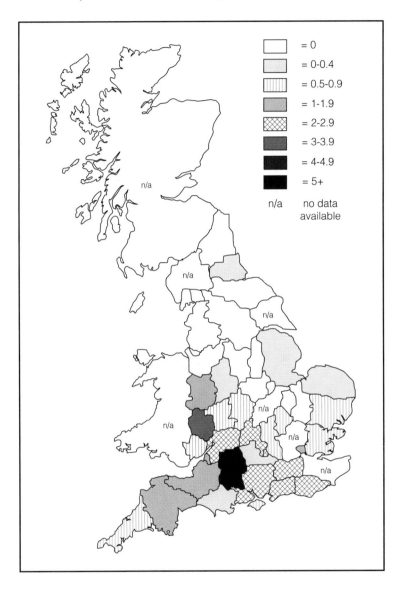

2.15   **Carpenter** (386)

Carpenter in the seventeenth century had the same distribution as in the twentieth; why was this occupational name not as widely used in the north?

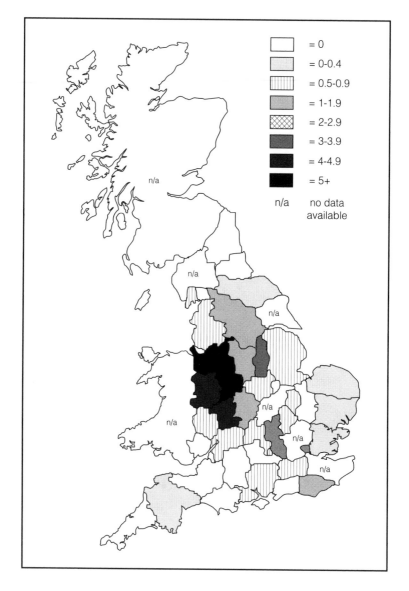

2.16   Cartwright (267)
The broad band from North Wales to the North Sea can still be seen in today's distribution of the surname Cartwright.

Oh yes, I almost forgot – one *Purston* did turn up – but in Shropshire, rather than Northamptonshire or Yorkshire, where it is a placename.

Part 3

The distribution of surnames in medieval England

Introduction

We are about to reach back into the earliest period of English surname history, a time when the simple practices which govern their later use were still developing, when many people still had only one name or, if they had a second, probably a non-inherited byename. A few, indeed, used more than one second name, either on different occasions or even in the same document. Furthermore, the sources of simultaneous information about the great majority of the population are few, and so far rarely published. Part 3 will describe those sources and spend some time summarising the main findings of considerable previous research into this early period, before seeing the results of a scan of names in the fourteenth century. We shall thus have a final check on the accuracy of the distribution analysis of Part 1 as a predictor of where those same surnames were found over six hundred years ago.

It is by coincidence that the principal sources of information about the distribution of surnames in the Middle Ages are as long before the seventeenth century as we are after it. In going back so far, we reach a time when, according to the textbooks, we cannot assume the same degree of continuity or stability which has been found on our trail so far. Even before the research starts, we are warned that surnames in the fourteenth century are likely to have certain characteristics which are not only disconcerting to the uninitiated, but should, more importantly, cause us to question the statistical bases of our enquiries. These problems are discussed after we examine the sources themselves.

We take for granted that a person's name will be in two parts – the first, or forename, which in this country has Christian baptism at its root, and a second which is normally inherited from a parent.

This was not always so, as the earlier history of this, and most other countries, shows; the personal name is the one given to each separate child, and what we now call a surname was a later development, being at first a subordinate description, almost as an adjective describes a noun. A curious, late survival of this relationship is the fact that a child was not given a surname on an entry of birth in England and Wales until 1 April 1969.

In their capacity as adjectives, surnames could be varied to suit whim and convenience, and could change with time even for the same person; they could also describe different aspects of an individual – colour, occupation, social or geographical position, relationship, character traits, all either in a straightforward manner or as a nickname, anything in fact which helped to distinguish one Edward, Henry or Robert from another. It is useful to bear in mind this subordinate role of medieval surnames when trying to uncover the mysteries of their early development.

Far more has been written about surnames in the Middle Ages than about any subsequent period. Interest in their meaning is of very long standing, and the subject cannot be properly researched without an exploration of their origins. Hence, any self-respecting dictionary of surnames will include the date and location of early examples, with variations. In addition to the introductions to such dictionaries, whole books have been written to try to account for the development of surnames, but only Reaney (OES) was an effective precursor to the researches of R. A. McKinley. Rarely have such works trespassed upon the seventeenth century, let alone the twentieth. Much of the research has been undertaken by Scandinavian scholars, notably Fransson (1935), Tengvik (1938), and Lofvenberg (1942), the last writing under severely restricting wartime conditions.

More recently, it has been realised that the subject has wider implications, particularly relating to social class, geographical mobility, and the origins of named settlements. Pioneering this type of research has been Richard McKinley (see Introduction). The first five volumes of the English Surnames Series, four written by McKinley himself, have established a pattern for the main issues in research first explored by Reaney – the development, county by county, of surnames according to type (locative, toponymic, occupational, patronymic, and nickname), and the relationship between those types, on the one hand, and social class and geographical

mobility on the other. Part 3 therefore owes a considerable debt to
the pattern, as well as to the detail, contained in that series, and
the results of the fourteenth-century scan are most appropriately
considered as the origins of the various surname types are
described.

Research has revealed a connection between surnames and
social status, in this case a relationship which is hardly surprising
as the name so often derived from the status. However, what
appears to be a common-sense approach to the meanings of names
can prove very misleading. Apparently high status names – King,
Prince, Lord, Bishop – probably started as nicknames rather than
being a true reflection of occupation. At best, they might have been
applied to someone who worked in a particular level of household.
(Servants as such gave rise to a number of names – Arlot, Boy, Day,
Ladd, Swain, for example; see OES, pp. 193–7. Not all persons are
ever listed in a medieval document, but some classes are more regularly missing than others, especially servants.) The reasons for
coming to that judgement lie in the very number of such names,
which far exceeds the number of offices which could have given rise
to them, and the fact that serfs were called Knight, Squire, Priest
or Chapman, all occupations which serfs would not have been
allowed to follow. (ESS2, p. 50; McKinley, 1990, p. 136; OES, pp.
168–70)

This difference between serfs (who held land in return for services
and restrictions on their movements) and freemen itself gave rise to
some hereditary names, most commonly Bond (though that can be
a personal name) and Freeman. Serf names were more common in
the south of England, where there were more of them, but on the
whole that status is encapsulated in fewer names (e.g. Cotterell)
than those who had their freedom (Akerman, Farmer, Frank, Fry,
Holder, Sokeman). Both Bond (with variant Band) and Frank
(Franche) are also to be found in a number of compound names –
Younghusband, Frankland, and so on (e.g. ESS5, p. 233). These
names were sometimes held by persons of the opposite status in the
fourteenth century, suggesting that they had risen or fallen in rank
since the time they were acquired. At first the majority of wealthy
families seem to have had locative names, with the lower orders
developing surnames based on nicknames, personal names or occupation names. Very few wealthy taxpayers in the fourteenth century had occupational surnames but by the sixteenth century these

distinctions had virtually disappeared.

Distinctive occupational surnames can also be used to judge migration, though McKinley is of the opinion that they were held by a relatively immobile section of the community. 'Occupational surnames were less prone to migrate from their original homes than were surnames in some other categories, particularly locative' (ESS3, p. 153). The absence of a fairly common but regionalised name like Walker from East Anglia (before 1500), Oxfordshire (before 1350) and Sussex (before the sixteenth century), for example, is of some significance. Stringer, common in Lancashire and Yorkshire in the seventeenth century, did not reach Sussex until the early sixteenth (ESS5, p. 255), and does not appear in the scan of admittedly defective fourteenth-century sources further south than Westmorland.

In contrast with the rather more fluid locatives, occupational names which were regional in origin are more noted for their extent of ramification within limited geographical areas. Some, of course, atrophied, even if they had started to become hereditary. Others, such as Crowther or Boardman in Lancashire, remained restricted in numbers as well as in area. A few were, genetically at least, very successful indeed, ramifying to such an extent that they become very common in some parts of the country by the seventeenth century while remaining virtually absent in others. Lancashire is particularly noticeable in this regard, with names such as Lord (in the Bury and Rochdale area) and Rimmer (north of Liverpool) becoming very numerous in certain districts. The same phenomenon can be found in other counties – Trinder ramified in Oxfordshire, for example, though it seems to be accidental that Walker should do so when Tucker did not.

Although only five volumes of the ESS have been published at the time of writing (covering Lancashire, Norfolk, Oxfordshire, Suffolk, Sussex, and the West Riding of Yorkshire), some national generalisations are already emerging, though with certain characteristics which are unique to, or distinctive about, each individual county. Pinpointing where families of specific surnames were living during the period of surname formation in the Middle Ages can prove very enlightening. As McKinley observes, 'Though much valuable work has been carried out on the etymology of topographical surnames, very little attention has been paid to their distribution' (ESS4, p. 187), a deficiency which his own writing will inspire many others to correct. George Redmonds gently admonishes Reaney (ESS1, p.1) for reaching conclusions about the origin of some names without investigating their distribution. Reaney himself had been doubtful about the usefulness of distribution studies, as we have noted.

Research for this book, therefore, has not been quite so blind into the unknown as for later periods. Patterns have already been established into which any conclusions drawn from an application of the Banwell method can be placed. The relatively rapid development of surnames calls into question certain aspects of that method, and it remains to be seen whether its conclusions are consonant with the findings of other, well-tried methods of investigation. The information might be so uncertain that the method has to be abandoned; as we have already noted in Part 2, the relatively small size of the total population even in the seventeenth century reduces its value as a research tool; that is compounded for the Middle Ages by a current lack of widely available sources which cover a large proportion of the population.

Sources of surname distribution in medieval England

Lay Subsidies   These were taxes on movable property paid by the laity (clergymen *per se* paying Clerical Subsidies), surviving records being in the PRO. The earliest to be called by this phrase was collected in 1275, and they were raised at regular intervals, and in different forms, thereafter until the seventeenth century. After 1332 (1334 in the case of Kent alone on a county-wide basis, though there are occasional later survivors – Horton and Stone in Buckinghamshire for 1336, for example) there are no individual names, only village totals for two hundred years until the Great Subsidy of 1524–5. Hence, the period from 1275 to 1332 is critical, located as it was at an important time in the development of surnames.

For detailed, historical accounts of Lay Subsidies, see Willard (1934) and Beresford (1963). The principle was to tax individuals as a fraction of the assessed value of their movable goods, the fraction varying from year to year and even (after 1294) from place to place. There was a difference between urban and rural areas as to which goods had to be assessed and which were exempt. In 1327, the fraction was one twentieth, whereas five years later it was one fifteenth in the countryside, and as high as one tenth in towns.

There is a well-researched connection between the Lay Subsidies and social class, as they contain always a minority of the population – those who were wealthy enough to be assessed – though Peter Franklin, editing the Gloucestershire Lay Subsidy of 1327, has recently advised against making assumptions which might automatically exclude all those of poorer rank. On each occasion, the poor were formally exempt, a minimum payment usually being set – in 1327 it was 6*d*. The church was also exempt, except in so far as some clerics owned lay property after 1291. Others who escaped the collection were 'moneyers' (workers in the royal mints), inhabitants of the Cinque Ports and, alas, the Counties Palatine, Cheshire and Durham. Tin miners in Cornwall and Devon were also exempt, but their names are included in the Devon subsidy roll of 1332. On the other hand, individuals having property in more than one small area (the 'vill') might appear more than once in the record. Simon Blake paid the 1327 tax on property in three different Essex vills, for example. In later centuries, when there was apparently no association between surname and social class, tax returns can be used as useful samples of the total population; in the fourteenth century, however, there *was* a strong connection as we shall see.

The Poll Tax This was technically another Lay Subsidy, but now classified separately because of the character of its format. It was levied in 1377, 1379 and 1381, the basis being slightly different in each case. In 1377, everyone over the age of 14 (except beggars) was to pay one groat (4*d*) to the Crown; in 1379 a grading, relating to social class, was introduced on everyone over the age of 16, and over 15 in 1381. This last collection sparked riots which caused the Crown to change its policy, and for the next century and a half only village totals, with no names, survive. Thus, the fourteenth-century treasure house of surname data came to an abrupt end, and anyone tracing families in the fifteenth century has to depend on alternative, and inferior, sources of information.

Poll Tax returns are available for almost all English counties, and normally include the names and payments of some 60 per cent of the whole population, several times more than may be found in the earlier Lay Subsidies. In some areas, occupations are also given in the record, a matter of some significance in relation to the development of surnames as we shall see.

Like the other Lay Subsidies, the records are all in the Public Record Office (Class E179), but so far relatively few have been published, presumably because of their very size. In some ways, therefore, they have the same significance for the surname detective as the index to the 1881 census – the information is there for what is by far the best source available, but only a small minority is yet available in published form. This will change in the next few years, as Oxford University Press is to publish them all for the British Academy, edited by Carolyn Fenwick.

Hundred Rolls   These are the results of enquiries into the rights and properties of the Crown. Although they are available for many counties from 1273, their main use for the surname detective lies in the fact that the 1279 surviving returns are extremely detailed in a few cases – Bedfordshire, Buckinghamshire, Cambridgeshire, Huntingdonshire, Leicestershire, Oxfordshire, Suffolk and Warwickshire – which list the names of all tenants, including the humblest. J. B. Harley's useful article (1961) includes a map indicating the extent of coverage within those counties, and which have been published. The documents are relatively early in the history of inherited surnames, and in some cases are available in the absence of published Lay Subsidies.

The three types of document above are the principal means by which we can try to see the distribution of surnames *at any one time* county by county. There are additionally a large number of other possible sources which may be called upon in certain circumstances.

- In counties for which none of the three exists in published form, there are more limited surveys of inhabitants, usually for the purpose of recording current tenancies in manors or other domains. They have been used in Durham, Northamptonshire, and Rutland for the purpose of the fourteenth-century surname scan, the results of which are built into Part 3.
- In even less fortunate counties, no simultaneous survey has been published or even exists, so recourse must be had to documents which cover a wide chronological period, in the same way that

the wills index to Berkshire was used in Part 2. These documents abandon the 'snapshot' principle, and offer greater risks of having bias as to social class and multiple references to the same person. Cheshire has been covered in this way.

- A large number of surnames will already have been found to originate in only one region or county, and the detective following those names may be more interested in the detailed history of a name within a very limited area over a long period of time. The surname scans which can provide a distribution snapshot every few hundred years may be quite inappropriate to such an exercise, which requires as many continuous sources of surnames as possible over that limited geographical area.

The footnotes provided by the ESS indicate the wide variety of documents used to satisfy these needs, though not all have been published by any means. The following list tries to cover only the main sources, and it is worth consulting the publications of local record societies (Mullins, 1958, 1983) in order to see what others might be available. (In particular, records relating to petty or serious offences may be a fruitful source of surnames.) Those series located in the Public Record Office are being published at regular intervals.

Charter Rolls in the PRO, 1199 to 1517 contain grants of land and privileges to organisations; discontinued in 1517 when they are to be found in the Patent Rolls. Calendars are available 1226–1517, with full texts 1199–1216.

Close Rolls in the PRO, from 1205 to 1903, a very wide variety of subjects including deeds, wills, leases, naturalisation, change of name. Most of the medieval period has been calendared, published to 1509, with full texts 1227–1272.

Curia Regis Rolls in the PRO, cases before the King's Bench and Common Pleas, containing many pedigrees establishing plaintiff's right. The printed calendar is from 6 Richard I to 1242.

Feet of fines 1182 to 1833 These record fictional lawsuits raised in order to establish the legal ownership of land. Many local calendars have been published, but they are in the normal legal language, Latin, until 1733.

Fine Rolls in the PRO, 1120 to the execution of Charles I, the earliest being known as 'Oblata' Rolls. 'Fines' in this case were payment for privileges – in this case, to enter land being inherited, liberty from knight service, safe conduct, pardons, etc. Calendars are published to 1509 in 22 volumes.

Freemen Rolls   Records of the granting of the freedom of a chartered borough or guild. Those surviving from before 1500 are: Chester, Newcastle upon Tyne, Wells and York.

Inquisitiones post mortem 1218 to 1645, investigations into the landholding of those who held land directly from the Crown, though many of the witnesses were of less exalted a status. Many calendars have been published relating to local cases, those held by the Public Record Office being calendared 1219–1422.

Manorial records   Free tenants gave military service or paid rent for 'their' land; bondsmen or villeins had to pay for the privilege by working on the land of the Lord of the Manor until that arrangement was commuted into cash payment. The Manor Court rolls record the passing of lands from one tenant to another, with the occasional surveys and 'extents' being taken, and the appointment of local officials. It is rare to find a long series of records available for any one manor, however.

Patent Rolls in the PRO, 3 John to 9 Geo VI contain grants to individuals and organisations concerning licences, wardships, and right to use land; more domestic matters such as sewers, keeping the peace and gaol delivery may also be found. Calendars are published 1226–1578.

Plea Rolls in the PRO, from 1273 to 1875 contain several pedigrees among the actions heard in the Curia Regis. Many of the early rolls have been published by the Selden Society.

Wills   Publications of indexes to series of wills can be most conveniently obtained from Gibson (1985). Those surviving from before 1500 are found in the national collections of the two Archbishops, and in Bedfordshire, Berkshire, Buckinghamshire, Cambridgeshire, Dorset, Essex, Hertfordshire, Huntingdonshire, Kent, Leicestershire, Norfolk, Suffolk, Sussex and Worcestershire.

Problems and pitfalls

Inheritance

Family historians are normally interested in surnames as long as they are inherited from one generation to another. Even though most names have been polygenic, so that not all bearers of a name are descendants of an original holder, there is an almost instinctive affinity between a Cartwright researcher now and those located three hundred years earlier. Sooner or later, however, you will find that automatic relationship between the inheritance of surnames and the inheritance of paternal genes is broken. The father of a Roger Cartwright in 1379 might have been called Adam Johnson, and *his* father John the Cooper. In this example, is the surname detective interested in Cartwrights, Johnsons or Coopers? Clearly still the first, but only in order to get an idea of the likely points of origin where 'Cartwright' was being used as a byename. Note that even when inheritance *had* become quite common, it did not necessarily follow that *all* children in the same family would adopt the same surname.

Evidence that surnames had been inherited can be adduced from several pieces of evidence – the fact that some had ramified so that several families in the same village bore the same surname; that individuals had surnames which did not relate to their own occupation or office; unmarried women having personal surnames with the suffix 'son'; and, as we shall see, surnames using Old English Christian names (OES, pp. 311–12).

Discontinuity

Sooner or later then, we arrive at a time when individuals appear to have no surname, and very little research is available on the process by which, even as late as the fifteenth century, they acquired one. Many took patronymics, the Christian name of their father, but we shall return to the related questions of whether this was associated with the late development of surnames in the north of England, leading to the preponderance of names ending in 'son' or even 'daughter' (noted in Part 1), and whether, just because a surname does not appear in a written record, the individuals concerned did not actually use one. Even today, an echo of those early Scandinavian practices can be seen in the Icelandic phone book, which is arranged in order of forenames.

Several writers have commented on the fact that, in the Poll Tax returns, servants appear to have no surname. Redmonds (ESS1, p. 32) noted 'a large number of people who still possessed no true surname'. All the larger villages assessed had some inhabitants with only a Christian name who were described simply as 'servants'. According to Reaney, 'in Yorkshire one man in six and in Lancashire one man in four had no surname' in the fourteenth century (OES, p. 90). However, Reaney does have a section concerning servants' surnames (OES, pp. 193–7). I wonder if adult servants were given surnames in a written record, but the numerous teenagers who earned their living serving in other households were restricted to a Christian name as they were when living with their own family. Surnames were given to half the servants who came before the Cheshire sheriffs in the 1360s and 1370s (from transcriptions kindly provided by Dr Paul Booth, University of Liverpool).

In one respect, however, I believe that the number of people in the West Riding who actually had no surname may have been greatly exaggerated. Many of them, if not the majority, were servants; but in the case of one or two townships, such as Carleton or Langcliffe, almost all servants *were* given a surname, and it rather looks as though the absence of servants' surnames in most cases might have been a clerical device, relating to status, by those recording the document. In terms of the adjectival basis of surnames, this is not surprising, as 'servant of' a named person was (just like 'wife of' or 'son/daughter of') a perfectly adequate means of identification. Servants were recorded without a surname in seventeenth-century Cambridgeshire, and in Fielding's *Tom Jones*, a servant complains that 'though my lady calls me Honour, I have a sir-name as well as other folks' (Book VII, ch. vi). And then there is the vestigial Jeeves who, of course, needed no other name.

It is hard to believe that two world wars in the twentieth century have had any significant effect on surnames, still less the Civil War in the seventeenth century. Those unnatural disasters were dwarfed by the Black Death of 1348–49 which killed over 30 per cent of the total population of England. Whole families, which had dutifully paid their taxes in the first half of the century, were wiped out before the second, and it is not too fanciful to wonder how many of the older surnames were wiped out with them. Using sources from before and after the 1348–49 watershed in the same scan, therefore, might be a more flawed technique than sources similarly separated by the same period of time in other centuries. It covered most of the British Isles, being particularly virulent in East Anglia. We should also expect that names which were thinly spread before the Black Death might suddenly appear to have had only one or two points of origin. Bride might be an example – implausible as a French locative as it usually appears as 'le bride', it is found in many parts of the country in the early fourteenth century, but seems to have survived largely in the East Riding through to the seventeenth. Similarly, whereas Part 2 has concluded that the origin of Quick lay in the south–west, we can find a family called Quike *at* Quick in Lancashire in the late thirteenth century (VCH Lancashire, Vol. 3, p. 407).

Translation and publication

There have been several processes between the medieval holder of a name, and its appearance in a modern, published index, and changes or even errors may have occurred at each stage. Whatever the original name used in speech, the clerk had to write it down, sometimes another had to copy it, a modern transcriber has to read the handwriting correctly, and has finally to publish and index it correctly. Did a resident of York in 1327 really call himself 'Ranulphus de Novo castro', as he appears in the subsidy list, or 'Ranulph Newcastle'?

Did people *really* call themselves 'Faber', the Latin for Smith, or was that merely the clerk's way of presenting the record? In the 1327 Lay Subsidy for Shropshire there are 32 Fabers and only 7 Smiths; similarly, the same document for the North Riding has 28 Fabers and only one Smith, a pattern found in Cumberland in 1332. In the Lay Subsidy of that year, however, there are apparently no Fabers in Buckinghamshire or Warwickshire, but 46 and 79 Smiths respectively. Not infrequently (Essex 1327, Kent 1334) the two names are indexed together. Fransson (1935, p. 33) found that in ten counties Smith was only the sixth most commonly occurring name before 1350, but I'm sure that is because so many appear as Faber. As a result, references to Smith and to Faber have been merged when reaching conclusions about the distribution of the name using the Banwell technique (see Map 3.13). When trying to distinguished between Weaver, Webb, Webber, and Webster when they are all translated as Textor or Textrix, however, that solution does not help.

What is the difference between John Smith, John the Smith, and John the smith, and have indexers always distinguished between them? Some earlier editors (e.g. J. C. Cox's introduction to the Derbyshire Lay Subsidy of 1327) believed that the last, and even the second, is merely the *occupation* of a man with no surname. This possibility cannot be denied; but when, in the Lay Subsidy for Warwickshire in the same year, *all* Smith taxpayers were called 'le Smyth', and there are no fewer than four among the 66 taxpayers in Blackwell, it cannot always be the case. Five years later in Warwickshire, on the other hand, there were 77 Smiths and only one 'le Smith'! Reaney (OES, p. 304) effectively disproves the theory that 'le' before an occupational surname implies an occupation rather than the name.

Additionally, because many of these records are written in Latin, it is by no means clear that, because a person was called Henricus filius Richardi in a tax return, he would have been *called* 'Henry Richardson' rather than 'Henry' whose father happened to have been called Richard. McKinley (ESS2, p. 129) suggests that, in thirteenth-century East Anglia at least, such a description was unlikely to be used as a surname, only an identifier through quoting a father's name. His conclusion is based on the numbers of such cases in Latin compared with the estimated (and much lower) numbers of patronymic surnames used at that time.

Furthermore, there is not universal agreement on the translation from Latin to English. Most would translate 'Bercarius' as 'Shepherd', for example, though both Bercarius and Shepherd can be found as surnames in the same document. W. F. Carter, editing the 1332 Lay Subsidy for Warwickshire, translates it as 'Barker', with quite a different meaning, and important for our consideration of Barker in the 100 surname study. Reaney accepts that Barker might originate as shepherd as well as tanner. In fact, the distribution of Barker itself leaves no doubt that it was in common use only north of Birmingham, being especially common in the North Riding though relatively rare in Lancashire (Map 3.1).

We are lucky to have (published in 1857) Bishop Hatfield's survey of the estates of the Bishopric of Durham (1377–80), for there are neither Lay Subsidies nor Poll Tax records available for that county in the fourteenth century. The index, however, includes only two names in seven, the editor believing that indexing the poorer tenants would have the effect of 'swelling out the book without any corresponding benefit'! The index to the Oxfordshire Hundred Rolls of 1279, on the other hand, has an index for both the text and its modern translation.

Lack of simultaneity

As the fourteenth century progressed, there was undoubtedly movement in practice from the use of Latin and French to English, from non-hereditary byenames to hereditary surnames, and from the practices of one social class to another. These changes were neither straightforward nor simultaneous, differentially affected by a matrix of surname type and geographical area. For example, the evidence hints that locative surnames became inherited a century or more before nicknames and occupational names, and that filial names (mostly those ending in 'son') rather later still. As important as type, however, is location, most writers suggesting that changes took place later in the north than in the south. Now I sometimes think that 'the north' to most people means 'further north than where I live', and it will be interesting to see whether distribution studies can shed any light on the significance of latitude on surname development. The editor of the 1332 Subsidy in Cumberland noted (p. 73) that the text was 'heavily charged with Christian names' as surnames – actually, there are well over 25 per cent in the county as a whole, though far less in the towns – and that 'Cumberland folk were considerably behind the rest of the country in the adoption of surnames'. At the same time, McKinley produces convincing evidence for the gradual but earlier spread of hereditary surnames in East Anglia, where some of the most important families had developed them by the twelfth century, small freeholders by the thirteenth, and almost everyone by the fourteenth.

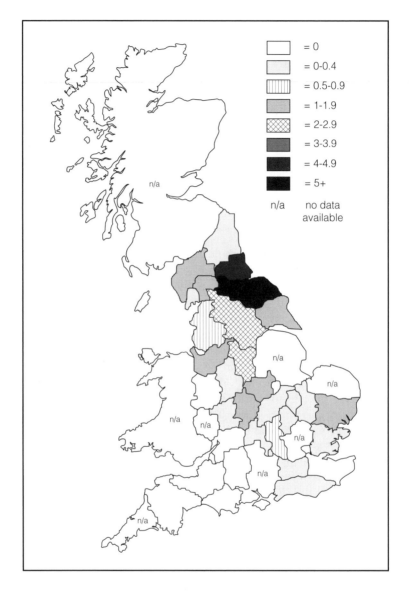

3.1   Barker (407)

A surname not yet found in the south-west – otherwise the modern pattern is already established in the fourteenth century.

Recognition

Parts 1 and 2 tried to encourage the amateur to use various techniques to explore the history of examples from the enormously wide range of available surnames. The recognition of many of those names, once we go back a further three hundred years, is not straightforward. The spelling changes, which become even more erratic, can alter the meaning and origin of a word. George Redmonds (ESS1, p. 35) notes Moxon, a filial name, becoming Moxham (*prima facie* a locative name); Tattersall, however, could become Tatterson, a change in the opposite direction. At least one medieval Cordwainer family eventually corrupted into Gardner. At Thrussington, Leicestershire, the 1377 Poll Tax recorded the name 'Margeta at the town's end' (i.e. Townsend); at Cleobury Mortimer (Shropshire, 1327) was 'Rog' Above the town' (i.e. Overton). At Somerset in the same year was 'Richardus Taillour Biwestestheterne' – was tailor the occupation of someone with a primitive version of the surname West, or was Tailor a surname with a residential location indicated; or did Richard have no surname? Many entries are ambiguous. We have met Blak in Part 2, not knowing whether it was Black or Blake; now, there are many more examples. Was 'Flessher' a Fletcher or a Fleshewer (Butcher)? Should we class 'Textor' as Weaver, Webb, Webber, or Webster?

Women's names

The utilisation of women's names presents even greater problems in the medieval period than in the twentieth century, and offers a perfect excuse (should one be required) to exclude women from surname studies altogether! The adoption of the bridegroom's surname by the bride did not become automatic until the fifteenth century. Before then, it is unclear whether to regard 'Maud the widow of Robert' as using 'Robert' as a byename in the same way as 'Henry the son of Robert'. Should 'Ricardus Carpentarius et uxor eius' count as one surnamed Carpenter or two? Did the answer vary from region to region, and from one part of the century to another?

McKinley's summary of women's names (1990, pp. 47–9) suggests that there was no general convention, either national or even regional, until the fifteenth century – women sometimes used their husband's surname, a byename (perhaps with the addition of the

suffix 's' as we shall see), or simply used their own maiden name
(see also ESS3, ch. 5, and OES, pp. 82–5). In these circumstances,
with so many unknowns, the surname detective trying to make
geographical sense out of as many examples as possible can sensi-
bly take one of four courses of action: (a) determine which convention pertained in the region and period concerned, and apply
that to each example; (b) ignore all women; (c) count all married
couples as one person (a line taken by McKinley (ESS4, p. 272)); or
(d) include all women using modern conventions of surname adoption, recognising that their presence signals a greater likelihood
that there will be other members of the family invisible in the
source concerned.

   In the fourteenth-century scan of 100 names, I have taken the
final option, though this greatly increases the apparent number of
individuals in those areas for which the Poll Tax is available.

Some technicalities

Sources available for the fourteenth century, here liberally interpreted as 1279–1379 in order to incorporate the maximum
number of published records, enable a scan of surnames to be
attempted comparable with that undertaken for the seventeenth
century. Where more than one county record is available, that
which contains the greatest number of names has been used. (Once
again, an approximate count is given in Appendix 3.) Thus, the
1379 Poll Tax for the West Riding has been preferred to any earlier Subsidy for the same area, but 1327 preferred to 1332 for
Worcestershire. There is a residual problem, more serious than the
same one three hundred years later, of what to use when neither
Lay Subsidy nor Poll Tax has been published. The temptation to use
transcriptions of the latter, lodged by Professor Beresford in the
library of the University of Hull, has been resisted in view of the difficulty which most would have in gaining access to them, but once
they are published, such a scan will be much easier and far more
complete.

   Although, as we have seen, there are other sources available,
none is as satisfactory or so easy to use – they contain entries either
spread out over long periods of time, or multiple references to the
same person. For this earlier period, it is even more important than

later for amateurs to rely on publications or transcriptions, for the difficulties of reading the originals, especially as most are available only in the PRO, are considerable. In the cases of Cheshire, Durham and Northamptonshire the assessment of total entries, as well as the counting of separate individuals, has been even more uncertain than in the Lay Subsidies.

Not for another two hundred years do we begin again to have a regular series of sources for surname distribution, making the investigation of hypotheses about the intervening development and movement of surnames very difficult to undertake. There is no doubt that the fourteenth-century scan which follows is therefore a much more opaque indication of the presence of surnames than its seventeenth- and twentieth-century counterparts, and the surname detective tracking down individual names must have recourse to a much wider range of sources. The Banwell method is beyond its usefulness for all but the most popular names through a combination of incomplete lists and the low population – perhaps 4.2 million before the Black Death.

One result is that some of the 100 names in my original list which I would have expected to find in medieval England (Ashburner, Bunyan, Darlington, Duncalf, Gorst, Lancashire, Linter, Restell, Trinder, and Winder) cannot be found at all. (A John Derlington became a freeman of Chester in 1397–8, and the surname appears in the Preston Guild Roll at the same time, indicating their presence in the north-west at an early period, and it would seem that the early examples of the name in its native Durham were found as 'Darnton'.) A number of names had migrated from outside England, of course, but others might be missing because not all counties are covered, or because the proportion of the total population found in the sources used is low.

The origin and distribution of surname types

Locatives

The most numerous of all the different types of English surname are those which derived from the names of particular places, whether they are countries, regions, counties, towns, villages, hamlets or even farmsteads. Interest in them is for several reasons – their relationship to social class and the relatively early period at which they became inherited, and to their usefulness as markers for studying geographical mobility.

Conclusions are subject to the many provisos described above and in Part 1. Recognition of what are essentially placenames is not straightforward, as those names have changed over time, many have disappeared, some are not easily recognisable as place names at all, and still others are of uncertain origin because there is more than one – often far more than one – place with that name (OES, pp. 38–45). McClure (1978) estimates that less than half of all English placenames were unique in the Middle Ages. We saw in Part 1 how the spelling of names is likely to vary most when distances from the point of origin are greatest. Some are badly misspelled in printed versions, as well as in the original. Those paying tax did so in relation to where their property was located, not necessarily where they themselves lived; thus, they might appear in more than one part of the return.

Relying on 'de' appearing before the name is an uncertain, though sometimes helpful, basis for identifying locatives. One of the problems raised in Part 1 was the possibility that, in the north-west at least, the name Weaver might be locative as well as occupational. Entries in all the fourteenth-century Cheshire sources searched for the name, such as the Ledger Book of Vale Royal Abbey which has four references to this surname between 1278 and 1350 as 'de Wevere', confirm that possibility. (It should be noted that in a Lay Subsidy document, 'de' also means 'from whom' the tax was being collected, and precedes all entries in some editions.) It was not entirely locative, however, as there were pockets of Weavers in Northumberland and in the south-east, though in Essex they seem to be editorial translations of 'textor' (Map 3.2).

Medieval placenames can be identified most readily through the volumes of the English Place Name Society, arranged by county. McKinley (1990, pp. 53–8) gives examples of the above difficulties – Arnold is a place name, for example, whereas Jerningham is not; Abram, near Wigan, used to be called Adburgham; Wooster looks like an occupation, rather than a variation of Worcester. By eliminating problem names from any statistical consideration, however, some generalisations have been drawn from those about which enough certainty does exist.

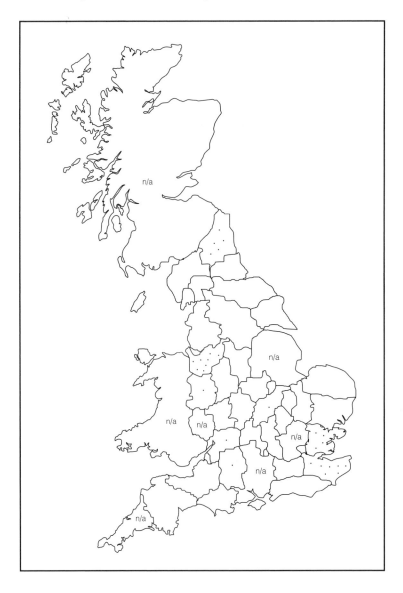

3.2 Weaver

(See Map 2.14) Weaver is now seen to have at least two sources, one locative in Cheshire, the other(s) almost certainly occupational.

- 'Most inhabited places, even very small ones, gave rise to loca-tive names' (McKinley, 1990, p. 56). We have already noted that the number of instances of a locative name appears at first glance to be in inverse proportion to the size of the place, but the number and small size of those points of origin still seem extra-ordinary. Two-thirds of all the locative surnames in the Lan-cashire Lay Subsidy of 1332 were of very small places, hamlets or smaller (ESS4, p. 186). The same pattern has been observed in Cornwall where in 1327 'the general impression is of a very strong feeling in the county that it is right to bear the name of your dwelling as a surname' (Padel, 1985). Many either never became hereditary, or survived for only a few generations before disappearing from the spectrum of English surnames.

- Not only are there a large number of locative surnames; the number of individuals bearing them is also substantial. McKinley (1990, p. 23) has a table indicating the percentages of people in sixteen counties with different kinds of surnames in the four-teenth century – locatives are the most common in three-quar-ters of them, being particularly widespread in Lancashire, Devonshire, Shropshire, Staffordshire, Warwickshire, and Gloucestershire, all in the west of England, with Kent, Leicester-shire, Surrey and the West Riding also having over 25 per cent. Of these, Lancashire tops the league, having a large number of small settlements and isolated farms, also noted in the West Riding by George Redmonds (ESS1, p. 61). We observed in Part 1 the number of quite popular names which have emerged from the old parish of Rochdale, to which McKinley (ESS4) devotes a whole section. The preponderance of locative names in Lan-cashire remained until the seventeenth century, but could scarcely survive the industrial revolution.

- Another generalisation to emerge from the six counties so far covered by the English Surnames Series concerns a relationship between locative surnames and social class. The class particu-larly acquiring them were those of middling wealth – perhaps the lesser landowners and free tenants. They were the substantial contributors to the lay subsidies (Poll Tax excepted) and are therefore 'visible' in those records, where they form a far greater percentage of the total than in later centuries. This is not to say that such surnames were not held by lesser mortals (though McKinley suggests that they had once been free but had fallen on hard times) or that other types of surname could not be found in their ranks; but whereas in Lancashire, where the contrast was probably greatest, they were held by 52 per cent of those paying the Lay Subsidy of 1332, locatives were borne by only 21 per cent of the unfree tenants on the Earl of Lancaster's manors fourteen years later, patronymics being much more common.

- This association with land in the place of residence is strong, and suggests a major reason why they originated in the first place – because individuals resided there rather than owned the place or had left it. The last remains a popular explanation, especially for those who had travelled some distance away from the settlement after which they were named. Lofvenberg, for example, believed that the presence of 'de' before a locative indicated that the person had migrated, whereas 'atte' (see below under toponymics) meant that the person had resided there (1942, p. xxi). It is noticeable, however, that those who were far removed from a possible point of origin were often called by a town, county or even country rather than a small village whose name was unknown beyond its immediate surroundings, suggesting that they were not bearing a surname inherited from parents.
- A common pattern for the adoption of locative surnames seems to have been that only one family at a time would be given a particular name. As time went on, of course, several families in the same area came to have the name, either because it became inherited by sons, leading to ramification, or because migration brought in families from other places of the same name. At first, however, it seems to have been a temporary 'adjective', replaceable if it became more appropriate to call the individual something else. Even so, some names were adopted so early that they provide the first evidence that a place, well enough known later, was so called in the fourteenth century or earlier.

One apparent exception is McKinley's finding, in areas as far apart as East Anglia, Lancashire and Oxfordshire, that those few who had travelled great distances carried the names of towns rather than villages. This might be misleading, however, if the migrant acquired the name after his journey, for he would be given a familiar name (e.g. York) rather than the name of the exact place (e.g. Holgate) of which no one would have heard. Even in that case (chosen at random) a Simon de Hollegate lived in Norwich in 1290 (OES, p. 309).

- Because land and tenancy were often inherited, so locatives were probably the earliest of all the different types of surname to be passed from father to son. The time at which this happened varied from place to place, McKinley believing that many had become hereditary in the thirteenth century as far north as Lancashire, though there is plenty of circumstantial evidence to show that many others were not, even in the 1330s. In the city of Oxford, for example, many of the locative names from the Hundred Rolls of the late thirteenth century were no longer present in 1327. In Sussex, where all towns, most villages, and many hamlets and farms had given rise to surnames, a large number were held by a single individual, the average being under 1.5 as 926 people held as many as 648 locative names.

Knowledge about the timing of the inheritance of names is of particular interest to genealogists, who get very excited when this is coupled with the view that only one family was given a locative name in any one place. Lofvenberg generalised, 'The rarer the surname is, the greater is the probability that the different persons bearing it hail from the same place' (1942, p. xxviii). I suspect that the timing of the development of the hereditary practice might have been earlier than the above circumstantial evidence suggests, for the reason which McKinley himself had observed (ESS2, p. 18) – 'It is also clear that even where a surname was well established in the manor and had apparently become hereditary, it was not necessarily inherited by all members of the family'. If only the eldest son inherited not only the land but also the surname, the dating of the inheritance of surnames could be earlier than thought by a factor of some generations.

Whatever the cause, locative surnames ramified slowly – the pace appears to have been greatest in the north of England, across Lancashire and Yorkshire (McKinley, 1990, p. 60). In 1332, 90 per cent of locative surnames in Lancashire were still located within ten miles of their geographical origin – over 50 per cent in Suffolk five years earlier. The fourteenth-century scan has revealed disappointingly little about the locatives among the 100 surnames, however. Heathcote is confined to three examples near Warwick, suggesting that county as the point of origin of the name, rather than the Heathcote in Derbyshire or the West Riding; in the the seventeenth century, however, Derbyshire had more Heathcotes than all other counties put together. Purslow seems to be missing from the 1327 Shropshire Lay Subsidy, and the earliest I can find so far is a William Pusselowe who signed the Shropshire Peace Roll in 1400. The only Pinchbecks (in the absence of a Lincolnshire source) and Sladens in the scan are in the West Riding, but of course the absence of evidence is not evidence of absence. A more detailed search of the county records would almost certainly establish their presence – there was a Quenilda de Sladen living in Rochdale in 1246, for example (VCH v., p. 227 n. 53).

Because the origin of locative names can be pinpointed in so many cases, they have been used in order to assess the timing, rate and direction of mobility – recently, for example, by Crosby (1993). It should be remembered, once again, that there are significant methodological problems in using this data, in terms of multiple possible origins of many, and the alleged predisposition of locatives to be given in cases of mobility, making them an untypical sample. We have already seen that, in the early fourteenth century, the majority were living within ten miles of the place of origin. Dispersal from that point was slow – names were far more likely to ramify within a few miles rather than scatter within or across county boundaries. Padel (1985) found that almost all identifiable locatives in Cornwall were living in the parish of origin, or in adjoining parishes, in 1327, but he also uncovered disconcerting evidence that when a man moved, he took not only his surname but also the name of the farmhouse from which it was derived! Most 'aliens' came from adjoining counties, though as many as 4 per cent of the immigrants to Sussex in 1332 had come from abroad fairly recently. Reaney has interesting maps (OES, pp. 333, 344) of the origins of locative surnames found in Norwich and London showing that they were far more attractive as places for migrants; evidence of movement out of Cornwall can be gleaned from those 'Pen...' and 'Tre...' names which are found, for example, in Gloucestershire in the early fourteenth century.

McKinley concludes (1990, p. 66) that 'It is unusual, in Britain, for any surname, of whatever type, which originates solely in one place or one area of limited size to disperse widely at any period before the nineteenth century'. He himself, however, notes some exceptions. The name Lancashire, as we have seen, is largely limited in the seventeenth century to areas close to the county itself and London, with only the occasional foray into distant parts – to

Gloucestershire by 1522, for example – whereas Kent was widespread even in the Middle Ages as far as Dorset in the west and Derbyshire and Yorkshire to the north (Map 3.3). In the latter case, however, it appears in Shropshire at least as 'le Kent', implying that it is a topographical name, perhaps the river, as well as that of a county. There is a suggestion that names of towns along major trading routes (Kendal and Pickering being singled out) will spread earlier and to greater distances, but this does not explain why many others on those routes did not do so, or why a port such as Liverpool had not attracted many from outside Lancashire by the time of the late fourteenth century Poll Taxes.

The absence of Scottish surnames even in the north of England in the fourteenth century should not be taken as evidence that the political relationship between the two countries had prevented migration. There were quite large numbers of people *called* Scot as far south as Yorkshire, the implication being that, as we have found with the surname French, it was often easier to call a person by a well-known word rather than try to use the name of their original home. French in the fourteenth century was almost entirely confined to the area south of a line from Gloucester to Norwich, six hundred years having made little difference to the main pattern of distribution (Map 3.4). Being much rarer, Dutch cannot be expected to have much connection with its later location, and in fact only one has shown up in the scan, in the North Riding.

The origins of England and English remain mysterious, but the fourteenth-century scan eliminates the outer rim of the country as the source (Map 3.5). England is already found in the West Riding, in the southern counties of East Anglia, and in the south-west; the rarer English is largely confined in a broad band from East Anglia to Devonshire. Both names are relatively rare near the Welsh and Scottish borders.

The English Surnames Series tries to look also at sixteenth- and seventeenth-century sources, finding that most ramification was still local, and that the spread of surnames was not nearly so great as an intervening two to three hundred years would have allowed. Most locatives in sixteenth century Norfolk, for example, were still found within a ten miles radius of their origin (ESS2, pp. 92–101).

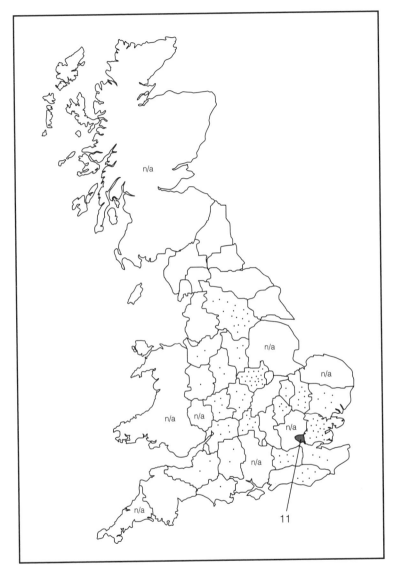

3.3   Kent

(See Map 2.9) Kent was already widespread in medieval England, though it had not yet ramified in Cheshire.

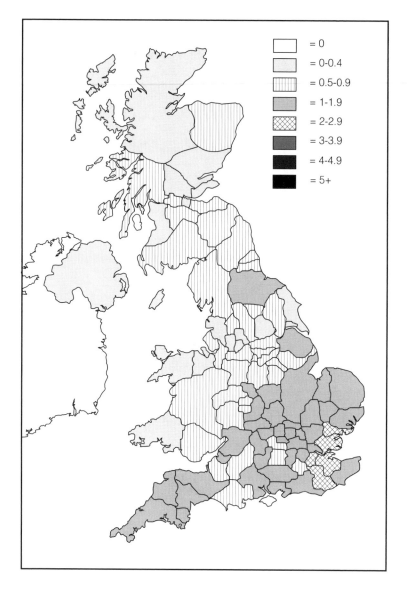

3.4a, b   French   20thC. (8,005) *above*   14thC. (190) *right*
French in the fourteenth century shows the same features as it was to do later.

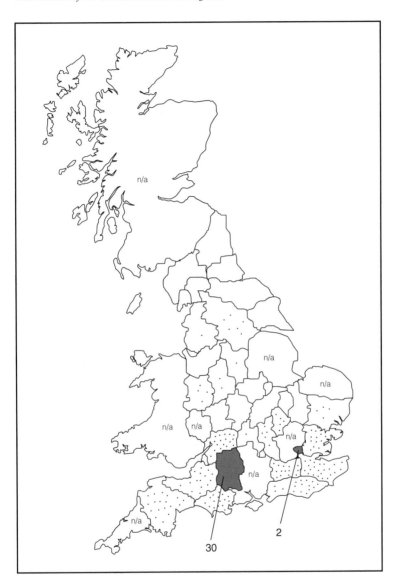

n/a

n/a

n/a

n/a

n/a

n/a

n/a

n/a

n/a

2

30

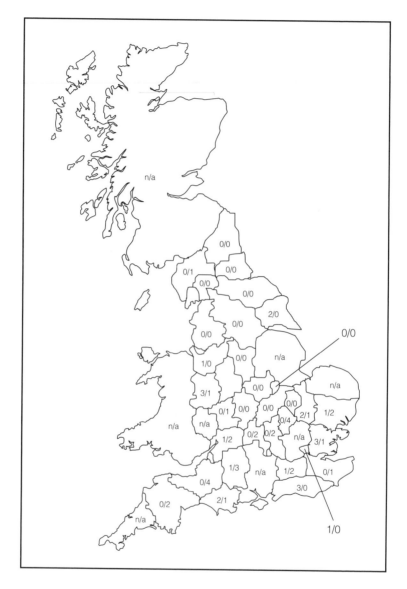

3.5   England/English

(See Map 1.17) Though the centres of these names have changed somewhat over time, the maps leave no doubt that they originated well within,
and widely across, England.

Toponymics

Toponymics, or surnames based on topographical features of the medieval landscape, are very numerous. One has only to think of Field, Green, Hall, Hill, Lake, Meadows, or Wall to realise that there were few natural or even man-made objects which have not at one time been adopted as surnames. Fransson (1935) included many in his dictionary of occupational names because so little attention had been paid to them until then. It might be thought that the identification of toponymics was straightforward, but there are several reasons why life is a little more complicated than that.

In the first place, many such features are also the names of places, so it becomes virtually impossible to tell whether some instances are toponymic or locatives surnames. Barrow, Birch, Dale, Ford, Grove, Mount, Park, Street, Townsend, and Wood, for example, are each the name of more than one place in England. Edridge, however, is a variant of Edrich (Aedric), a Scandinavian personal name.

Meanings of words have changed so that, while the majority are still recognisable as toponymics, the reason they were adopted in the first place might not be. Once again, quests originated in Part 1 have to be modified in the light of this new evidence. Before the sixteenth century, for example, 'furlong' meant part of an open field rather than a unit of distance; and it looks as though Well, Wells (also a common locative), Weller and Wellman should have been investigated alongside Spring, having originally the same topographical meaning (see McKinley, 1990, pp. 75–7). Spring in the fourteenth century is found mainly in three separate groups, one in Devon/Somerset, another in Sussex/Kent, and a third in the North Riding/Durham/Northumberland (Map 3.6). The continuity evident between the seventeenth and twentieth centuries was therefore not there during the previous three hundred years, making something of a nonsense of the attempt in Part 1 to relate the present distribution to topographical features. Note, however, that only eighteen examples of Spring have come to light during the fourteenth century, and we should therefore not be surprised by the evident lack of continuity, as the name is rare.

The localised use of words in the thirteenth or fourteenth century now sometimes finds its sole vestigial echo in these toponymics. Bysshe, now celebrated solely as Shelley's middle

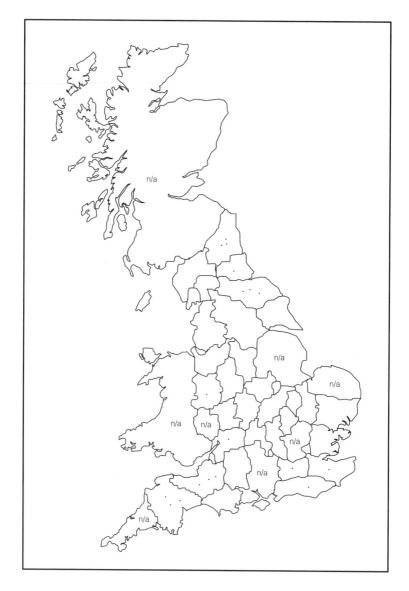

3.6   Spring
Spring, a rare name, shows little relationship to its later distribution.

name, in south-east England meant a thicket. McKinley quotes Fogg, mainly a Lancashire word for new grass growing after the cutting of hay, Hamme, an Oxfordshire word for a meadow, which appears to the exclusion of Meadow as a surname in surrounding areas, and Yeo, a word for a stream in south-west England, the only place in the country where no one needs to ask my colleague Ron Yeo how to spell his surname! Ham, however, is also the name of at least sixteen places in England, one of which in Somerset gave rise to an ancestor of Eric Banwell whose map shows a significant skew for the name towards the south-west. Heath, in Kent and Sussex, was pronounced Hoath or Hoad, suggesting that those names should have been included as variations of Heath in the scans in Parts 1 and 2 (OES, p. 352). The distribution of 158 Heaths in the fourteenth century (Map 3.7) was remarkably similar to the pattern three hundred and six hundred years later, in contrast to the much rarer Spring, noted above (Map 3.6).

Two particular suffixes ('er' and 'man') can cause confusion with occupational names. For example, was Bridger or Bridgeman someone whose residence was near a bridge, or whose occupation had something to do with construction, upkeep or toll collection? These suffixes have been the subject of extensive investigation. Adding 'er' rather than 'man' to a topographical feature seems to have no regional implications – they appear in the same locality, sometimes even held by the same individual in different documents. Equally, there seems to be no connection with the social status of the individuals concerned. These particular variations of toponymics developed relatively late, being rare before the end of the fourteenth century, and slow to develop in Oxfordshire even before 1500. It is possible, however, that their earlier use in English vernacular has been hidden by the use of Latin if the subtleties of the suffix have not been fully translated; it is possible, for example, that Pontus might have been used indiscriminately for Bridge, Bridger and Bridgeman. In the north of England, 'er' or 'man' were more likely to be used for occupational names, however, and, as an added complication, 'er' was also added to placenames in Sussex in the same way that we would incorporate it in 'Londoner', especially in the case of an individual who had moved away from their place of origin (ESS5, p. 184).

Other suffixes make toponymics sound like nicknames, but they are sometimes locatives! In particular, those ending with 'bottom'

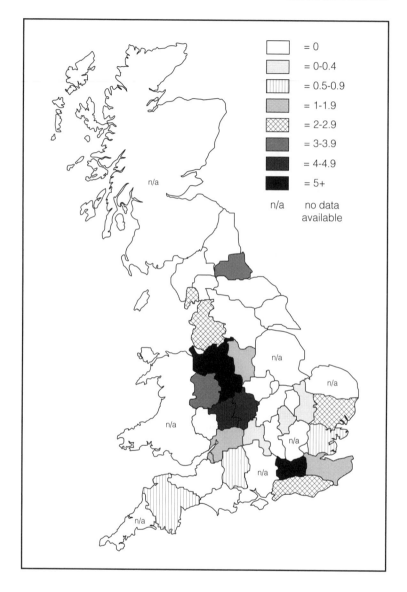

3.7   Heath (158)
(See Map 1.24) Evidently generated across the two broad areas, the north-east midlands, and the south-east, where they are most numerous today.

and 'head' are largely based on places in valleys on either side of the Pennines. See, for example, Hey (1993, p. 21) for the name Broadhead. Whitehead is too thinly scattered in the fourteenth century, from the Bristol Channel to the North Sea, to accept this as a locative surname, but seventeen are found in the West Riding Poll Tax, supporting the view that, like Weaver, the name had more than one type, as well as more than one point, of origin (Map 3.8).

Another difficulty in the identification of toponymics concerns prepositions which were used with them. Just as locative names were preceded by 'de' in Latin and French, or 'of' in English, so toponymics were usually accompanied by the giveaway 'at' ('ad' in Latin), though sometimes this was replaced by 'at the', 'atte', 'atten' (usually before a vowel), 'atter', 'above', 'among', 'beyond', 'by', 'besides', 'binethe' (beneath), 'close', 'from', 'in the', 'near', 'over', 'under', 'up', or their Latin equivalents. 'Rog' Above the tonn' lived in Cleobury Mortimer, Shropshire, in 1327; 'Emma ad pontem' at Tilton, Leicestershire in 1377; 'Robert Attetounheued' at Graysothen, Cockermouth in 1332. (So, there was at least one example of Townhead as a surname, questioned in Part 1.) 'Alice and Emma atte ye bek' paid the Poll Tax as labourers in the East Riding in 1379. 'In the hay' was a surname recorded in the Essex Lay Subsidy of 1327.

The use of such prepositions survived in Surrey and Sussex until as late as the sixteenth century. Their presence two hundred years earlier cannot be taken for granted, however; there were seven taxpayers called Stone in that same Essex return – five were described as 'atte Stone', two were merely 'Stone'. Similarly, in 1379 William and John Atte Cotes lived at Barmby in the East Riding, where there was also Alic' Cotes at the same time; Wiliam of ye Wilows and Robert Wyllows can be found in the same area. Furthermore, these prepositional prefixes have merged and abbreviated over time – it is easy to see Attwells were once living 'at the well', but others are more difficult to spot. Nash, for example, comes from 'atten Ash'; similarly 'de Ash' has become Dash. Again, the presence of a prefix does not guarantee that the name is a toponymic, for there are plenty of locatives, such as Byfleet, Overton or Underbarrow, which also have them, which could cause confusion if their 'de' was omitted.

Finally, some evidently topographical names remain a mystery – de Cimiterium at Aldridge in Somerset, 1327, for example seems to

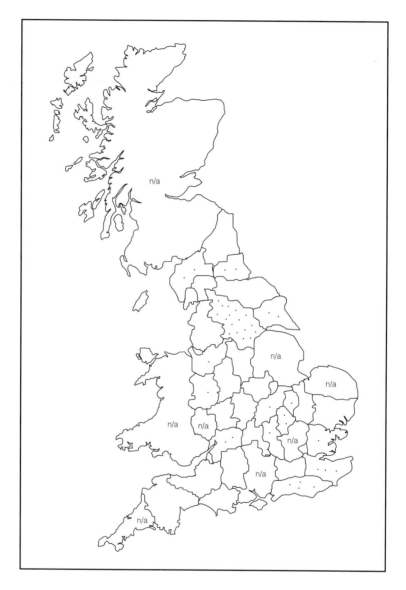

3.8   Whitehead
Whitehead, like Weaver, appears to be most common where it is a locative name.

have no modern counterpart; Churchyard seems close, but I don't know when people were first buried outside the fabric of parish churches. (Cimentarius, by the way, was Mason.) Some, of course, might have been nicknames anyway – shades of my old diminutive landlady, Mrs Mountain.

As with locatives above, McKinley's conclusions were reached after eliminating ambiguities and unresolvable problems from his statistics. There is a great disparity between different parts of the country in the *proportion* of surnames which are topographical in origin (see ESS5, p. 11; 1990, p. 23). They are very common in the south-east, particularly in Sussex where over a quarter of all tax-payers in 1332 had them, but much rarer in Lancashire. One theory to explain this difference is based on the fact that there were more nucleated settlements in the former, more named single farm-house settlements in the latter where, in consequence, locative names from tiny places were far more common. McKinley links this with the popularity of the suffix 'house' in Lancashire (ESS4, p. 210; 1990, p. 73).

The size of the difference in percentages across sixteen counties in the fourteenth century (as well as that in the seventeenth for comparison) can be found in McKinley (1990, p. 23), a factor of nine separating the county where the greatest proportion lived (Sussex) from that with the fewest (West Riding). The difference is only one of degree, however, and toponymics are common every-where; so are certain ones such as Green which, like Smith, have developed from many families simultaneously and are therefore unlikely to be genetically related to each other. There were 49 Greens living in 38 places in Norfolk in 1332, for example.

Many toponymics, on the other hand, are limited either region-ally or even locally in their spread, and we must look to one of three explanantions as to why this should have been so.

- By definition, dialect consists of words which are not universally used, and when such words have a topographical meaning, they can give rise to localised toponymics. Marsh can be found wherever there were marshes and Saltmarsh is a name which can be found in Gloucestershire in 1327 and the East Riding in 1379; but Carr had a very specific meaning in East Anglia, sig-nifying where trees grew by the side of a fen. Similarly, in the same area, local words for fields or enclosures – Herne, Tye and

Wong – all became surnames. Leyne in Sussex was a piece of arable land, giving rise to a local surname.

As we have already noted, Booth has a strongly northern connection, no fewer than 39 appearing in the West Riding Poll Tax return of 1379, but the very size of that source should be taken into account when comparing numbers across counties (Map 3.9). I have seen it no further south than Staffordshire before 1350, though McKinley found a 'stray' in Norfolk in the late thirteenth century. Its meaning, a cow keeper's hut, had a counterpart in Scale or Scole, a northern name with a similar meaning, normally encountered in the plural. Summerscale(s) seems to have been confined to the West Riding in the four-teenth century, where there are interesting variants Wynter-scalle in Dent and Waterscale in Bentham.

- The geology and geography of an area results in highly skewed distributions of surnames. The name See appears to have been generated on the south-east coast, McKinley finding them in Sussex, and there was one in Essex at the same time. John Forest was a servant at Metham in the East Riding in 1379. From the original survey of 100 names, the occasional Haven is noted in Gloucestershire and Wiltshire, so it might have originated from the Christian name Evan, as Weekley believed, but the use of 'atte Haven' in thirteenth-century Somerset and Sussex suggests a toponymic origin. Gorst has been found only in Cheshire and Gloucestershire, and only in very small numbers. Among the commoner names, however, both Clay and Heath (Maps 3.10, 3.7) show such strong similarities to their modern distribution that, numbers apart, it would be difficult to distinguish between the two maps. There seems little doubt that their epicentres remain where they originated.

- The local economy generates toponymics as well as occupational surnames. Mill exists alongside Miller, for example. Clement Swynhird paid the Poll Tax at Melton in the East Riding in 1379. Six hundred years ago, Bacon was concentrated in a band from Dorset and Gloucestershire to East Anglia – further north, they were found in the West Riding rather than in Derbyshire as at present, but again the similarities are unmistakable (Map 3.11). Temple seems to have proliferated in the north-east in a way which is unpredictable from its distribution in the fourteenth century, but once again we are talking of a rare name.

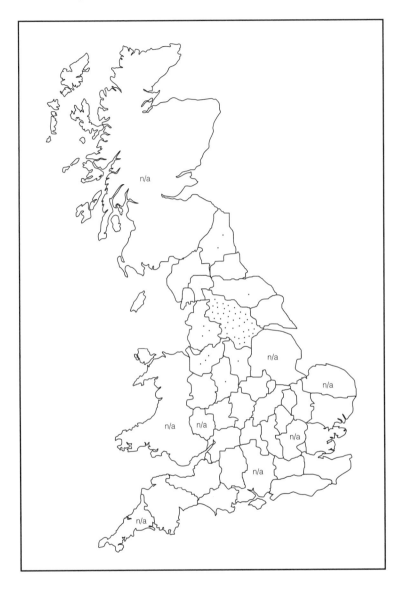

3.9 Booth

The numbers in the West Riding are a reflection of the size of the source, but the name was already rare both to the north and south of Lancashire, Cheshire and Yorkshire in mediaeval times.

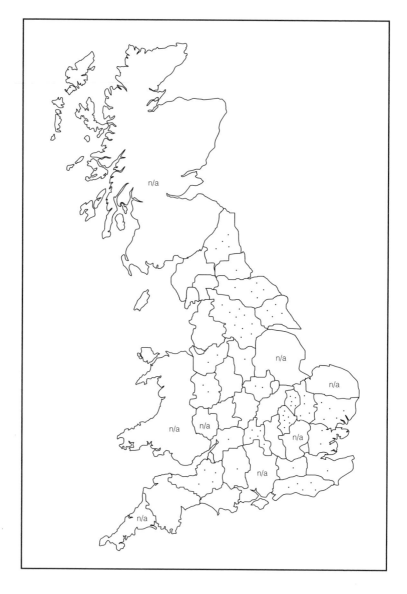

3.10 Clay

Clay (see Map 1.23) is difficult to compare with later centuries in the absence of early sources from Lincolnshire and Nottinghamshire.

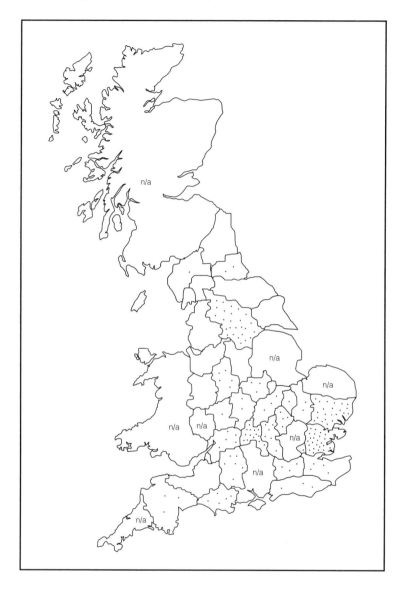

3.11 Bacon
Bacon had widespread points of origin, particularly in south Yorkshire, East Anglia and the south midlands.

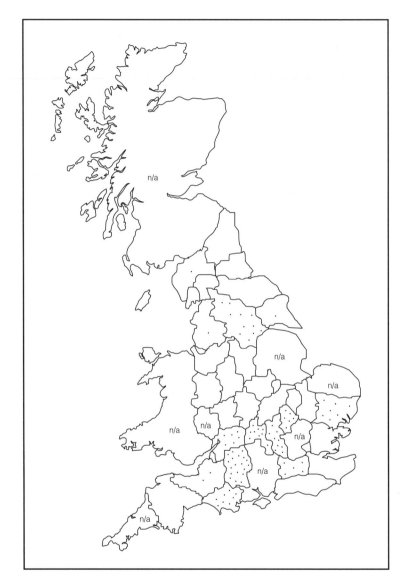

3.12a–d **North** (94) *above* **South** (35) *right* **East** (83) *p. 186*
West (341) *p. 187*
(See Maps 1.18–1.21) All four names found popularity originally in a wide
arc from south Yorkshire through the east midlands and across to the
south coast, a pattern still distinguishable today.

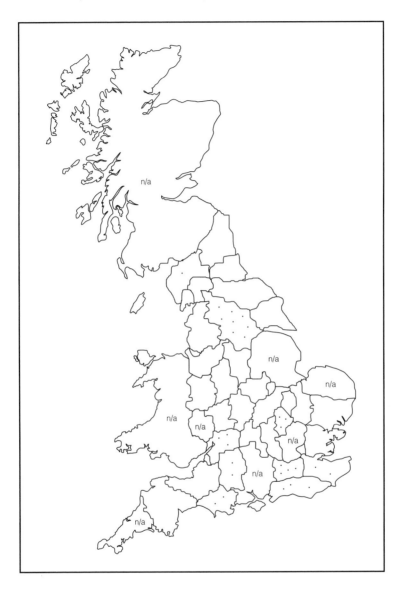

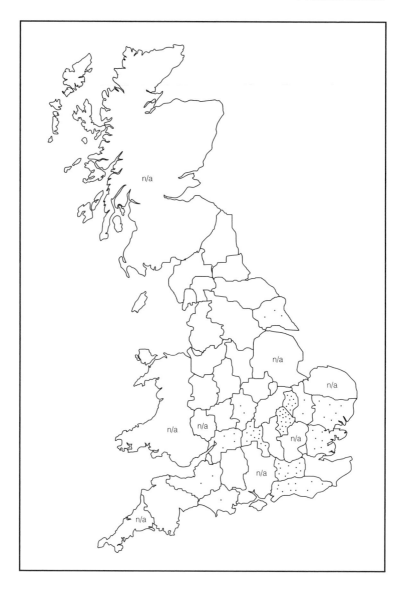

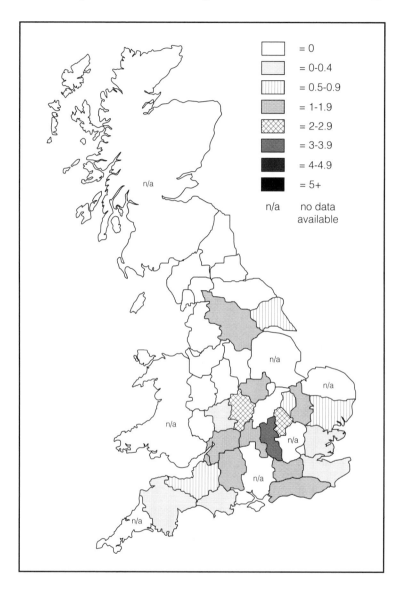

	= 0
	= 0-0.4
	= 0.5-0.9
	= 1-1.9
	= 2-2.9
	= 3-3.9
	= 4-4.9
	= 5+
n/a	no data available

Of all the toponymics in the 100 survey, North, South, East and West have proved the most curious (Maps 3.12a–d). Most writers have something to say on the issue – see Reaney (OES, pp. 53–4) and McKinley (ESS5, pp. 180–2) who found the four names highly localised within Sussex before 1400, though none was based on a single family origin. The names appear to be related to unusual topographical features within the county. East (usually written Est) lies mostly south of a line from the Humber to Dorset, being particularly numerous in Surrey and Sussex; North (and the less numerous South) are also found more commonly towards the south-east, from the West Riding to Somerset, though not in Kent; West was the commonest of the four as it still remains six hundred years later, and shows a similar pattern as North and South. All four names are conspicuously rare in the north-west, from Shropshire to Lancashire. Comparison of the maps from the fourteenth and twentieth centuries, however, is frustrated by the absence of data for fourteenth-century Lincolnshire and Nottinghamshire, but one can predict a significant presence for these names in the Poll Tax returns for those counties.

There is a relationship between at least the commonest toponymics and the social status of their original bearers, McKinley finding that in Oxfordshire they 'are predominantly the surnames borne by the unfree section of the population'. There are some exceptions, particularly where there is a strong connection with occupations which are unlikely to have been followed by a serf, such as Mill. The main conclusion, confirmed by his research into Sussex, is based on an early period when hereditary surnames had yet fully to be developed, and in consequence many had disappeared by 1400 (ESS3, pp. 41–44; 1988, p. 143).

Geographical mobility can be detected through a detailed study of some rarer toponymics. As we have seen, Booth appeared in Norfolk by 1300, where the slow spread of Fen names with general population movement can be seen over the next two centuries (ESS2, p. 112).

Perhaps the most interesting result of McKinley's researches, however, is the development of the additional 's' to many toponymics which seems to have taken place nationwide and at a relatively late date – the sixteenth and even seventeenth centuries. Bank and Birch became Banks and Birches in Lancashire, Grove became Groves in Oxfordshire, Rede became Redes in Sussex, Mill became Mills in Norfolk. This change had scarcely begun before 1400 – I can see none in the Essex tax list of 1327, for example. In some cases (Meadows, Wells), the additional 's' has superseded the original; in perhaps the majority, both forms survive (Wood, Woods); yet in others (Dale, Green) the additional 's' has never taken hold. There is no apparent reason for the development of this pluralising of toponymics, which does not seem to be in imitation of the genitive 's' added to Christian names in patronymics (see pp. 217–20).

Occupational

Surnames which originated as a way of describing individuals according to how they earned their living are the commonest – as well as the rarest – in the vast spectrum of surviving names, and some scholars are interested in them mainly because they provide the first available evidence that such a word existed at that time. As with all other categories, their identification is not always straightforward. Some, such as Barker or Winder, are also place-names; others, such as Monk, probably originated as nicknames. One theory ascribes the survival of any Latin version of a normal surname – Faber, Pistor, or Sutor, for example – to their original use as a nickname, having derived from the written form (McKinley, 1990, pp. 142–3). McKinley and Thuresson consider surnames of status and office together with those of occupation, and there are good reasons for doing so. Bailey, Constable, Provost or Reve could all be regarded in either category. However, as the former's own researches make clear, many names such as Bishop, Deacon, King, Priest, or Squire are much more likely to have originated as nick-names.

A common problem in the fourteenth century, and earlier, is the uncertainty which is inherent in translating a name written in Latin when there are several possible Middle English names then in normal use. How do we stop the name *as we translate it* from becoming a self-fulfilling prophesy of surname distribution? Is 'Fullo' translating Blakester, Bleacher, Fuller, Tucker or Walker? 'Tannator' can be both Barker or Tanner, and indeed there are examples of the same person being called by these two names on different occasions anyway! McKinley noted another problem which affects the treatment of this, one of my original hundred surnames. Both he and W. F. Carter believed that the Latin 'Bercarius' has been used not only for the normal Shepherd, but also to translate Barker (ESS2, p. 34).

We have also already seen that the suffix 'er' can be deceptive as a signifier of an occupational name; Simister is a locative!

Many of the common occupational names already existed, as byenames rather than as hereditary surnames, in the eleventh century (see below, p. 225). They were held by up to 20 per cent of people in the extant fourteenth-century returns. This overall, national norm was a little higher in the south, but very much lower in Shropshire (only 5 per cent in the 1327 Lay Subsidy) and in Leicestershire (10 per cent in 1327). It is unclear whether county differences reflect the actual spread of names in the early fourteenth century or merely the fact that the obligation to pay the subsidy was more restricted in Shropshire to that class which had a large proportion of locative surnames, but that county also had the lowest percentage of the fourteen counties surveyed in seventeenth-century sources (McKinley, 1990, p. 23). McKinley also reveals that his county figures mask an uneven local spread of occupational names during the Middle Ages, there being significantly more per head of population, as well as a greater variety in this category, in urban areas.

Enough research has now been done on different parts of medieval England for a number of generalisations to be offered with little fear of future substantial revision.

- Agricultural activity has generated far fewer occupational surnames than non-agricultural, despite having far more people engaged in it. There are a few popular names based on traditional rural occupations, particularly livestock rather than arable, most notably Shepherd. (Also among the former, for example, are Coward (cow herd), Horseman, Palfreyman; tillage generated Ploughman, Tiller, and Thresher, while harvesting produced Mower and Stacker.) Rarer ones, such as Biker or Cocker, are no longer readily recognisable as such. (For many more examples, see ESS2, pp. 33–6.)

    In terms both of numbers of bearers of surnames and of numbers of names, the industrial far outstripped the agricultural. The reason normally offered for this phenomenon is that so many people had the same agricultural occupation that it was an inadequate adjectival basis for distinguishing one person from another. Particular trades, on the other hand, were pursued by relatively few people within any one area. Coopers, haywards, smiths (Map 3.13), tailors were everywhere (and everywhere long before the fourteenth century), but there were perhaps only one or two in each village. Three hundred and eighty-five Chapmans have been found across every English county in the scan except Shropshire, Westmorland and Northumberland. Their present day concentration in the east of the country was already evident (Maps 3.14a & b).

To the south of York, Fullers were to be found almost entirely in East Anglia, Kent, Surrey and Sussex, but the word was evidently also in use in the North Riding, Cumberland and Northumberland to an extent which makes their present rarity in those counties quite surprising (Map 3.15). Of the 56 Tuckers found by the current scan, however, 53 were in Devon and Somerset.

- In almost all cases, popular occupational surnames had a number of variations, some obvious, others rare and obscure. Best known are the Fuller, Tucker, Walker trio, but even Smith finds counterparts in Marshall, a smith specialising in horse care, and in the south-west, Angove or Gove. Most of those with the suffix 'ster' will have synonyms used as surnames from the same root, but Baker and Baxter also have Whitbread. The word baxter must have been in use as far south as East Anglia, but was much commoner in the north of England, exactly as predicted from the phone book maps in Part 1 (Maps 3.16 a & b).

- At the other end of the scale from Smith, many of these early names never became hereditary or (like Iremonger in Oxfordshire, a name which can be found in many other counties in early medieval England) died out shortly afterwards. Others survive today by a slender thread of genetic descent which has at times relied on a single family for its existence, for example Spinner, which can be found in only ones and twos in Leicestershire, Somerset, Staffordshire, Suffolk, Warwickshire, Wiltshire, and the West Riding; in the seventeenth-century scan, however, they were found only in Devon and Worcestershire! (Note, incidentally, that the word 'spinster' came to mean an unmarried woman only in the late Middle Ages.) Others, such as Dring, seem to be particular to one area – in that case, Oxfordshire.

Widely dispersed rare names have been clearly generated in several parts of the country independently, by individuals probably
not related to each other.
- Of all the industries extant during the centuries when surnames
  were being developed, none generated more than the later stages
  of textiles where, as Fransson observed, specialisation or the division of labour was greatest.

The distribution of occupational names   The etymology of most surnames has been thoroughly investigated over a number of years,
but the English Surnames Series has attempted to explain the geographical anomalies revealed by distribution studies. There are a
number of reasons why occupational surnames are not evenly
spread, one being dialect, which, as we have already seen in the
case of toponymics, results in different words being used for the
same thing in different parts of the country. Part 1 indicates how
these differences, some seven hundred years old, are still visible in
modern phone books (see maps for Fuller and Tucker, Barker and
Tanner, for example). A milward in Oxfordshire was a miller; a
bowker in Lancashire was a bleacher – that is, yet another Fuller,
Tucker or Walker!

Because dialect is well understood as a source of diversity, the
uneven spread directly related to the location of those occupations
which gave rise to them is probably more interesting. Everyone
accepts that Smiths were once smiths, and the skewed distribution
noted in Parts 1 and 2 might have been due to the prevalence of
synonyms in certain areas as indicated above. However, dialect can
hardly explain why Smith was three times more common in
Oxfordshire than it was in Sussex. McKinley professes himself to be
mystified by the uneven distribution of many popular occupational
surnames, believing that it cannot be due to dialect, ramification,
or even the uneven distribution of the trades themselves (ESS5, pp.
228–9). His suggestion that there were more smiths in Sussex, the
Weald being an iron producing area, thus making it less distinctive
to use as a surname, seems improbable.

Doubt has been cast on a demonstrable, direct relationship
between the location of industry and associated surnames, McKinley having concluded that, in East Anglia at least, 'in most cases it
is not possible to draw conclusions about the distribution of any

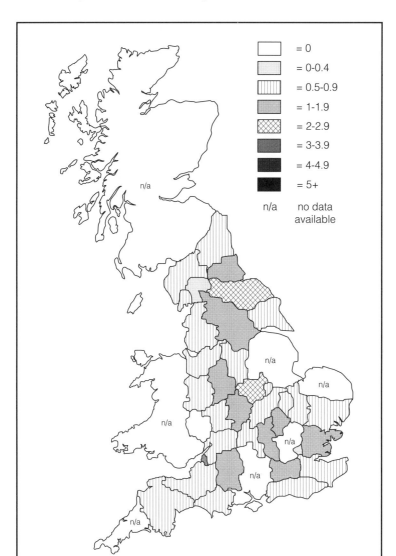

3.13   Smith (2,899)

(See Maps 1.15, 2.5) The absence of more than average concentrations in the west is already noticeable, but the later pattern of the surname in the east has not yet been established.

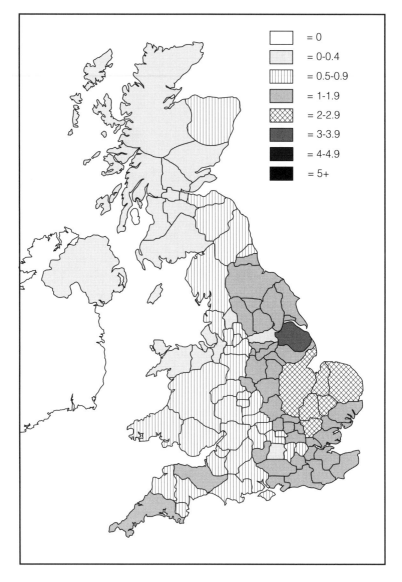

3.14a, b   Chapman   20thC. (21,958) *above*   14thC. (385) *right*
Not common in the north and west, but its absence from Cambridgeshire
in 1279 is hard to explain. The name shows the same overall pattern as
in the twentieth century, despite the absence of data from Lincolnshire,
Norfolk and Nottinghamshire.

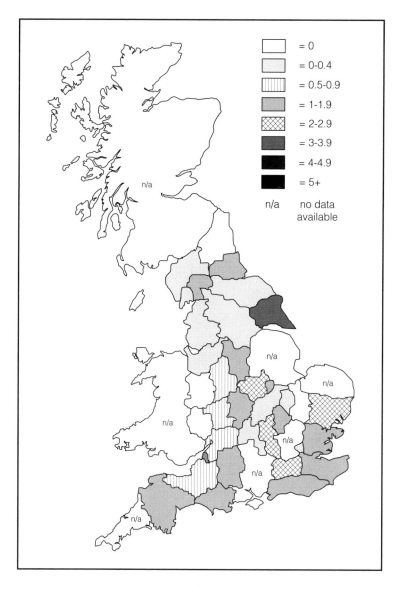

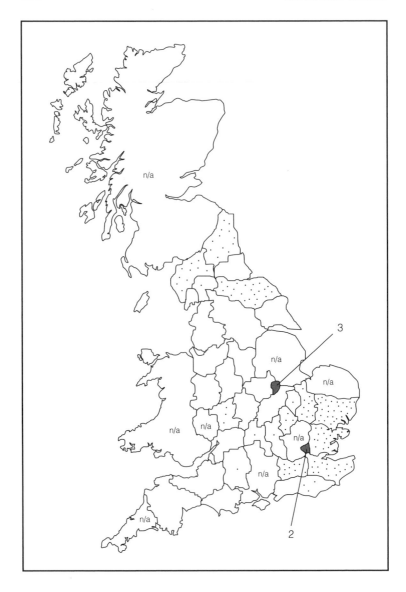

3.15   Fuller
(See Map 1.9) Fuller is common in the south-east, as predicted, but surprisingly numerous in the north of England.

industry from the occurrences of occupational surnames' (ESS2, p. 53). For example, the silk name Thrower was not found in urban areas as would have been expected (ESS2, p. 40), though Fransson (1935, p. 84) suggested that the name might also signify a potter. This tentative doubt has been somewhat dispelled by McKinley's own later researches in other counties, however. Oxfordshire names originating from various crafts and trades associated with the production of books, such as Bookbinder, some of which had died out by the sixteenth century, were located only in the city of Oxford itself two hundred years earlier. The name Shepherd was found to be located in the sheep rearing areas of Oxfordshire in the late thirteenth century (ESS3, p. 134). The majority of Coggers, Shipmans and Shipwrights were found on or near the Sussex coast. (Salter was not so found, but they might have been traders rather than processors. This surname was to be found inland in Cambridgeshire, Staffordshire, Wiltshire and Worcestershire in the thirteenth century. To add to the confusion, it might also mean psalter, a musician!) Surnames derived from commerce were generally to be found where common sense would expect them to be – in towns during the fourteenth century, but largely dispersed among the population more generally during the next few hundred years.

Other industries, such as iron or glass in Sussex, were examined but not found to have generated surnames in any numbers. Similarly, Glaswryght appears as a name in Gloucestershire in 1327, but is very rare. Bearing in mind the assumption about the earlier development of names in the south of England, the explanation will depend on the timing of the development of those industries in relation to the adoption of names and their inheritance. A counterargument might be that the early location of surnames might be the first evidence of an industry, though this might be difficult to establish.

By the seventeenth century, the original distribution patterns of occupational surnames have been somewhat dispersed, as names like Capper, Fleshmonger, Leadbeater, Mower and Thrower (as well as Walker) appear in Sussex for the first time, for example. Nevertheless, the circumstances of birth of occupational names can still be seen reflected in our modern phone books, supporting McKinley's overall conclusion about their *relative* immobility. Using these rare names to study migration is still difficult, however. Names like Alderman and Constable are widely, though thinly, scattered in the

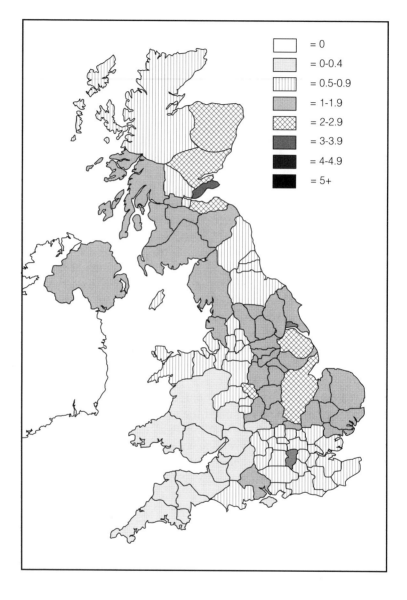

3.16a, b Baxter   20thC. (9,912) *above*   14thC. (143) *right*
Baxters, six hundred years apart – the similarity of distribution is striking.

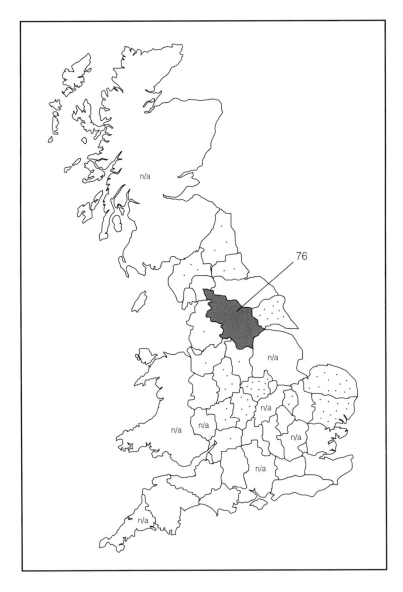

fourteenth century, and the sudden appearance of the latter in, say, Leicestershire, could be the result of a move from Gloucestershire, East Anglia, or even Northumberland.

Occupational names in the Yorkshire Poll Tax of 1379   The 1379 Poll Tax returns for the West Riding of Yorkshire, as well as representing a very substantial number of people, some 35,000 individuals, have another great advantage – though little help is obtained through the very thin introduction to the volume. Occupations are given against the names of a minority, but as the document covers so many persons these form a significant number.

There are strong indications from these individuals that, although the acquisition of inherited surnames was still incomplete, it was not a particularly recent innovation in Yorkshire at that time. The surnames of 333 whose occupation was given as 'smith' or 'faber', can be analysed. It is an occupation which requires skills and implements best inherited from a parent, and in the Poll Tax return there is more than one Smith, the son of a Smith, both being smiths. Forty-five (or 13.5 per cent) have an occupational surname *other than Smith or Faber* – Chapman, Cooper, Cutler, and so on, though among them are the occasional Arrowsmith or Goldsmith which are closely related, and several Marshalls, a name which originated in looking after horses. A further 78 (23.5 per cent) have names based on places, the majority being locative, most of those places being far from the residence in 1379, as far away as Leicester. As we have already noted that the majority of such names were given when the individuals first taking them were living in the places concerned, it would appear that at least one third of the Smiths had inherited their surnames from at least one generation earlier. This is in line with Gustav Fransson's overall conclusion after studying ten English counties, including Yorkshire – that after 1350 'in most cases people have not those occupations that their surnames denote' (1935, p. 16).

Seventy (21 per cent) of smiths were *called* Smith, a very high proportion compared with what would be expected in subsequent generations and it is clear that, despite the last paragraph, we have moved back to a time not too distant from its origins. (Reaney, incidentally, says that 22 *men* called Smith were smiths in the West Riding Poll Tax of 1379; OES, pp. 312–3.) The remainder (140 or 42 per cent) had surnames which were either based on Christian names, or were not easily identifiable. Even so, it would not be unreasonable to suggest that at least half of all Smiths had inherited that surname from their parent.

In conducting this sort of analysis, we may solve (or stumble across a solution to) problems opened out in Part 1. We would expect twenty carpenters to be called Carpenter if they showed the same proportion as smiths in having the same word as a surname. In fact, there is none, although the proportion of carpenters having *any* occupational surname (38 per cent) is not far removed from that of the smiths. However, whereas almost two-thirds of all the occupational surnames of smiths was Smith itself, about the same proportion of carpenters were called Wright (one even Wrightson). This suggests very strongly that the reason why there are so few Carpenters in the north of England even in the late twentieth century is because carpenters were known there as wrights in the early Middle Ages, whereas in East Anglia wrights of all kinds appear to have been given the Latin form Carpentarius with few actually being *called* Wright! (However, this theory does not explain the virtual disappearance by the seventeenth century of Carpenter as a surname in the North Riding and Cumberland where the name was plentiful in the early fourteenth – see Map 3.17.)

'Both the surname Wright, and surnames formed from compounds of "wright", are rarely found before the late thirteenth century, probably because the very common Latin word Carpentarius was used to translate such names' (ESS2, p. 57). An analysis of those in Yorkshire whose *occupation* was given as wright indicates correspondingly fewer (only some 5 per cent) having this as a surname – instead, 11 per cent have occupational surnames, some of which are closely related. There are several Carters in particular, with Cooper, Carpenter, and Turner also figuring. Redmonds (ESS1, p. 49) points out that Wright is a common West Riding name especially when used as a suffix, and Reaney examines those compounds in OES, pp. 206–8.

Another problem left over from Part 1 was why so few people appear to be called Shoemaker, when that occupation must have been relatively common. Isolating all those described as 'shoemaker', 'cordwainer' or 'sutor' (the Latin form) in 1379 indicates the overwhelming majority having that meaning as a surname were *called* Sutor (or variant, such as Souter or Sowter). However,

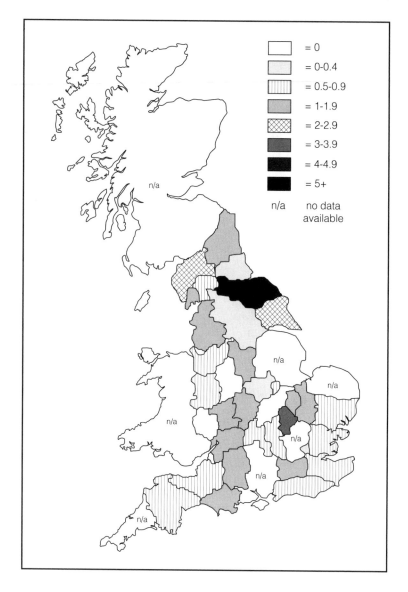

3.17   Carpenter (730)
(See Map 2.15) Carpenter had already been overtaken by Wright as a surname in the West Riding, though it was still well used as a byename further north.

there were relatively few of them, only 6 per cent – twice as many had come into this from many other occupations, either themselves directly, or more likely from an ancestor. We find people called Baker, Cartwright, Fisher, Husteler, Marshall, Milner, Palmer, Shepherd, Walker and Webster all carrying on trade as shoemakers in the West Riding. It is noticeable here, as in other parts of the country, that it is largely the 'industrial', especially the processing parts of textiles, rather than the agricultural occupations which have given rise to surnames. As suggested above, this was because so many earned their living on the land that agricultural surnames were scarcely efficient as identifiers.

The occupation webster shows remarkable statistical similarities to smith. Exactly the same proportion (48, or 21 per cent) were called Webster, despite a large number being women who were often both 'huswyf' and 'webster' or 'textrix'. (Of one Webster senior and junior pair, only the junior was described as a 'webster'.) Fifteen per cent had occupational names other than Webster, and once again had come from a remarkably wide range of other occupations, including Carter, Clerk, Chaloner, Hunter, Lytster, Miller, Palmer, Piper, Slater, Souter, Taylor, Turner, Walker and Wright.

The 1379 Poll Tax for the East Riding, published for only one of the hundreds, Howdenshire, has a much greater proportion of occupations listed against individuals, and a scrutiny of all surnames which are occupational reveals only a small minority following those same occupations. Three of the fourteen Milners were actually millers; of fifteen Taylors, six then followed that occupation; a quarter of Wrights were carpenters; but no Barker, Chapman, Clerk, Gardiner, Merchant, Shepherd, Smith, or Spicer earned their living in the way their surnames suggest. Of a total of 228 whose occupations are given, only twenty had the same occupation as a surname. Six occupations are supplied in the London Subsidy Roll of 1319, but none had the same as a surname.

Writers on medieval surnames have correctly stressed the fluidity of inheritance patterns well into the fifteenth century, employing well-documented examples to show that individuals still did not necessarily adopt the surname of their parent as their own surname. The findings of the present research reveals regional differences even within counties, and it is evident from the 1379 Poll Tax returns that the West Riding itself was not proceeding at the same rate. Some parts – especially Staincliff, Ewcross and the Ainsty

– had significantly higher proportions of people whose occupation was the same as their surname, suggesting a particularly late development of inheritance. All nine Smiths and Cartwrights appearing before the Cheshire sheriffs in the 1360s and 1370s followed that same occupation – but of sixteen other occupational surnames, only one did so (Madoc le Wright of Stanney, who was a carpenter!)

Nicknames

Perhaps the most fascinating of all the categories of surname, those originating in nicknames, have had a distinctive history. They grow in importance with each successive volume of the English Surnames Series, and have been the subject of separate articles and books (Jonsjo, 1979; McClure, 1981; Reaney devoted five chapters of the OES to them). Defining nicknames in terms of the origin of surnames is no easy task, however, as there is a sense in which *every* byename was once a nickname. Defining them as 'familiar, pet, or derisory names' or 'a shortened or familiar form of a person's name' is an inadequate basis for their use and development as surnames.

So we can *recognise* them even though we cannot *define* them. Or can we? We probably can recognise the majority – but there is a significant minority which, as noted earlier, can be easily confused with other categories of surname, or exist side by side with quite different origins and meanings. Whitehead is one of the many locative names ending with 'head' (Hartshead, for example) which can be a placename as well as a nickname. Haddock might be a fish, but it is also a corruption of Haydock in Lancashire. Was Tranchmore (one who 'slices through the sea') an occupation or a nickname (McKinley, 1990, p. 163)? Wagstaffe, and all other Shakespeare-like names, was evidently occupational in origin for a constable or other staff-wielding dignitary, but was so widespread across the mid-north of England that it hardly pertained to specific individuals, being almost a variant on the occupational name (rather like calling a wireless operator 'Sparks' during the war). In the south of England particularly, nicknames are often preceded by 'le/la' or 'the', which helps to distinguish them from placenames. 'Dictus' ('called') is also used, not quite 'alias' which was also in use at that time.

Others on the fringes of being nicknames are combinations, or

compounds, of a genuine occupation with an additional, idiosyn-
cratic adjective: Hoggeprest and Whitegroom in Sussex, for
example (McKinley, 1988, p. 362).

Nicknames were generated at a time when people's beliefs,
assumptions, lifestyles, imagination, expectations and relationships
were quite different from those we are used to. Nevertheless, they
obviously had just as strong an appeal as they do today, for they
were created in very large numbers. It is, however, extremely rare
to discover the reason why any nickname was originally applied,
for it is in their nature to be at the same time complimentary or
insulting, genuine or ironic, true or false, according to the particular circumstances and individuals concerned. From the names in
the 100 surnames with which this quest started, who can now tell
whether a man was called Bellamy (bel ami) because he was
friendly or just the opposite, Bassett (from bas = low) because he
was short or tall? The distribution of the name (Map 3.18 a, b)
probably has more to do with the use of the French language than
with genetics. Was Drinkwater a drunkard or abstemious, an ale-
housekeeper, or even suffering from a disease which caused a
thirst? (It is sobering to point out that the fourteenth-century scan
shows the name only in Kent, Sussex and Wiltshire, but other
sources also reveal it in Dorset, Lincolnshire, London, Shropshire
and Suffolk.) A Robert Drinckemilk paid the Lay Subsidy of 1296
in Northumberland.

Was Fox a person of a certain appearance, habits, or craftiness?
(That name, by the way, had the same distribution across the north
of England six hundred years ago as it has today (Maps 3.19a and
b).) Spruce might have been in origin a Prussian, the explanation
given in the only surname dictionary to contain a reference to it, a
person of neat appearance or the opposite, or one living near to, or
as physically or morally straight as, the tree? Happily, the other
meaning of the word, a deceiver, appears to be twentieth century
in origin. (On that score it is perhaps worth adding that a useful
source of information on whether a word conveyed a particular
meaning at a given date is the full Oxford English Dictionary,
though most of its sources are literary and therefore later than the
period we are currently discussing.) Wiseman, a name not confined
to Suffolk where it was very common (Map 3.20), but also found
in Cambridgeshire, Derbyshire, Essex, Huntingdonshire, Kent,
Leicestershire, London, Northamptonshire, Oxfordshire, Sussex,

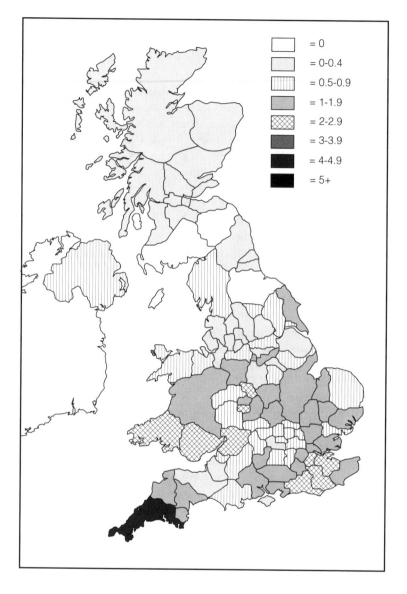

3.18a, b **Bassett**   20thC. (2,508) *above*   14thC. (98) *right*
The maps show a slow evolution of the distribution of the name, but it is
clearly in the south six hundred years.

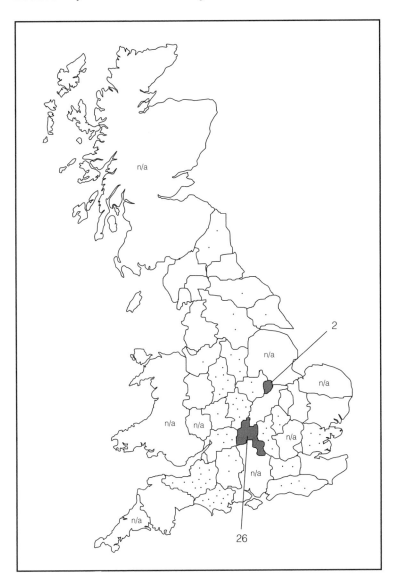

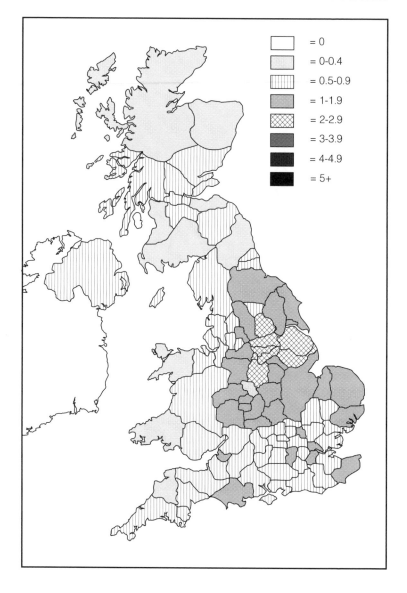

3.19a, b   Fox   20thC. (15,184) *above*   14thC. (279) *right*
Already in a broad band across the north of England, Fox is predictably
popular in Lincolnshire and Nottinghamshire once sources are available for
those counties.

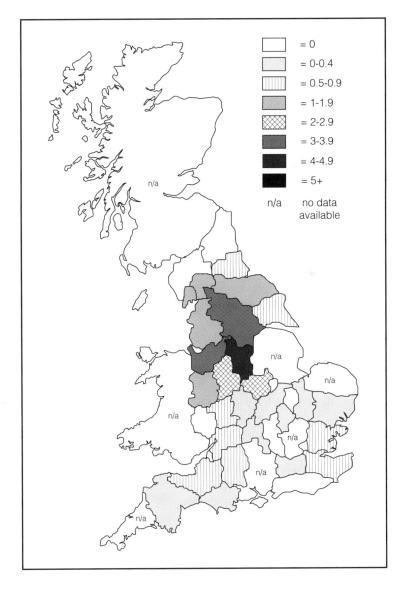

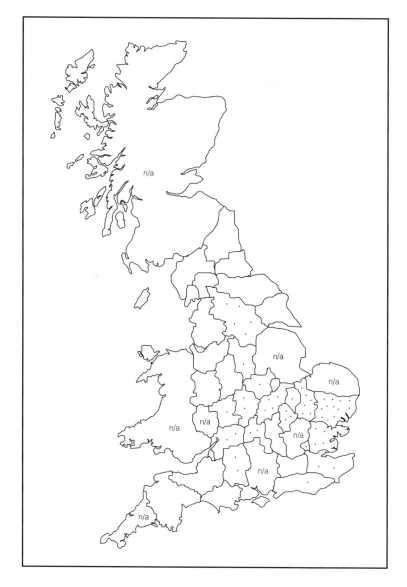

3.20   Wiseman

Wiseman has had a continuous presence in Yorkshire and East Anglia, but its later ramification in seventeenth-century Gloucestershire has not been predicted.

Warwickshire, Wiltshire, Worcestershire and Yorkshire, might have been an egghead or a blockhead.

Finally, there are those which defy attempts to understand their meaning, thus rendering questionable their status as nicknames – what of Adam Fivewinterald (1246 in Lancashire), Robert Forpens (1379 in the West Riding), and many others – Always, Hurlbutt, Kay, Munday and Quartermain, all attracting possible but seemingly unlikely explanations so far.

No effort has been spared to group nicknames into various subcategories according to appearance, dress, speech, mental or morals traits, personal habits, social status, wealth or age, each of which can contain praise or criticism of the individual concerned by being compared to objects in the natural world (birds, animals – some, like wolf or beaver, are now extinct in this country, but the existence of the surname is no guarantee that the animal lived here when surnames were being created – topographical features, coins, and even dates) by the use of normal adjectives, metaphors, quotations (usually oaths), antonyms or hypochoristics. In the case of compound nicknames, one element might come from English, the other from French, Scandinavian, or another 'foreign' language. It is this fluidity of sources and purposes which give nicknames their fascination, their subtlety, and, of course, their obscurity. How many would immediately recognise Touchpricke as signifying a skilful archer?

Happily, many give fewer problems, although, as already noted, most can have more than one interpretation. One group of names might have an explanation not so far found in textbooks – those based on a date. I have had Peter Munday as a neighbour, Peter November as a colleague, and Brian Christmas as a correspondent, for example. The generally accepted view is that the most likely explanation of these fascinating names is that individuals had been born on a particular day of the week or time of the year; alternatively, they owed a service to the lord of the manor at that time. Without denying the possibility that these are correct in some cases, it must be said that to anyone used to studying names in a much later period they have all the hallmarks of being foundlings. Admittedly, only Monday and Friday seem to have survived in the dictionaries, but a Will Seterday can be found in Yorkshire in 1365. The same explanation could be offered for 'Fivewinterald' and other names which are based on a person's age – those surnamed

'Lef(t)child' in the Essex Lay Subsidy of 1327 and Carte Nativorum of Northamptonshire, the clerk 'John Twoyereold' in Lydney, Gloucestershire in 1522, or 'Elena Mydnyght' at Preston in the West Riding in 1379.

The development, as well as the origins, of surnames based on nicknames has a history distinct from that of other categories. The practice of giving such names to individuals long predates the Middle Ages, and seems to have been used by both French and Scandinavian traditions. It was based on a common understanding of vocabulary, expression and metaphor over a wide area, but was also subject to incident and accident. In consequence, these names were:

- very numerous. Over 1,000 different nicknames have been found in Sussex alone before 1650, 480 of them from before the middle of the fourteenth century;
- each held by relatively few individuals in any one area. They are often widespread, though low in numbers of persons holding them, only 5 per cent in the Salford Hundred of Lancashire in 1524 (ESS4, p. 363; see also McKinley's comments on the names Sherwen and Spendlove, ESS5, p. 362–3). Up to one third were held by only one person in each county's sources before 1400 (ESS5, p. 361);
- at the mercy of elimination with the death of individuals to whom they had been given. This seems to be true especially of long, compound names, names based on French (ESS5, p. 395), those given to serfs rather than to free men (ESS5, p. 397–8), and quotations;
- subject in some cases to regional dialect. Hogg in most areas implies something to do with pigs, but on the coast of Sussex, where most of that county's fourteenth-century examples seem to have been, it is more likely to be connected with a seafaring vessel of that name (ESS5, p. 365); Moyl meant bald in a Cornwall which did not yet speak English;
- liable to be adopted by, or rather given to, all classes of society except the highest;
- candidates nevertheless for significant ramification once over the initial hurdle of the acquisition of genetic inheritance. Lancashire has some remarkable examples of this development, with names like Lightfoot, a name found commonly across the north of Eng-

land in the fourteenth century (McKinley, 1981, pp. 369–70),
Lord (1981, pp. 272–3), Tyson (p. 371) and Whitehead. Redhead in the fourteenth century produces no surprises – they are
almost all found in counties north of Derbyshire, and in East
Anglia (Map 3.21). The ramification of rare names such as Fist
in Sussex (1988, p. 167) provides a very useful platform for the
study of mobility;
• usually acquired fairly early in the development of inheritance,
but occasionally much later. Proving this is impossible in the
absence of any complete listing of individuals in the Middle Ages,
but it does seem as if a few did not exist earlier than the fifteenth
century.

Personal names

For almost a thousand years, English people have used byenames
or surnames which originally described them as being the son or
daughter of a parent's personal (i.e. first, baptismal or Christian)
name. The practice of having byenames which were personal in
nature was a first step towards hereditary surnames because,
unlike most others, it was basically genetic; nevertheless, progress
towards our present system was not smooth – nor did it result in
uniformity of type, timing or distribution. The phone books in Part
1 can now be seen to show the marks of those differences in early
development which followed the gradual adoption of personal surnames from byenames after 1250.

McKinley (ESS2, pp. 130–1) reports that, although byenames
based on Christian names were commonly used even in eleventh-
century East Anglia, such usage died out there during the period
1150 to 1250 and were held by only a small percentage of people
in later centuries – in the lay subsidies, only 20 individuals in Norfolk (1329/30) and 19 in Suffolk (1327). Reaney devotes a major
section of OES (pp. 98–127) to Old English names, with similar conclusions.

The earliest such names predate the Norman Conquest, being
either Old English or Scandinavian, though none seems to have
become hereditary at that time. About one in five of those named
in the Domesday Book of 1086 had a personal byename, but the
Conquest was probably of much greater significance through its
impact on the type rather than the popularity of personal names in
use. Pre-Conquest personal names normally had two elements and

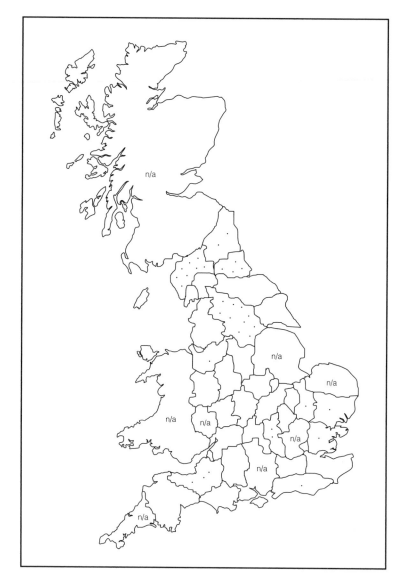

3.21   Redhead

(See Map 1.11) Redhead was present in the north and east as expected, but a surprising number of odd individuals could be found in other parts of fourteenth-century England.

were, in consequence, very numerous; personal names introduced after 1066 tended to be Biblical (Andrew or Thomas, for example), or names currently in vogue in France, including some Greek names, especially those which were favoured by royalty. McKinley specifically pinned the change from Old English and Scandinavian to French in Oxfordshire to between 1180 and 1220 (ESS3, p. 213; OES, ch. 7). The newcomers gradually superseded the older names as people imitated the landowning classes among whom they were quite common, and only Edward and Edmund survived among the popular byenames and surnames of the fourteenth century. Both male and female new Christian names were far fewer in number than those which had been used before the Conquest, an apparently insignificant change but one which had two important consequences.

- Having fewer Christian names led to an increased need to use byenames in order to distinguish between individuals, and it is no coincidence that the development of diminutive forms of personal names and hereditary surnames was contemporary with the decline in the use of pre-Conquest personal names at baptism. The thirteenth century was a watershed in this respect, though the evolution occurred at different times in different regions of the country. The loss of those names which predated 1066 was not simultaneous; parts of the north and East Anglia which had been in the Danelaw continued to use them for another century or so, obviating the need to develop surnames. Hence the Scandinavian name Sagar, which was examined in Part 2, could not be expected to have developed in the west midlands or the south-west, though Segar is to be found in the Gloucestershire Lay Subsidy of 1327.
- The existence of Old English or Scandinavian personal names used as surnames is a major clue to the timing of when names became hereditary, for they would not have been adopted after their use as baptismal names had died out.

The English Surnames Series is revealing regional differences in the timing and distribution of three main types of personal surname – those which remain unchanged (the 'uninflected'); those which have the letter 's' or 'es' added as a suffix; and those which have 'son' added. Before describing them, however, there is an issue to be raised concerning the data usable in any survey of individual

names. Henry, Harris, and Harrison present no problem of cate-
gorisation, as examples of the three types. How should we treat
'Richard son of Henry', however – as a byename or a surname?
There is ample statistical evidence to suggest that it was not a surname in the way that Richard Harryson would have been. On the
other hand, to ignore the geographical implications of the distibu-
tion of Christian names being used as bynames in early periods
would be to have an incomplete picture of the likely origins of the
name. Accordingly, and in the knowledge of the methodological
pitfalls potentially involved, I included all such references in an
attempt to see where Roger, for example, developed as a byename,
qua incipient surname.

The result, however, produces such a lack of continuity with
later centuries that I am now convinced it should not have been
adopted. When 'Rogers' and 'son of Roger' are counted together,
the name is far more common in the north than in the south where
Rogers later predominates. It might be argued that 'son of Roger'
is more likely to be a precursor to Rogerson, but McKinley has effectively disproved that hypothesis (see below). 'Son of Roger' appears
from this survey to carry no significance for the later distribution
of Rogers or Rogerson, and the only good thing to emerge from that
little fiasco is to note with some satisfaction the complete absence
of anyone called Rodgers in the Middle Ages.

Uninflected personal names   Until the thirteenth century, this was
by far the commonest of the three types, some even becoming
hereditary before 1200. Many would now no longer be recognised
as first names, as they died out of use some six to seven centuries
ago; most did not survive as hereditary surnames, but there are a
few vestigial remnants of those early days. We would therefore
expect to find examples of this type mainly in the south-east if
hereditary surnames developed there so early that Scandinavian
Christian names were still in use. Edrich, for example, a variant of
Aedric, is almost always found to the south of a line from the west
midlands to East Anglia (Map 3.22). At first, they were predominantly Old English or Scandinavian, as the newly introduced names
were rarely adopted as uninflected bynames or surnames in England (in contrast with Wales). Thus, we do not find Robert, Thomas
or William as English surnames in the late Middle Ages except in
Cornwall, however common they might have been as Christian

names. (Paradoxically it is those very personal names, which became uninflected surnames, which did not themselves survive as Christian names.) Thurston remained a popular first name in Lancashire until the late seventeenth century, though it did not develop as a surname; conversely Ottiwell, while dying out in Lancashire, remained a not uncommon Christian name in Cheshire into the seventeenth century.

Oddly, however, this did not apply to the hypochoristic, diminutive forms which were also growing in popularity as a mechanism for increasing ways to distinguish individuals by name. They were based on rhyming variations on all or, usually, part of the original, often with the addition of a suffix such as 'cock' (OES, pp. 209–13), 'et', 'in', 'kin' (OES, pp. 213–17), 'mot', 'on', or 'ot'. Colet, for example, is a hypochoristic of Nicholas. In some areas, uninflected surnames remained the most popular of the three forms – in Suffolk, for example, they formed some 23 per cent in 1523. In Lancashire, on the other hand, uninflected names were very rare, lending yet more support for the view that hereditary surnames developed late in that county.

Uninflected names can be used in order to study ramification and migration, but only when their origins can be pinpointed, which is possible in a remarkably large number of cases. McKinley found no fewer than 160 held by only one person in Sussex before 1500, but of course many of these will have died out.

In no part of England has McKinley found uninflected names to be characteristic of any social class.

Personal names with an added suffix 's'   There can be few first names which cannot be turned into common surnames by adding the letter 's' on the end, but why that came about remains a mystery. It happened in two waves, the first in the thirteenth and fourteenth centuries, the second over the next three hundred years, in parallel with that identified for toponymics above, remaining a permanent feature of our spectrum of surnames (OES, pp. 91–6). The first wave had several distinctive features.

- It applied to byenames which had arrived after the Conquest rather than before, so the practice of turning byenames into hereditary surnames had already begun. Edwards and Edmunds are the main exceptions to this generalisation. They are hard to

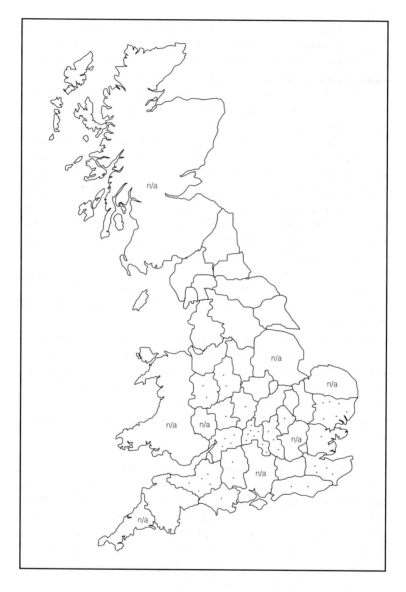

3.22   Edrich

Edrich provides a good test for the theory that surnames which are Old English personal names should be found mainly in the south.

spot when a source document has been written in Latin, but it is believed that the genitive is used where the nominative or accusative would be expected (e.g. Robertus Rogeri instead of Robertus Rogerus).

- McKinley's survey of 11 counties (ESS3, p. 231) shows that there was a pronounced geographical skew to the new practice which was most common in the south-west midlands and Oxfordshire (where a quarter of the personal names in 1327 have an added 's'), and especially in counties bordering Wales – Gloucestershire, Herefordshire and Shropshire. Correspondingly, they were fewer in south-east England (where most surname development had already taken place when this phenomenon started), and in the north. McKinley concluded that 'it is doubtful if such hereditary surnames developed in the northern counties at all' (1990, p. 119). They had appeared in East Anglia before 1200, but formed only 0.5 per cent of names in Lancashire in the seventeenth century.

- Most of those who acquired names with an additional 's' were small tenants, either bond or free – in the Oxfordshire Poll Tax returns there are far fewer than expected, it is thought because the surnames of servants were not given. (ESS3, p. 218; see also above, p. 154)

- A substantial proportion of people bearing these names before 1350 were married or widowed women. It is generally believed that the 's' was probably genitive (nowadays apostrophied), implying that women 'belonged' to their husbands, or that they were the widow 'of', but why men should be given them is not clear unless they were employed by the person of that name. Perhaps it was another form of differentiation of individuals. There are no men with the added 's' in the Kent return of 1334, but it was not a general rule that women's names had this form. In the 1327 Essex Lay Subsidy, there were women whose surnames were Godfrey, Henry, Jacob, Vincent, for example, who were not given the suffix 's'.

- Hypochoristics were particularly prone to the acquisition of the final 's'. They are probably more noticeable in the early sources because diminutives could not be translated into Latin.

The first wave was not permanent in areas where it did not become common, such as Sussex. The second wave defies explanation as, through the fifteenth, sixteenth, and even seventeenth centuries, names which had been hereditary for some generations began to add an 's' for no apparent reason. As with the earlier wave, the same phenomenon can be observed in occupational names, nicknames, a few toponymics (perhaps a genitival reference to the place of someone's tenancy), and even the occasional locative. The first wave probably had meaning, the second merely fashion.

Scandinavians do not appear to have developed this particular suffix, though they have 'son/sen' of course. Oddly, the Dutch did, and in their case it was used genitivally – Hans the son of Melle was called 'Hans Melles' as late as the eighteenth century.

My belief that these names developed as abbreviations of names with the suffix 'son', to which we now turn, has now been abandoned, as I have found no substantiating evidence for such a change.

Personal names with an added suffix 'son' Most of the personal names which formed the basis of those in the last section can also be supplemented with the suffix 'son', and the histories of the two types have considerable parallels. Still a well-known feature of Scandinavian surnames, the addition of 'sunu' was known in pre-Conquest England, but never became hereditary. Within a generation of 1066, individuals were described as being the 'son of' (or, more generally, the Latin filius/filia), and most writers have assumed that, for example, 'filius Rogeri' could be the equivalent of Rogers or FitzRoger (e.g. the Introduction to the published Kent Lay Subsidy of 1334). However, McKinley has shown quite convincingly that this phrase was almost certainly not a translation of a personal name with 'son' as a suffix. This conclusion, interestingly enough, is based on studies of the geographical distribution of examples of this type of name.

Names with the suffix 'son' were rarely found before the middle of the thirteenth century, but within a hundred years they had become very common, and hereditary, especially in the north of England; they continued to be a popular form of newly acquired inherited surnames until the sixteenth century if not later. Wherever they were found, they were adopted by small tenants, free and unfree, but rarely by 'substantial landowners'. As far south as the middle of Staffordshire, 'son' rather than 's' was the normal

suffix (1990, pp. 112–13). I have been unable to find the name
Dawson further south than Warwickshire in the fourteenth century, the vast majority of examples being in the West Riding (Map
3.23). Some were areas to which the Danelaw had not extended,
calling into question the belief that they were the result of strong
Scandinavian influence. Furthermore, most were based on male
and female names newly introduced after 1066, although some
(Ormson, Swainson) were Old English. Hypochoristic forms were
particularly prone to this development also, so we get Wilson as
well as Williamson.

The north of England has been portrayed as being up to a century behind the south in the development of inherited surnames,
and that the simple 'son of...' or 'daughter of...' as (or instead of) a
surname was much more widely used, resulting in that pattern
even in the twentieth century of far more holders of names ending
with 'son' in the north of the country. There is no doubting that
assertion. A comparison of two counties, Northumberland and Bedfordshire, at the opening of the fourteenth century reveals the difference – whereas in the former just over 30 per cent of all
taxpayers were 'son' of or 'daughter of', the same figure for the
latter was less than 4 per cent.

McKinley (ESS5, pp. 332–4) has a useful summary of the
regional differences between 's' and 'son' names over almost half
the country, developing the overall theme in Reaney (OES, pp.
86–90). The former were particularly numerous, as a proportion of
the population, in the south-west midlands during the fourteenth
century, and particularly in the Welsh border counties south of
Cheshire by the seventeenth. On the other hand, 'son' had spread,
albeit to a less extent, in Lancashire and Leicestershire in the fourteenth century, but had ramified far more extensively than 's' in
counties from Staffordshire to Nottinghamshire northwards. The
normal explanation for the main geographical skew is the fact that
surnames became inherited much earlier in the south, but that is
unsatisfactory – the names were simply not developed in sufficient
numbers in the thirteeenth century *to become* hereditary.

In the south, 'son' names were not unknown but were much
rarer, some suspecting their presence to have been the result of
migration from the north. Half of the ten in Gloucestershire in
1327 were based on women's names – Emmeson, Margerison, or
Marieson, for example. There were only five in the Essex Lay

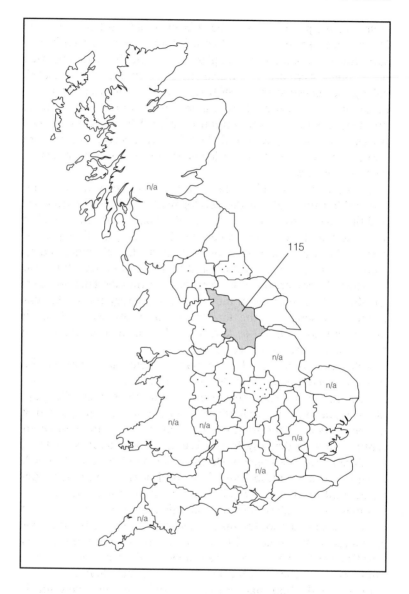

3.23   Dawson

A personal name with 'son' suffix, like Dawson, should be found mainly in
the north.

Subsidy of 1327 – Leveson (from an Old English personal name, there being six in the Oxfordshire Hundred Rolls and one paid the Gloucestershire Lay Subsidy of 1327), Hobson, Stevenson, Parsonson and Revesson, the last two being occupational rather than personal. Only 3 per cent of the 1523 Suffolk Lay Subsidy had this form. Only eighteen 'son' names are to be found in the Isle of Wight Hearth Tax return of 1674, compared with ninety-three ending with 's', though some of the latter are toponymics. In contrast, in one parish there were nineteen with 'son' suffixes in one of the rare published lists from fourteenth-century Lancashire which cover a large percentage of the population (persons who promised to subscribe to the stipend of the priest of the altar of Our Lady at Ormskirk in 1366, published by the Record Society of Lancashire and Cheshire, Vol. 31, App. B, 1896), but none with a personal name with the suffix 's'. All the Moxons in the fourteenth-century scan are found in the West Riding, from which they have scarcely moved in six hundred years. (They appeared under their original metronymic forms Megotson, Magson, or Mokesson.)

In the north, particularly Lancashire and Yorkshire, the suffix 'daughter' was also used, being found (albeit rarely, even into the sixteenth century. A further form associated particularly with south-west Lancashire, is the double 'sonson'. McKinley says that these 'seem to have gone out by about 1500'. In the West Riding there was a servant called Johannes Adamson Tomson at Appletreewyck in 1379, not an isolated example. In Gloucestershire there is yet a further refinement, as 's' is added to 'son' making such names as Johnsons or Pearsons (ESS3, p. 231).

As noted in Part 1, not all names ending with 'son' were of this type. Some (e.g. Clarkson, Mason) are occupational; others (John and Richard Knaresboroughson at Carleton in the West Riding, 1379) are locative; and one in the 100 name survey, Tyson, is a nickname (according to Kneen, McKinley and Tengvik), though other writers (Black, Reaney and Weekley) have suggested 'son of Denis' as an explanation, which would fit in with its geographical distribution as it is largely confined to the Lake District and the North Riding. Ballardson is found in Lancashire (ESS4, p. 325).

Conclusion

We should now be in a position to review how far the present day distribution of surnames is an indication of their place of origin; whether, by looking into the nominal telescope of phone books, we are seeing the light of their beginnings uncontaminated by intervening mass migrations.

There are obvious problems about tracking names which are rare, for quite different reasons. We have seen how those which originated from a single point can move dramatically over time. It is also clear that, the rarer the name, the less likely it is that the distribution of its early examples will be visible in the fourteenth-century sources until the Poll Tax becomes widely available; this is particularly true of names which are not locative. Some thinly scattered names evidently did not survive the Black Death, with the result that a few later examples may be preceded by many earlier instances. There is also the suspicion that the late development of inherited surnames in the extreme north of England (certainly north of where I live) can have a distorting effect on distribution patterns based on fourteenth-century sources.

Distribution studies are of even more limited value in relation to determining the meaning of surnames. It has been possible to show, for example, that Weaver is a locative name, and that England/English is not a geographically peripheral nickname; similarly, Box is unlikely to be solely a locative, as it can be found in many counties from Yorkshire to Kent to Devon in the fourteenth century. However, the fact that Fox is distributed across the north of England, or that Nightingale is largely found away from nesting sites even in the fourteenth century, does not help to confirm them as nicknames.

To a large extent, however, the optimism of Part 1 has been justified by the maps in Part 3. With a few exceptions, common surnames of all types still appear to be concentrated where they were six hundred years ago. Furthermore, as there is nothing unusual about the hundred names investigated, the expectation is that this broad generalisation is true of most of the others.

Epilogue

We have now tracked back English surnames to the beginning of their time. If we try to regress still further, we do not simply reach an earlier, connected sequence – we break through into a different dimension, a world of nominal fantasy in which a wonderful variety of byenames flash before our eyes, each one short-lived, but the whole offering a kaleidoscope of words, some familiar, others quite alien.

By strange coincidence, this world may be viewed a further three hundred years before the last. Domesday Book, compiled in 1086, was a massive attempt to list all lands held by and of the Crown, and the names of royal tenants. We therefore have lists of people, county by county, admirably reproduced in published form by Phillimore and with a name index to the whole country. Once again, therefore, we have available, for a period of almost a thousand years ago, the equivalent of a pre-war phone book! By no means all householders, let alone all people, are listed; nevertheless, it is an excellent source of data, without parallel at that time.

Most have only one name, and only a few of those with more might seem familiar at first glance – a Bassett here, a Carpenter there, though only three Smiths in the whole country! Instead, we enter the world of Edric the Bald, Edric the Blind, Aldred brother of Odo, Burnt Albert, Harold's Concubine, Walter the Crossbowman, Hugh Donkey's daughter, Ralph the Fat, Alfyeat Ghost, Ketel Friday, Roger God-save-ladies, Humphrey Goldenbollocks, Ralph Haunted, Robert the Lascivious, Ralph Passwater, Ralph Pierce-hedge, Alwin the Rat, Akile Suffering, Edlufu Thief, Godwyn Weak-feet, Alric Wintermilk, and the Half-men of Suffolk.

References and further reading

Addison, Sir W. (1978) *Understanding English surnames.*

Anderson, M. (1971) *Family structure in nineteenth century Lancashire.*

Bardsley, C. W. (1901a) *English surnames.*

Bardsley, C. W. (1901b) *Dictionary of English and Welsh surnames.*

Baring-Gould, S. (1910) *Family names and their story.*

Beddoe, J. (1885) *The races of Britain.*

Benjamin, E. A. (1987) 'The Welsh patronymic custom', *The Local Historian*, 17.7.

Beresford, M. W. (1958) 'The Lay Subsidies 1290–1334', *The Local Historian*, 3.8.

Beresford, M. W. (1963) *Lay subsidies and poll taxes.*

Black, G. F. (1946, repr. 1965) *The surnames of Scotland.*

Boyce, A. J. (1984) *Migration and mobility.*

Brett, D. (1985) 'The use of telephone directories in surname studies', *The Local Historian*, 16.7.

Buckatzsch, E. J. (1951) 'The constancy of local populations and migration in England before 1800', *Population Studies*, 8.

Camsell, M. (1986) 'Devon locative surnames in the fourteenth century', *Nomina*, 10.

Chapman, C. (1991) *Pre-1841 censuses and population listings.*

Christmas, B. W. (1991) *Sources for one-name studies and for other family historians.*

Clifford, S. C. (1987) 'The origins of surnames', *Family Tree Magazine*, 3.6–7 (April, May).

Coleman, D. A. (1979) 'A study of migration and marriage in Reading, England', *Journal of Biosocial Science*, 11.

Cottle, B. (1967, 1978) *The Penguin dictionary of surnames.*

Crosby, A. G. (1993) 'Migration to Preston in the fourteenth century: the evidence of surnames', *Lancashire Local Historian*, 8.

Dolley, M. (1983) 'Toponymic surnames and the pattern of pre-1830 English immigration into the Isle of Man', *Nomina*, 7.

Ecclestone, M. (1989) 'The diffusion of English surnames', *The Local Historian*, 19.2 (see also his letter in 20.3).

ESS – see McKinley and Redmonds below.

Ewen, C. L'E. (1931) *A history of surnames of the British Isles*.

Ewen, C. L'E. (1938) *A guide to the origin of British surnames*.

Feeson, F. (1965) 'The history and technique of surname distribution studies', *Family History*, 3.

Fransson, G. (1935) *Middle English surnames of occupation, 1100–1350*.

Gibson, J. S. W. (1985) *A simplified guide to probate jurisdictions*.

Gibson, J. S. W. (1988) *Census returns 1841–1881 on microfilm*.

Gibson, J. S. W. (1990) *The hearth tax, other later Stuart tax lists, and the Association Oath rolls*.

Gibson, J. S. W. (1993) *General Register Office and International Genealogical Indexes*.

Gibson, J. S. W. and Creaton, H. (1992) *Lists of Londoners*.

Gibson, J. S. W. and Dell, A. (1989) *Tudor and Stuart muster rolls*.

Gibson, J. S. W. and Dell, A. (1994) *Lists of people in the 1640's* (provisional title).

Gibson, J. S. W. and Medlycott, M. (1989) *Militia lists and musters 1757–1876*.

Gibson, J. S. W. and Medlycott, M. (1992) *Local census listings*.

Gibson, J. S. W. and Mills, D. (1984) *Land tax assessments c1690–c1950*.

Gibson, J. S. W. and Rogers, C. D. (1990a) *Poll books c1696–1872*.

Gibson, J. S. W. and Rogers, C. D. (1990b) *Electoral registers since 1832; and burgess rolls*.

Giller, A. M. (1992) *A study of the history of the surname Eveleigh* (unpublished M.A. thesis, University of Sheffield).

Glasscock, R. E. (ed.) (1975) *The lay subsidy of 1334*, British Academy Records of Social and Economic History, NS 2.

Goss, C. W. F. (1932) *The London directories, 1677–1855*.

Gottlieb, K. (1980) 'Surnames as markers of inbreeding and mobility', *Human Biology*, 55.

Guild of One Name Studies (1991) *Register of one name studies*.

Guppy, H. B. (1890, 1968) *The homes of family names of Great Britain*.

Hair, P. E. H. (1976) 'Family and locality: an encouraging exercise in Herefordshire records', *Local Historian*, 12.1.

Hanks, P. (1992–3) 'The present-day distribution of surnames in the British Isles', *Nomina*, 16. (An important article published too late to be used.)

Hanks, P. and Hodges, F. (1988) *A dictionary of surnames*.

Harley, J. B. (1961–63) 'The Hundred Rolls of 1279', *Amateur Historian*, 5.

Hassall, W. O. (1967) *History through surnames*.

Hey, D. (1987) *Family history and local history in England.*

Hey, D. (1992) *The origins of one hundred Sheffield surnames.*

Hey, D. (1993) *The Oxford book of family history.*

Hitching, F. K. and S. (1910) *References to English surnames in 1601.*

Holt, J. C. (1982) *What's in a name? Family nomenclature and the Norman Conquest.*

Jonsjo, J. (1979) *Studies in Middle English nicknames 1. Compounds.*

Kaplan, B. A. and Lasker, G. W. (1983) 'The present distribution of some English surnames derived from place names', *Human Biology*, 55.

Kent, J. R. (1981) 'Population mobility and alms: poor migrants in the Midlands during the early seventeenth century', *Local Population Studies*, 27.

Kneen, J. J. (1937) *The personal names of the Isle of Man.*

Kuchemann, C. F. et al. (1967) 'A demographic and genetic study of a group of Oxfordshire villages', *Human Biology*, 39.

Lasker, G. W. (1978) 'Relationships among the Otmoor villages and surrounding communities as inferred from surnames contained in the current register of electors', *Annals of Human Biology*, 5.

Lasker, G. W. (1983) 'The frequencies of surnames in England and Wales', *Human Biology*, 55.

Lasker, G. W. (1985) *Surnames and genetic structure.*

Lasker, G. W. (1988) 'Application of surname frequency distributions to studies of mating preferences', in Mascie-Taylor, C. G. N., and Boyce, A. J. *Human mating patterns.*

Lasker, G. W. and Kaplan, B. A. (1983) 'English place-name surnames tend to cluster near the place named', *Names*, 31.

Lasker, G. W. and Mascie-Taylor, C. G. N. (1990) *Atlas of British surnames.*

Latham, J. 'What's in a name – or why Macs are rife', *New Society*, 11 Dec., 1975 (34.688).

Leaver, R. (1990) 'Families on the move: personal mobility and the diffusion of surnames', *The Local Historian*, 20.2.

Leeson, F. (1964) 'The study of single surnames and their distribution', *The Genealogists' Magazine*, 14.12.

Leeson, F. (1965) 'The history and technique of surname distribution studies', *Family History Magazine*, 3.14/5.

Leeson, F. (1970, 1971) 'The development of surnames', *The Genealogists' Magazine*, 16.8, 16.10.

Lofvenberg, M. T. (1942) *Studies on Middle English local surnames.*

MacLysaght, E. (1985 ed.) *The surnames of Ireland.*

Mander, M. (1984) *How to trace your ancestors.*

Marker, I. J. and Warth, K. E. (1987) *Surname periodicals, a world-wide listing of one-name genealogical publications.*

Mascie-Taylor, C. G. N. and Lasker, G. W. (1984) 'Geographic distribution of surnames in Britain: the Smiths and Joneses have cline like blood group genes', *Journal of Biosocial Science*, 16.

Mascie-Taylor, C. G. N. and Lasker, G. W. (1985) 'Geographical distribution of common surnames in England and Wales', *Annals of Human Biology*, 12.5.

Mascie-Taylor, C. G. N. and Lasker, G. W. (1990) 'The distribution of surnames in England and Wales: a model for genetic distribution', *Man*, 25.

Matthews, C. M. (1966) *English surnames*.

McClure, P. (1978) 'Surnames from English placenames as evidence for mobility in the middle ages', *The Local Historian*, 13.2.

McClure, P. (1981) 'The interpretation of Middle English nicknames', *Nomina*, v.

McKinley, R. A. (1969) 'The survey of English surnames', *The Local Historian*, 8.8.

McKinley, R. A. (1975) *Norfolk and Suffolk surnames in the middle ages* (English Surnames Series Vol. 2).

McKinley, R. A. (1976) 'The distribution of surnames derived from the names of some Yorkshire towns', in Emmison, F. and Stephens, R., *Tribute to an antiquary: essays presented to Marc Fitch by some of his friends*.

McKinley, R. A. (1977) *The surnames of Oxfordshire* (English Surnames Series Vol. 3).

McKinley, R. A. (1981) *The surnames of Lancashire* (English Surnames Series Vol. 4).

McKinley, R. A. (1988) *The surnames of Sussex* (English Surnames Series Vol. 5).

McKinley, R. A. (1990) *A history of British surnames*.

McLure, P. (1979) 'Patterns of migration in the late middle ages: the evidence of English place-name surnames', *Economic History Review II*, 32.

Moore, A. W. (1890) *The surnames and place-names of the Isle of Man*.

Morgan, T. J and P. (1985) *Welsh surnames*.

Mullins, E. L. C. (1958 and 1983) *Texts and calendars* (2 vols).

Norton, J. E. (1950) *Guide to the national and provincial directories of England and Wales, excluding London, before 1856*.

OES – see Reaney below.

Ordnance Survey (1987) *Gazetteer of Great Britain: all names from the 1:50,000 Landranger Map Series*.

Padel, O. J. (1985) 'Cornish surnames in 1327', *Nomina*, 9.

Porteous, J. D. (1982) 'Surname geography: a study of the Mell family name c. 1538–1980', *Transactions of the Institute of British Geographers*, NS 7.2.

Porteous, J. D. (1985) 'Place loyalty', *The Local Historian*, 16.6.

Porteous, J. D. (1987) 'Locating the place of origin of a surname', *The Local Historian* 17.7.

Porteous, J. D. (1988) *The Mells*.

Prideaux, R. M. (1989) *A west country clan*.

Reaney, P. H. (1967 and 1976) *The origin of English surnames*.

Reaney, P. H. and Wilson, R. M. (1991) *A dictionary of British surnames*.

Redmonds, G. (1972a) 'Surnames and place-names', *The Local Historian*, 10.1.

Redmonds, G. (1972b) 'Surname heredity in Yorkshire', *The Local Historian*, 10.4.

Redmonds, G. (1973) *Yorkshire West Riding* (English Surnames Series 1).

Rogers, C. D. (1986) *Tracing missing persons*.

Rogers, C. D. and Smith, J. H. (1991) *Local family history in England*.

Rogers, K. H. (1991) *Vikings and surnames*.

Sharrock, J. T. R. (1976) *The atlas of breeding birds in Britain and Ireland*.

Shaw, G. and Tipper, A. (1989) *British directories: a bibliography and guide to directories published in England and Wales (1850–1950) and Scotland (1773–1950)*.

Sims, J. (1984) *A handlist of British Parliamentary poll books*.

Sturges, C. M. and Haggett, B. C. (1987) *Inheritance of English surnames*.

Tengvik, G. (1938) *Old English bynames*.

Thomas, C. (1973) 'Irish colonists in south-west Britain', *World Archaeology*, 5.1.

Thuresson, B. (1950) *Middle English occupational terms*.

Titterton, J. (1990) 'Pinpointing the origin of a surname', *The Local Historian*, 20.1.

Todd, J. E. and Dodd, P. A. (1982) *The electoral registration process in the United Kingdom*.

Ullathorne, G. (1992) *The history of a Westmorland name* [Ullathorne] (unpublished M.A. thesis, University of Sheffield).

Verstappen, P. (1980) *The book of surnames*.

Watson, R. (1975) 'A study of surname distribution in a group of Cambridgeshire parishes, 1538–1840', *Local Population Studies*, 15.

Weekley, E. (1914 ed) *The romance of names*.

Weekley, E. (1916) *Surnames*.

Willard, J. F. (1934) *Parliamentary taxes on personal property 1290 to 1334*.

Willis, A. J. and Tatchell, M. (1984) *Genealogy for beginners*.

White, G. P. (1972/1981) *A handbook of Cornish surnames*.

Appendix 1

List of prefixes and suffixes suggesting place names

This guide is neither definitive nor complete, and none is a foolproof indication that the name concerned originated from a place. The best of the early guides is to find the name preceded by de or d' during the Middle Ages, though Weekley (1916, p. 14) advises us to beware of poor transcribers who have misread an original 'le' as 'de'!

Prefixes – Eas(r)..., Nor(th)..., Pen..., Pol..., Tree..., South..., Wes(t)...

Suffixes – ...acre/aker, ...bottom/botham, ...bourne, ...bridge, ...b(o)rough, ...burgh, ...burn, ...bury, ...by, ...chester, ...clough, ...combe, ...cote/cott, ...croft, ...dale, ...den, ...don, ...field, ...firth, ...fold, ...ford/forth, ...garth, ...gate, ...halgh/haugh/hough, ...head, ...ham/um, ...hill, ...holme, ...house, ...hurst, ...leigh, ...l(e)y, ...mouth, ...pole, ...ridge, ...shaw, ...stead, ...stone, ...thorpe, ...thwaite/white, ...ton/tun, ...twistle, ...wich/ich/ick, ...wood, ...worth(y)

Difficulties of recognising the origins of locative names are discussed by McKinley (1990, pp. 52–9).

Appendix 2

Published name maps and where to find them

Col. 1. *Lasker and Mascie-Taylor (1990)*
Col. 2. *Lasker (1985)*
Col. 3. Elsewhere in this book
Col. 4. Eccleston (1989)

(Variants are not listed separately)

Surname	1	2	3	4	Surname	1	2	3	4
Adams		●			Black		●	●	
Allen		●			Blake			●	
Allwright	●				Blood	●			
Alp	●				Booth			●	
Amey	●				Breward	●			
Anderson		●			Brown		●		
Appledore	●				Brush	●			
Arculus	●				Burwood	●			
Attwell	●				Campbell		●		
Ayliff	●				Camper	●			
Bacon			●		Campion	●			
Bailey		●			Careford	●			
Baker		●			Carpenter				●
Balsdon	●				Carter		●		
Banham	●				Cartwright				●
Banwell	●				Caunce	●			
Barker		●	●		Chapman		●	●	
Barnes		●			Chilton	●			
Bassett			●		Churchward	●			
Baxter			●		Clark		●		
Bell		●			Claxton	●			
Bellingham	●				Clay				●
Bennett		●							

Surname	1	2	3	4	Surname	1	2	3	4
Colegate	●				Fletcher			●	
Collins		●			Formston	●			
Cook		●			Fosbrook	●			
Cooksey	●				Foster		●		
Cooper		●			Fox			●	
Cox		●			French			●	
Crabb	●				Fuller			●	●
Crafer	●				Furmston	●			
Crawforthe	●				Gabb	●			
Crayford	●				Gander	●			
Crippen	●				Garforthe	●			
Crowfoot	●				Garlick			●	
Crudginton	●				Gillard	●			
Cuff	●				Glaister	●			
Cufley	●				Goodbody	●			
Culfe	●				Gothard	●			
Culley			●		Gotts	●			
Danks	●				Gouge	●			
Darlington			●		Grafman	●			
Davies		●			Gray		●		
Dawson			●		Green		●		
Dawton	●				Griffiths		●		
Denley	●				Grigg	●			
Derbyshire	●				Hall		●		
Drinkwater			●		Harman	●			
Dunkley	●				Harris		●		
East		●	●		Harrison		●		
Ebden	●				Heath			●	
Edrich			●		Heaven	●			
Edwards		●			Hebden	●			
Ellis		●			Henney	●			
England			●		Hennings	●			
English			●		Hibbs	●			
Evans		●			Hill		●		
Fake	●				Hodgkinson	●			
Fautley	●				Hogwood	●			
Feake	●				Hollows	●			
Fenna	●				Holmes		●		
Fieldsend	●				Hore	●			
Firmston	●				Hughes		●		
Fisher		●			Hunt		●		

Surname	1	2	3	4
Ibbs	●			
Inch	●			
Jackson		●		
Jacob	●			
James		●		
Jenkins		●		
Johnson		●		
Jones	●	●		
Kaur		●		
Keats	●			
Kellyu		●		
Kent			●	
Kerfoot	●			
King		●		
Le Bootillier	●			
Lee				
(see also				
Leeson, 1964)		●		
Lewis		●		
Long		●		
Longmire	●			
Lovegrove	●			
Mallory	●			
Marker	●			
Marshall		●		
Martin		●		
Mason		●		
Mewis	●			
Mewse	●			
Miller		●		
Mills		●		
Mistry		●		
Mitchell		●		
Mitham	●			
Moore		●		
Morgan		●		
Morris		●		
Mowbray	●			
Murdoch			●	
Murphy		●		
Musk	●			

Surname	1	2	3	4
North		●	●	
O'Brien		●		
Offley	●			
Olivey	●			
O'Neill		●		
Owen		●		
Palgrave	●			
Palmer		●		
Pannett	●			
Parker		●		
Patchett	●			
Patel		●		
Patenden	●			
Pearson		●		
Perrin	●			
Philcox	●			
Phillips		●		
Phoenix	●			
Pilling	●			
Pinchbeck			●	
Pook	●			
Potter				●
Powell		●		
Price		●		
Proudfoot	●			
Purslow			●	
Redhead			●	
Reesby	●			
Restorick	●			
Richards		●		
Richardson		●		
Roberts		●		
Robinson		●		
Rogers		●	●	
Rumsey	●			
Sambridge	●			
Sandison	●			
Scoins	●			
Scott		●		
Seabury	●			
Shakespeare	●			

Surname	1	2	3	4	Surname	1	2	3	4
Shalliker	●				Trevor	●			
Shaw		●			Tucker			●	
Sherrell	●				Turner		●		
Short		●			Turpin			●	
Shuttle	●				Ulph	●			
Simpson		●			Underhay	●			
Sladen			●		Venables	●			
Smelt	●				Walker		●	●	●
Smith	●	●	●	●	Waller	●			
Sneddon	●				Ward		●		
Snelgrove	●				Warth	●			
South			●		Watson		●		
Southern		●			Weaver			●	
Southwell	●				Webb			●	
Spear	●				Webber			●	
Spilling	●				Webster			●	
Spring			●		West		●	●	
Spruce			●		Wheeler				●
Stagg	●				White		●		
Stitson	●				Whitehead			●	
Stott	●				Whitlock	●			
Sullivan		●			Wigzell	●			
Sutcliffe		●			Wilkinson		●		
Swale	●				Willerton	●			
Tanner			●		Williams		●		
Taylor		●			Wilson		●		
Tedd	●				Windebank	●			
Thomas		●			Winder			●	
Thompson		●			Wiseman			●	
Thompstone	●				Wood		●		
Tinker			●		Woodger	●			
Tiplady	●				Woodier	●			
Tooke	●				Wright		●		
Towner	●				Worsdell	●			
Treleaven	●				Young		●		
Treling	●				Zouch	●			
Treliving	●								

Appendix 3

Sources of names for (substantial parts of) counties prior to 1700

Figures in brackets after the county names are the populations enumerated in 1881.

Figures in brackets after a source are an indication of the number of people named therein.

In bold, those used in the scans of the fourteenth and seventeenth centuries.

Bedfordshire (149,473)

> An early Bedfordshire taxation [1237], ed. H. Jenkinson, Beds. Rec. Soc. 2. 1914

> The taxation of 1297 – local rolls of assessment, ed. A. T. Gaydon, Beds. Rec. Soc., 1959

> **Two Bedfordshire subsidy lists: 1309** and 1332, ed. S. H. A. Hervey, Suffolk Green Books, 1925 (1309, 5,680; 1332, 4,360)

> Bedfordshire Muster Lists 1539–1831, ed. N. Lutt, Beds. Rec. Soc., 1992

> **Hearth Tax 1671** in Beds. Rec. Soc., Vol. 16, 1934, repr. 1990 (9,500)

Berkshire (218,363)

> The muster Certificates for Berkshire, 1522, ed. J. Brooks and N. Heard 1986–87 (unindexed, but index in Berkshire RO; West Berkshire only)

Buckinghamshire (176,323)

> 1327 and **1332** subsidies, in **A. C. Chibnall, 'Early taxation returns'**, Bucks. Record Society 14 (1966) (2,314)

> The certificate of musters for Buckinghamshire, 1522, ed. A. C. Chibnall, Bucks. Rec. Soc. 17 & 18, 1973 (c.13,000)

> Subsidy roll for the county of Buckingham anno 1524, ed. A. C. Chibnall and A. V. Woodman, Bucks. Rec. Soc. 8, 1950

> **Buckinghamshire contributions for Ireland**, 1642, ed. J. Wilson, 1983 (c.8,000)

Cambridgeshire (185,594)

> **Hundred Roll 1279**, in *Rotuli Hundredorum* (1818) (c.23,000)

> **Lay Subsidy Roll 1641**, in W. M. Palmer, 'Cambridgeshire Subsidy Rolls 1250–1695' (1912, repr. from the *East Anglian* 1898–1909) –

(2,142)

Cheshire (644,037)

  Poll Tax 1660 (Northwich Hundred), in Rec. Soc. of Lancs & Ches, Vol. 119, 1979 (5,756)

  Hearth Tax 1664 (Northwich Hundred), in Rec. Soc. of Lancs & Ches, Vol. 119, 1979 (2,585)

  Hearth Tax 1665 (City of Chester), in Rec. Soc. of Lancs & Ches, Vol. 52

  Hearth Tax (Eddisbury, Wirral Hundreds), in Cheshire Sheaf, 3rd ser., Vols. 7ff

  (Total of above in bold type – 10,937)

Cornwall (330,686)

  The Cornwall Military Survey 1522, ed. T. L. Stoate, 1987

  Cornwall subsidies in the reign of Henry VIII [1524 & 1543], ed. T. L. Stoate, 1985

  The Cornwall Muster Roll 1569, ed. H. L. Douch, 1984

  Protestation 1641/2, ed. T. L. Stoate, 1974 (30,653)

  Poll tax 1660 and Hearth Tax, in T. L. Stoate (ed.), Cornwall Hearth & Poll taxes 1660–74, 1981 (14,470 in 1674)

Cumberland (250,654)

  C. P. Steel (ed.), Cumberland Lay Subsidy ... 6th Edward III [1332], 1912 (3,379) (Carlisle excluded)

  Transcription of 1664 Hearth Tax available in CRO

Derbyshire (461,914)

  1327 subsidy, in *Journal of the Derbyshire Archaeological Society*, 1907 (1,463)

  Various muster rolls 15th to 17th century, in Vol. 2 of Yeatman's *Feudal History of Derbyshire*

  Muster rolls 1585, 1587, in *Derbyshire Arch. Jnl.*, 17, 1895

  Muster Book of 1638, Derbyshire Record Society (to be published 1994?)

  Free and Voluntary Present, 1661, ed. D. Clay, 1992 (4,853)

  Hearth Tax Derbyshire Rec. Soc., Vol. VII, 1982 (16,200)

Devonshire (603,595)

  The Devonshire Lay Subsidy of 1332, ed. M. Erskine, Devon & Cornwall Rec. Soc., NS 14, 1969 (10,600)

  Tudor Exeter tax assessments 1489–1595, ed. M. M. Rowe, Devon & Cornwall Rec. Soc., 1977

  Military survey of the City of Exeter 1522, in *Tudor Exeter: tax assessments 1489–1595*, ed. M. M. Rowe, Devon & Cornwall Rec. Soc., NS 22, 1977 (1,363)

  Devon subsidy rolls 1524–27, ed. T. L. Stoate, 1979

  Devon subsidy rolls 1543–1545, ed. T. L. Stoate, 1986

  The Devon muster rolls for 1569, ed. A. J. Howard and T. L. Stoate,

1977 (15,000)

Protestation 1641/2 in T. L. Stoate (ed.) 'The Devonshire Protestation returns 1641', 1973 (63,254)

Hearth Tax, in T. L. Stoate (ed.), 1982 (22,919)

Dorset (191,028)

The Dorset Lay Subsidy Roll of 1327, ed. A. R. Rumble, Dorset Rec. Soc. 6, 1980 (7,399)

The Lay Subsidy roll of 1332, ed. A. D. Mills, Dorset Rec. Soc., vol. 4, 1971 (more complete than the former)

Dorset Tudor Subsidies 1523, 1543, 1593, ed. T. L. Stoate, 1982

Dorset Tudor Muster Rolls 1539, 1542 and 1569, ed. T. L. Stoate, 1978

Protestation 1641/2, ed. E. A. Fry, 1912 (22,000), indexed in B. W. Fagan, Dorset Records 2 (1912, repr. 1960)

1662/4 Hearth Tax, in C. A. F. Meekings, 'The Dorset hearth tax 1662–64', 1951

Durham (867,258)

1377–80 survey of Bishopric estates (Surtees Soc. 32, 1857 (2,800)

Protestation 1642, Surtees Soc. 135, 1922 (17,200)

Essex (576,434)

J. C. Ward, The medieval Essex community: the lay subsidy of 1327, ERO publ. 88, 1983 (8,326)

Hearth Tax 1662 – issued on microfiche, Soc. of Genealogists, 1989 (c.20,000)

Gloucestershire (572,433)

1327 Lay Subsidy, in P. Franklin, (1993) *The taxpayers of medieval Gloucestershire* (c.9,000)

The military survey of Gloucestershire, 1522, ed. R. W. Hoyle, 1993 (8,881)

1608 muster roll, in J. Smith 'Men and armour for Gloucestershire in 1608', ed. J. Smith or Smyth, 1902/1980 (19,402)

The inhabitants of Bristol in 1696, Bristol Record Soc. Vol. 25, 1968 (12,800)

Hampshire (593,470)

Central Hampshire lay subsidy assessments 1558–1603, ed. D. F. Vick (1987)

East Hampshire lay subsidy assessments 1558–1603, ed. D. F. Vick (1988)

West Hampshire lay subsidy assessments 1558–1603, ed. D. F. Vick (1987)

The Hampshire Lay Subsidy Rolls 1586, Hampshire Rec., Ser. IV, 1981

Hearth Tax 1665, Hampshire Record Series, Vol. 11, 1991 (c.20,000)

Hearth Tax 1664–74 Isle of Wight only, ed. P. D. D. Russell, 1981 (2,510)

Herefordshire (121,062)

Militia Assessments 1663, Camden Soc., 4th Ser., Vol. 10, 1972 (7,291)

Hertfordshire (203,069)

Huntingdonshire (59,491)

Hundred Roll 1279, in *Rotuli Hundredorum*, 1818 (c.9,700)

1332 lay subsidy, in J. A. Raftis and M. P. Hogan, 'Early Huntingdon-shire lay subsidies', 1976

Protestation 1641/2, *Trans. Cambs & Hunts Arch. Soc.*, 5, 1937 (8,270)

Kent (977,706)

H. A. Hanley and C. W. Chalkin, **'The Kent Lay Subsidy Roll of 1334/5'**, Kent Records XVIII, 1964 (11,016)

Hearth Tax 1664 (eastern half); Kent FHS Record publ. No. 14, 1983 (3,300)

Lancashire (3,454,441)

Lay subsidies 1216–1307, ed. J. A. C. Vincent, Lancs & Ches Rec. Soc. 27, 1893

The Exchequer lay subsidy roll ... AD 1332, ed. J. P. Rylands, Lancs & Ches Rec. Soc. 31, 1896 (2,571)

Taxation in the Salford Hundred 1524–1802, ed. J. Tait, Chetham Soc., NS 83, 1924 (incl. lay subsidies of 1524, 1543, 1563 and 1600; also **Hearth Tax 1672**, 3 hearths and over only)

Subsidy rolls for the Hundreds of Salford 1541, 1622 and Leyland 1628, ed. J. P. Earwaker, Lancs & Ches Rec. Soc. 12, 1885

Musters of the Hundreds of Leyland, West Derby, Salford and Blackburn, in Chetham Soc., OS 49, 50, 1859. (Many musters, but few names)

Association Oath 1696 (all county except the Hundreds of Amounder-ness, Blackburn, Leyland, and Salford), ed. W. Gandy, 1921, repr. 1985 (8,484)

Leicestershire (321,258)

Poll tax returns (1377–81) and earlier subsidies in Farnham (below) (9,437)

Hearth Tax 1666, in G. F. Farnham, *Leicestershire Medieval Village Notes*, 6 vols, 1920s (5,383)

Lincolnshire (469,919)

Protestation 1641/2, ed. W. F. Webster, 1984 (c.33,000)

London

E. Ekwall 'Two early [1292, **1319**] London subsidy rolls' (1951) 1327 (1,852)

1332 subsidy, in M. Curtis, 'Finance & trade under Edward III', 1918 (1,636)

Index to London inhabitants within the walls, 1696, London Rec.

Soc., Vol. 2, 1966 (60,000)

Middlesex (2,920,485)

Norfolk (444,749)

1355 City of Norwich Militia Arms & Array, in Norfolk & Norwich Arch. Soc., 14, 1901

c.1523 Militia list for Hundred of North Greenloe in Norfolk Rec. Soc., 1, 1931 (141 names)

c.1523 Militia list for Hundred of Holt, in N. & N.A.S. 22, 1926

The Norwich census of the poor 1570, Norfolk Rec. Soc., 40, 1971

The Muster Returns for divers hundreds, ed. H. L. Bradfer–Lawrence and P. Millican, in Norfolk Rec. Soc. 6, 7, incl. Clackrose 1569, Kings Lynn and Clackrose 1572, Thetford and Hundreds of Giltcross & Shropham 1574; and Kings Lynn and 15 hundreds 1577 (5,000)

Lay subsidy 1581 for certain Norfolk hundreds, Norfolk Rec. Soc. 17, 1944

The Norwich rate book 1633–1634, ed. W. Rye, 1903

Hearth Tax 1664, in *Norfolk Genealogy*, Vol. 15, 1984 (18,700)

Norfolk & Norwich Hearth Tax Assessment 1666, Norfolk & Norwich Gen. Soc., 1988

Northamptonshire (272,555)

Carte Nativorum, ed. C. N. L. Brooke and M. M. Postan, Northants Record Soc. XX, 1960 (4,000)

Book of musters 1540/1, in *Northampton Mercury*, 6, March 1876 (100)

Muster rolls for 1588, Eastern Division only, in Northamptonshire Lieutenancy Papers 1580–1614, ed. J. Goring and J. Wake, Northants Rec. Soc. 27, 1975

Muster rolls for 1591 (Northampton and ten southern hundreds) and 1612 in Musters, Beacons, subsidies, etc., in the county of Northampton, Northants Rec. Soc. 3, 1926 (1,548)

Muster rolls for various eastern hundreds 1605, 1613–19, in *The Montague Musters Book*, ed. J. Wake, Northants Rec. Soc. 7, 1935

Northumberland (434,086)

Lay subsidy of 1296, Soc. of Antiquaries of Newcastle upon Tyne Record Series (1968), ed. C. M. Fraser; (see also an article 'The lay subsidy roll of 1296', ed. F. Bradshaw, *Arch. Aeliana*, 1916 (4,250)

Muster Roll 1539, in Fencible inhabitants of Newcastle upon Tyne, *Arch. Aeliana*, 1st ser., 4, pt 2 1852; and Muster for Ward of Coquetdale and Bambrough in pt 3, 1854 (874)

Hearth Tax, Northumberland & Durham FHS 8.3, 9.1,2,4, 10.1–11, etc., (3,470)

Hearth Tax, Newcastle upon Tyne, *Arch. Aeliana*, s. 3, vol. 7, 1911 (2,510)

Nottinghamshire (391,815)

Inquisitions for the aid of 40s ... ed. N. Higson, Thoroton Soc. 14, 1951

Muster rolls 1595 for the Newark hundred, in *Trans. Thoroton Soc.* 10, 1906/7

Protestation 1641/2, ed. W. F. Webster, 1980 (18,501)

Hearth Tax 1664 and 1674, Thoroton Soc. Rec. Ser. vol. XXXVII, 1988 (1674 has 11,888)

Notts subsidies 1689, Notts FHS Rec. Ser. 24 (2 pts), unindexed (c.3,800)

Association Oath Rolls 1695, Notts. FHS Rec. Ser. 50

Oxfordshire (179,559)

Hundred Roll 1279, in *Rotuli Hundredorum*, 1818 (20,000)

Protestation Oxfordshire Record Society 36, 1955 (11,800)

Hearth Tax 1662 (Oxfordshire Rec. Soc., forthcoming)

Hearth Tax 1665 (indexed separately by J. Grere)

Rutland (21,434)

The Oakham Survey of 1305, Rutland Record Soc. Occasional Publ. 1988 (450)

Military Survey 1522, ed. J. C. K. Cornwall and Lay Subsidy 1524, Rutland Rec. Ser. 1, 1980

Hearth Tax 1665, ed. J. Bourne and A. Goode, Rutland Record Soc. Occasional Publ. 6, 1991 (2,901)

Shropshire (248,014)

1327 Subsidy roll, ed. W. G. D. Fletcher in the Shropshire Antiquarian & Natural History Soc., 1907 (4,897)

1539, 1542, 1579 muster rolls of various hundreds in *Trans. Shropshire Arch. & Nat. Hist. Soc.* 2, 1890 and 8, 1908.

Hearth Tax 1672, Shropshire Archaeological and Parish Register Society, 1949 (16,380)

Somerset (469,109)

Lay Subsidy 1327, ed. F. H. Dickinson in Somerset Rec. Soc. 3, 1889 (11,100)

Certificates of musters in the county of Somerset 1569, ed. E. Green, Somerset Rec. Soc. 20, 1904 (6,000)

1586 trained bands, in E. Green, 'The preparation in Somerset against the Spanish Armada', 1888 (1,200)

Protestation 1641/2, in T. L. Stoate (ed.) 'The Somerset Protestation returns and Lay Subsidy Rolls 1641/2', 1975 (also available on microfiche)

Hearth Tax 1664/5, Dwelly's National Records, Vol. 1, 1916 (5,400) (note that Vol. 2 of this series has indexes to earlier records)

Staffordshire (981,013)

The Exchequer subsidy of AD 1327, ed. G. Wrottesley, William Salt

Arch. Soc. 7, pt 1, 1886 (4,378)

The poll tax of AD 1379–81 for the Hundreds of Offlow and Cuttlestone, Wm Salt Arch. Soc. 17, 1896

Muster rolls for 1539, hundreds of Offlow, Cuttlestone & Pirehill and Seisdon & Totmonslow in The Muster Roll of Staffordshire 1539, William Salt Arch. Soc., NS 4,5

Subsidy Roll 1640, Pirehill Hundred, ed. S. A. H. Burne, Staffs Rec. Soc., 1941/2

Hearth Tax, Staffs Record Soc.: Collections for a History of Staffordshire, 1921, 1923, 1925, 1927; also for Lichfield in Collections of the William Salt Arch. Soc., 1936 (20,142)

Suffolk (356,893)

Suffolk in 1327 Subsidy Return, Suffolk Green Books, 1906 (11,721)

Military survey of 1522, Suffolk Rec. Soc. 28, 1986 (Babergh Hundred) (2,000)

Suffolk in 1524 Subsidy Return, Suffolk Green Books, 1910

Muster rolls 1534–40 in Muster rolls of the territorials in Tudor times, ed. E. Powell, *Proc. Suffolk Inst. of Arch.*, 15, 16, 1915–27, various hundreds

Suffolk in 1568 Subsidy Return, Suffolk Green Books, 1909

Poor relief in Elizabethan Ipswich (incl. a register of the poor, 1569–83), Suffolk Rec. Soc., Vol. 9, 1966

Musters of 1579 (Babergh Hundred) and 1584 (Blackbourn Hundred) in P.S.I.A. 18

Muster roll 1631, hundreds of Hoxon and Plomesgate, in East Anglian Notes & Queries, NS 13, 1909–10 (200)

County Muster Roll, in 'Able Men of Suffolk 1638', ed. C. E. Banks, Anglo-American Record Foundation, 1931 (24,000)

Hearth Tax 1674, in Suffolk Green Books, No. XI, Vol. 13, 1905 (29,125)

Surrey (1,436,899)

Surrey taxation returns ... 1332 assessment and subsequent assessments to 1623, ed. J. F. Willard and H. C. Johnson, Surrey Rec. Soc. 11, 1922–32 (5,471)

Muster rolls 1544–1684 in Surrey Musters, ed. T. Craib, Surrey Rec. Soc. 2, orig. 1914–19

Hearth Tax 1664, Surrey Rec. Soc., Vol. 17, 1940 (16,306)

Association Oath Rolls for Surrey, trans. C. Webb, West Surrey FHS Microfiche ser. 3, 1990

Sussex (490,505)

The three earliest subsidies for the county of Sussex in the years 1296, **1327** and 1332, ed. W. Hudson, Sussex Rec. Soc. 10 (1910) (7,210, 7,234, and 6,973 respectively)

M. J. Burchall (ed.), **East Sussex contributors to the relief of Irish Protestants 1642**, Sussex Genealogical Centre, 1984 (4,000)

Protestation 1641/2 (West Sussex only), Sussex Record Society 5, 1906

Warwickshire (737,339)

Inhabitants of Birmingham, Edgbaston & Aston possessing goods to the value of 10/– and upwards in the year 1327, ed. W. B. Bickley, 1885

The lay subsidy roll for Warwickshire of 6 Edward III 1332, ed. W. F. Carter, Dugdale Soc. 6, 1926 (5,457)

Hearth Tax returns, Vol. 1, Hemlingford Hundred – Tamworth and Atherstone Divisions, Warwicks. County Records, 1957 (c.3,000)

Westmorland (64,191)

Lay subsidy 1332, in W. Farrer, 'Records belonging to the Barony of Kendale', Vols 1 & 2, 1923, southern half only (572)

Muster roll 1539, whole county, in Cal. State Papers: letters and papers Henry VII 14 pt 2.

Protestation 1641/2, in Cumberland & Westmorland Arch. & Ant. Soc. Tract Ser. No. XVII, 1971 (3,378)

Hearth Tax 1669, in W. Farrer, 'Records belonging to the Barony of Kendale', 1923

Wiltshire (258,965)

D. A. Crowley (ed.), **The Wiltshire tax List of 1332**, Wiltshire Record Society 45, 1989 (9,600)

Muster rolls of North Wiltshire 1539, publ. 1834 (4 known copies, incl. BL and Wilts RO)

Two sixteenth-century taxation lists 1545 & 1576, ed. G. D. Ramsay, Wilts Rec. Soc. 1954

Protestation 1641/2, Wiltshire Notes & Queries 7 (5,312)

Worcestershire (380,283)

Lay subsidy roll for the county of Worcester c. 1280, ed. J. W. W. Bund and J. Amphlett, Worcs. Hist. Soc., 1893

Lay subsidy roll for the county of Worcester 1 Edward III [1327], ed. F. J. Fled, Worcs. Hist. Soc., 1895 (4,644)

Lay subsidy roll for the county of Worcester AD 1332–3, ed. J. Amphlett, Worcs. Hist. Soc., 1900

Lay subsidy rolls AD 1346 and 1358 for the county of Worcester, ed. J. Amphlett, Worcs. Hist. Soc., 1901

Lay subsidy rolls 6&7 Henry VI AD 1427–9 for the county of Worcester, ed. J. Amphlett, Worcs. Hist. Soc.,1902

Lay subsidy roll AD 1603 for the county of Worcester, ed. J. Amphlett, Worcs. Hist. Soc., 1901

The hearth tax collectors' book for Worcester, 1678–80, ed. C. A. F. Meekings, Worcs. Historical Soc., NS 11, 1983 (2,301)

Yorkshire whole county
   Yorkshire lay subsidy ... 1297, ed. W. Brown, Yorks Arch. Soc. Record
      Ser. 16, 1894 (3,402)
   Yorkshire lay subsidy ... 1301, ed. W. Brown, Yorks Arch. Soc. Record
      Ser. 21, 1897 (mostly North Riding) (8,699 persons)
Yorkshire ER (315,460)
   East Riding Poll Tax 1381 for Howdenshire, in East Riding Antiquar-
      ian Society, Vol. XV, 1908/9 (c.3,500)
   Muster roll 1584, various wapentakes, in Yorks Arch. Soc. Rec. Ser.
      115, 1951
Yorkshire NR (346,260)
   Lay subsidy rolls of 1 Edward III 1327 North Riding & the City of
      York, ed. J. Parker, Yorks Arch. Soc. Record Ser. 74, 1929 (3,848)
   Hearth Tax 1672, wapentakes of Ainsty, Langbarugh East and West,
      Whitby Strand, Rydale, Pickering Lith, Scarbrough, Birdforth and
      Bulmer, Ripon Hist. Soc.
Yorkshire WR (2,224,844)
   Two subsidy rolls of Skyrack, temp. Edw. III, ed. J. Stansfeld, Thoresby
      Soc. 2, 1891
   **The returns for the West Riding of the County of York of Poll tax
      laid in 2 Richard II 1379**, 1882 (c.35,000)
   Muster roll 1535, Claro Wapentake in Thoresby Soc. 15, 1909
   Muster roll 1539 Skyrack Wapentake in Thoresby Soc. 4, 9, 1895, 1899
   Lay subsidies, Skyrack, Agbrigg & Morley Wapentakes, 1545–6,
      Thoresby Soc. 9, 1899
   Lay subsidy, Wapentakes of Skyrack, Agbrigg & Morley, ed. W. Brigg,
      Thoresby Soc. 15, 1909
   Subsidy rolls of the Wapentake of Skyrack 1610, 1629, Thoresby Soc.
      22, 1915
   Subsidy rolls of the Wapentake of Skyrack 1621, 1627, Thoresby Soc.
      2, 1891
   Subsidy roll of the Wapentake of Skyrack ... 1621, ed. J. Stansfeld,
      Thoresby Soc. 2, 1891
   Hearth Tax 1672, Hundred of Skyrack, Thoresby Soc., 2, 43, 1891,
      1895 (3,245)
   Hearth Tax 1672, Wapentakes of Abrigg, Morley, Stainscliffe, Ewcross
      and Claro, Ripon Hist. Soc.
   The hearth tax returns for south Yorkshire, 1672, ed. D. Hey,
      1991 (7,933 in the Wapentakes of Strafforth & Tickhill, and Stain-
      cross)

Appendix 4

List of names studied for background to this book

Alderman
Ashburner
Bacon
Ballard
Barker
Bassett
Baxter
Bellamy
Black/Blake
Booth
Box
Bunyan
Carpenter
Cartwright
Chapman
Clay
Constable
Culverhouse
Darlington
Dawson
Death
Dempster
Drinkwater
Duncalf
Dutch
East
Edrich
England/English
Faber
Fairfax
Fletcher
Foot
Fox
French

Fuller
Furlong
Garlick
Hatter
Haven
Heath
Heathcote
Ingram
Jagger
Jessop
Jolliff/Jolly
Kemp
Kent
Lancashire
Lightfoot
Merryweather
Moxon
Murdoch
Nightingale
North
Oliphant
Outlaw
Packer
Pinchbeck
Pipe
Piper
Pollard
Purslow
Quick
Redhead
Restell
Rich
Ro(d)gers
Rust

Setter
Sladen
Smith
South
Spicer
Spindler
Spinner
Spooner
Spring
Spruce
Stalker
Stringer
Summerscale
Tanner
Tasker
Temple
Tinker/Tinkler
Trinder
Tucker
Turnbull
Turpin
Tyson
Wagstaff
Waugh
Weaver
Webb
Webber
Webster
West
Whitehead
Winder
Wiseman

Surname index

(Page numbers in bold refer to maps; figures in brackets refer to the number of instances, if more than one, on each page.)

General index

Abram 162
Abson 79
Adburgham 162
agricultural names 190, 203
Ainsty 203
Aldridge 177
alias 204
Anglesey 87
animal names 66, 204, 205, 211
Appletreewyck 223
Arnold 162
Association Oath 111, 112, 114

Banwell (system) 10, 22, 25(3),
  27, 45, 90, 91, 100, 114–16,
  124, 148, 156, 161
Barmby 177
Barnsley 69, 85
Bassetlaw 114
Bath 11
Bedfordshire 39, 57, 87, 92, 107,
  150, 152, 221
Bentham 180
Berkshire 108, 112, 113, 151,
  152
Birmingham 11, 15, 21
Black Death 154, 155, 161, 224
Blackburn 49, 69, 95(2)
Blackwell 156
Bolton 65
Bradford 32, 100
Brecknockshire 87

Brett (system) 21, 22
Bristol 11, 67, 113, 116
Bristol Channel 33
British Telecom 85
Buckinghamshire 110, 148, 150,
  152, 155
Burnley 95(2), 100(2), 102, 112
Burton on Trent 45, 66
Bury 147
businesses, locations of 17
byenames x, 3, Part 3 *passim*

CD-ROM 10
Cambridgeshire 65, 87, 92(4),
  108, 150, 152, 154, 197, 205,
  232
Cardiganshire 87
Carleton 154, 223
Carmarthenshire 87
carpenters 201, 204(2)
census 81, 82, 85–9, 100, 101
Channel Islands 86
Charter Rolls 151
Cheshire 33, 38, 52, 84, 105,
  108, 115, 116, 128, 138(3),
  149, 151, 154, 161, 162, 180,
  204, 217, 221
Chester 43, 84
Chinese names 65
Cinque Ports 149
civil registration 93, 101
clay 71